D1522382

A Gentleman
as Well as a Whig

A Gentleman
as Well as a Whig

Caesar Rodney and the
American Revolution

Jane Harrington Scott

National Society of
The Colonial Dames of America
in the State of Delaware

DELAWARE

Newark: University of Delaware Press
London: Associated University Presses

Associated University Presses
440 Forsgate Drive
Cranbury, NJ 08512

Associated University Presses
16 Barter Street
London WC1A 2AH, England

Associated University Presses
P.O. Box 338, Port Credit
Mississauga, Ontario
Canada L5G 4L8

The paper used in this publication meets the requirements of the American National Standard for Permanence of Paper for Printed Library Materials Z39.48-1984.

Library of Congress Cataloging-in-Publication Data

Scott, Jane, 1931–
    A gentleman as well as a Whig : Caesar Rodney and the American Revolution / Jane Harrington Scott.
        p.   cm.—(Cultural studies of Delaware and the Eastern Shore)
    Includes bibliographical references (p.   ) and index.
    ISBN 0-87413-700-4 (alk. paper)
    1. Rodney, Caesar, 1728–1784.   2. Statesmen—United States—Biography. 3. United States—History—Revolution, 1775–1783.   4. United States. Declaration of Independence—Signers—Biography.   5. United States. Continental Congress—Biography.   6. Legislators—Delaware—Biography.   7. Delaware—History—Revolution, 1775–1783.   8. Kent County (Del.)—Biography.   I. Title.   II. Series.
    E207.R6 S38   2000
    973.3—dc21

99-055926

Cultural Studies of Delaware and the Eastern Shore

1973
Carol Hoffecker, ed., *Readings in Delaware History*

1977
Harold Hancock, *The Loyalties of Revolutionary Delaware*

1983
C. A. Weslager, *The Nanticoke Indians—Past and Present*

1984
John A. Munroe, *History of Delaware* (2nd edition)

1984
Jay F. Custer, *Delaware Prehistoric Archaeology: An Ecological Approach*

1986
Claudia L. Bushman, Harold B. Hancock and Elizabeth Moyne Homsey, ed., *Proceedings of the Assembly of the Lower Counties on Delaware 1770–1776, of the Constitutional Convention of 1776, and of the House of Assembly of the Delaware State 1776–1781.*
Jay F. Custer, ed., *Late Woodland Cultures of the Middle Atlantic Region*

1988
Claudia L. Bushman, Harold B. Hancock and Elizabeth Moyne Homsey, eds., *Minutes of the House of Assembly of the Delaware State, 1781–1792*

1989
Jay F. Custer, *Prehistoric Cultures of the Delmarva Peninsula: An Archaeological Study*
John A. Sweeney, *Grandeur on the Appoquinimink: The House of William Corbit at Odessa, Delaware*

1993
John A. Monroe, *History of Delaware* (third edition)

1995
Carol E. Hoffecker, Richard Waldron, Lorraine E. Williams, and Barbara E. Benson, eds., *New Sweden in America*

1999
Toni Young. *Becoming American, Remaining Jewish: The Story of Wilmington, Delaware's First Jewish Community, 1879–1924*

2000
Jane Harrington Scott, *A Gentleman as Well as a Whig*
Carole E. Hoffecker, *Honest John Williams: US Senator from Delaware*

2001
William W. Boyer, *Governing Delaware: Policy Problems in the First State*

Contents

8   CONTENTS

Acknowledgments

THIS BOOK COULD NOT HAVE BEEN WRITTEN WITHOUT THE HELP AND support of many people. Chief among them are the members of The National Society of the Colonial Dames of America in the state of Delaware, who sponsored the project and James A. Stewart, Administrator of the Bureau of Museums and Historic Sites in Dover, who had the idea in the first place.

James B. Jackson of Dover, an eminent Rodney scholar and collateral descendent, generously shared his meticulous and exhaustive research about Caesar Rodney's life and times. I could not have done it without him. He also read and corrected the manuscript as did two of Delaware's foremost historians, Dr. John A. Munroe, Professor Emeritius, and Dr. Carol Hoffecker, Associate Provost of Graduate Studies, both of the University of Delaware. I also relied heavily on Dr. Munroe's books: *Colonial Delaware, a History* and *Federalist Delaware, 1775–1815.*

John Biggs, III, Esq. of Wilmington and Bruce C. Ennis, Esq. of Dover provided valuable information about Delaware's early government and sent me copies of Caesar's will and other legal documents. John J. Burchenal, former Board member of the Historical Society of Delaware, did research on Dr. Charles Ridgely, Dr. Thomas Bond and Jonathan Rumford. Mary H. Watkins, Recording Secretary of the National Society of The Colonial Dames, sent me material on the Tories of Sussex County, among other things, and Colonial Dames members Ann A. Biggs, Marion L. Laird and Beverly W. Rowland also contributed information and valuable suggestions. James Stewart and Mary Watkins also helped find the illustrations. I am indebted to them all.

A Gentleman
as Well as a Whig

1
Rodney Roots and Beginnings

A NOBLE STATUE OVERLOOKS THE CENTER SQUARE OF WILMINGTON, Delaware; a man in a tricornered hat mounted on a galloping horse. It represents Caesar Rodney who, at midnight on July 1, 1776, left his home in Dover, and "Tho detained by Thunder and Rain" traveled eighty miles to Philadelphia to cast his vote for independence.[1]

It is a heroic figure, and, in that sense, speaks the truth. Yet it is wholly inaccurate as an image of Caesar Rodney, himself. The bronze rider is strong and vigorous; the man who rushed to Philadelphia that night was a frail forty-six year old, with a body wasted by chronic asthma and a face scarred by cancer. Nor is it certain that he made the journey on horseback. Like most eighteenth-century gentlemen, Rodney usually traveled by carriage.

Nevertheless, it was a dramatic journey and a courageous act. Like all his fellow signers, Caesar put his life on the line that day. Yet, it was only one of many journeys that he took along the road to revolution.

Why did he do it? Caesar Rodney was never a radical. He was an essentially modest man from a well respected and long established Anglican family. He had an affectionate sense of humor and a cast of mind so balanced and ageeable that even those who disagreed with his political views continued to like and trust him. He was also in very poor health.

Nor were any of the classic causes of rebellion present in Delaware at the time: no mass poverty, no seething discontent, no oppressive church or titled nobility. The Rodneys and their friends and neighbors enjoyed a comfortable life by the standards of the time, and life was improving for most of their fellow Delawareans as well. What, then, led them to revolution?

The Rodneys, like many Anglican families in the New World, thought of themselves as English, entitled to all an Englishman's rights and privileges, even though, by the 1770s, they had lived in

13

Delaware for three generations.[2] At the same time, whatever position they had once occupied in English society, and however devoted they had once been to traditional English mores, they had traveled a vast distance. Much farther, perhaps, than they themselves realized. Just how important it was to Caesar and his compatriots to be able to make their own laws and govern their own community became evident only when they found themselves involved in a power struggle with the mother country.

Caesar's family, originally known as DeRodeney, was both ancient and privileged. The family seat, known as "Rodeney Stoke," was in Somerset County, England, near the city of Bristol, but much of its original holdings of land were lost, like so many in that part of England, during Cromwell's Puritan Revolution.

Caesar Rodney's paternal grandfather, William Rodeney, was the first member of the family to settle here permanently. His father, however, worked for a time as a Royal prosecutor and surveyor of customs in New York and died on Long Island Sound in 1679 while on a ship bound from the West Indies. William, the eldest of six children, was baptized in Bristol on March 14, 1660. If, as seems likely, he was also born in that year, then he was in Delaware by the time he was twenty, for he is listed as the foreman of a Kent county jury in December, 1681. (Thomas Rodney, writing over a century later, said he was born on March 4, 1652, but the year seems doubtful given the baptismal record.)[3]

1681 was the same year that King Charles II's brother, the Duke of York, granted Pennsylvania to William Penn in payment of a debt he owed to Penn's father. In August of the following year, 1682, Penn received two additional grants: a twelve mile circle of land around the town of New Castle and, to insure a safe passage from Philadelphia to the sea, the western shore of Delaware Bay from the southern edge of that circle to Cape Henlopen. These lands had been first settled by the Swedes and then by the Dutch; now the Duke of York claimed them as part of his spoils from the occupation of New Amsterdam, despite a conflicting claim by Charles Calvert to the whole of the peninsula between the Chesapeake and Delaware Bays. It was a dispute that would take many years to settle, but William Penn eventually prevailed and the Delaware colony became the Three Lower Counties of Pennsylvania.[4]

On November 30, 1688 William Rodeney declared his intention to marry Mary Hollyman, a member of the Philadelphia Monthly Meeting where it is noted in the minutes that he had formerly lived among Friends in Maryland. If so, he was probably one of the nearly fifty thousand young men who came to the Chesapeake Bay tidewater country in the seventeenth century. Like Rodeney, many were Anglicans from the environs of Bristol.[5]

The young couple's first three children, William, Jr, Rachel and Thomas, were born in Lewes in Sussex county. Soon after, the family moved to St. Jones county (now Kent county) where he had received a grant of five hundred acres. Sadly, Mary Hollyman died in 1692, possibly in childbirth and was buried on a plantation belonging to Griffith Jones.

In February of 1693, William Rodeney married for the second time, choosing Sarah Jones, daughter of Daniel Jones, a prominent Kent county landowner. They had six children. Caesar Rodney's father, also called Caesar Rodney, was the youngest, born on October 12, 1707.[6]

It is possible that William Rodeney found Delaware's Anglican rural society more congenial than the earnest Quakers of Philadelphia. In any case, he soon became a prominent member of the colonial government. From the time of Penn's first assembly in 1682, delegates from the Three Lower Counties, fearful of being overwhelmed by the more populous Pennsylvania, had agitated for more power to make laws for their colony. Their effort culminated in the first Delaware Assembly that met in New Castle in November 1704. William Rodeney was elected as the first speaker of this body, thus firmly establishing a Rodney family tradition of public service.[7] Although the speaker's power was largely ceremonial, he was looked up to as the most important citizen of the colony.

William Rodeney died in 1708, at the age of fifty-six and was buried in the family grave site at "Byfield" near Dover, Delaware. At the time, Caesar Rodney, Sr. was just a year old, but he would eventually outlive his four brothers and one sister to inherit his father's estate.

On October 18, 1727, when he was about twenty, Caesar Rodney, Sr. married Elizabeth Crawford, the daughter of a Church of England missionary named Thomas Crawford. Thomas Crawford, performed the ceremony and the next day he, himself, married his third wife, Katherine French. The "fidling and dancing" went on for two days as the newlyweds together with their "brides Men & Brid Maids" went from house to house with a "Drum and two Viol Ends Playing" before them.[8]

Thomas Crawford, who would become our Caesar Rodney's maternal grandfather, had been sent by England's "Society for the Propagation of Gospel in Foreign Parts" to serve Dover and the surrounding countryside. Like many eighteenth century women of her class,[9] his daughter Elizabeth was a cultivated woman who would impart to her eldest son a firm moral character and a deep respect for learning.

Caesar Rodney, the first child of Caesar Rodney, Sr. and Elizabeth Crawford Rodney was born shortly after midnight, on October 7, 1728. It is thought that his young parents were living in a small house owned by Elizabeth's father, not far from the Rodney farm at Byfield.[10]

According to Caesar Rodney, Sr.'s diary, the young father immediately sent for a midwife "and other women," but "Before aney came ye Child wass Born and it wass a SON." As "There was no sole with her but myself—being I believe just about midnight," he "ran away for Isabelah Hughes." Apparently all was well, for his entry for the following day, October 8, tells us that he: "Past ye Day away with Eating and Drinking and at Night I got super Went to Bed fair and Good helth—My wife and Child Continues Brave and well thanks be to God."[11]

The new baby, Caesar, would be the oldest of eight children. Two years later in 1730, his sister Elizabeth was born, followed the year after that, 1731, by George. Sarah, born in 1733, died before she was a year old. Mary came in 1735, William in 1738, Daniel in 1741 and finally Thomas in 1744. All grew up at Byfield.[12]

In 1745, when young Caesar Rodney was seventeen, his father died and the orphan's court appointed Nicholas Ridgely as his guardian.[13] At that time, his sister Elizabeth was fifteen and his brother George, fourteen. (George died a few years later at the age of eighteen or nineteen.) His second sister Mary, would have been ten years old, and his younger brothers William and Daniel, seven and four years respectively. The baby Thomas was eleven months.

Doubtless many of the burdens of helping his mother raise this growing family and running Byfield plantation fell on young Caesar's shoulders. Although Elizabeth Crawford Rodney would later marry Thomas Wilson and have two more children—Sarah, known as Sally, and John—she apparently continued to live at Byfield. In 1762 when Thomas Rodney was eighteen years old, he mentioned that "having lived chiefly with my Mother and father-in-law [step father] til this year, I moved from them [at Byfield] to my brother Caesar's, who then lived at Lebenon Farm."[14] Elizabeth Crawford Rodney Wilson died the following year.

By that time, Caesar, was a thirty-five year old bachelor and already well known in public life. That he felt deeply responsible for his brothers and sisters seems evident. In 1763, the same year his mother died, he wrote his brother Daniel; "Ever since you came to man's age, you have conducted yourself in such an idle, indolent

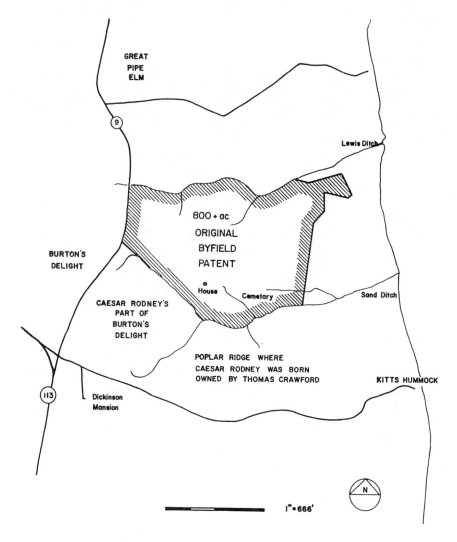

GREAT
PIPE
ELM

⑨

Lewis Ditch

800 + ac

ORIGINAL

BYFIELD

PATENT

BURTON'S
DELIGHT

a
House   Cemetery

Sand Ditch

CAESAR RODNEY'S
PART OF
BURTON'S
DELIGHT

POPLAR RIDGE WHERE
CAESAR RODNEY WAS BORN
OWNED BY THOMAS CRAWFORD

KITTS HUMMOCK

⑾⑶

Dickinson
Mansion

N

1" = 666'

Map showing location of Byfield drawn by Jeroen van den Hurk according to
information supplied by James B. Jackson.

manner as has & still doth give your friends great concern."[15] Daniel died the very next year, leaving a daughter, Sarah.[16] He was twenty-three years old.

Of all his siblings, Caesar was closest to his half sister, Sally Wilson, who, despite being married with two children of her own,[17] kept house for him in later years, and to his youngest brother, Thomas, a often foolish and hotheaded man, whose public career would closely follow his own. "Tommy" also managed Caesar's lands and took care of his financial affairs while he was involved with matters of state. Unfortunately he seems to have had little head for business and the results were ultimately disastrous.

In a diary entry of 1791, Thomas wrote that his father (Caesar, Sr.) and grandfather (William Rodeney), as well as "most of my unkles & brothers are buried on Byfield Farm." Originally the property of William Rodeney's father-in-law, Daniel Jones, the Rodney farm at Byfield consisted of about 850 acres on Jones Neck, between what is now the Dover Air Base and Delaware Bay, about a mile from the John Dickinson mansion. Thomas Rodney described its location as "between two branches, one called Jones' branch, which falls into the Bay through the Sand ditch; the other, hog pen branch which falls into the Bay through the black bank or Meadow ditch."[18] (The land is now part of a corporate farm: there is no sign of the family graveyard or of the house where Caesar Rodney grew up.)

Caesar inherited Byfield from his mother and owned it throughout his life, although he apparently never lived there as an adult. Over the years the property was enlarged by the acquisition of part of two neighboring farms: "Great Pipe Elm," on the northern boundary and "Burton's Delight" to the southwest as well as "other farmland and marsh."[19] These farms would provide Caesar with his main source of income throughout his life.

In seventeenth and eighteenth century Delaware, the Rodneys of Byfield were among the most comfortable in Kent County, although their life would have been considered plain in comparison to that of similar gentry in England. Their clothes were made from farm-raised wool or flax, and all their beef, pork and poultry, as well as vegetables, fruit, milk, butter and cheese came from the farm.

The local economy provided those tools and goods that could not be made at home, as well as special services like carpentry and brick making. Local gentry such as the Rodneys also patronized local silversmiths, cabinetmakers and hatters.

In the eighteenth century, Delaware's creeks and rivers were deeper and more navigable than they are today, and supplied the principal transport. The roads were notoriously bad, full of deep ruts in dry weather, and sticky mudholes in wet. Bridges were made of wood and frequently contained broken or rotten boards. With the exception of the King's Highway, which began in Sussex County and ran northward through Milford, Dover, Duck Creek, (now Smyrna) New Castle and Wilmington, most roads were merely rutted lanes leading to a landing place on the river or bay.[20]

The Rodneys and their fellow landowners sent their grain to market at Wilmington and Philadelphia on double-ended, shallow draft boats called shallops that came up the nearby St. Jones river. These shallops were able to sail far up the narrow creeks to take on cargo because they simply reversed sails, oars and rudder for the return trip, eliminating the need to turn around. Apparently they were also seaworthy enough to navigate Delaware Bay, for both shallops and and the larger vessels called sloops, brought such imported Philadelphia luxuries into Kent County as tea; coffee; bolts of cloth; "Jersey cheese;" Virginia twist tobacco; wine and furniture.[21]

Like all the early landowners in Delaware, the Rodneys kept slaves. In fact, there were already slaves in Delaware when Caesar's grandfather arrived in the 1680s, having been brought in by the Dutch from the West Indies some thirty years before. After dropping to about five percent of the population at the beginning of the eighteenth century, their numbers swelled during Caesar Rodney's time as tobacco farmers from the Eastern Shore of Maryland moved onto the virgin land of lower Delaware.[22]

It was the ownership of slaves, of course, that made it possible for the early families of Delaware, the Rodneys, Dickinsons, Loockermans, and Ridgelys to emulate the lives of English squires and, in many cases, afforded them the freedom to enter politics. Even so, none of these families owned anything like the number of slaves kept by some of their compatriots in the Chesapeake Bay region. By the eve of the Revolution, most members of the Delaware Assembly owned about twenty slaves, whereas Thomas Jefferson owned two hundred, George Washington two hundred and seventy-seven and Edward Lloyd IV of Wye House, on the nearby Eastern Shore of Maryland, about three hundred.[23]

Wheat and corn were grown as commercial crops, yet, according to Thomas Rodney, "the largest farmers . . . did not sow over twenty acres of wheat, nor tend more than thirty acres of Indian corn so all the families in the county had a great deal of idle time."[24] Thomas, himself, certainly seems to have enjoyed life as a young man about town. In a diary entry of September 1, 1769 he tells us that, after dinner at Duck Creek [Smyrna] at three in the afternoon he "play'd a Schore of Long Bullets [The firing of guns was a popular pastime for young men at the time.] and "then Sett of[f] home—on the way Mett with a Large Company of people horse-raseing . . .—This kept us So long, that I Didn't Reach home Till Near Sun sett—after I come home I went to one of the Taverns and Spent three Hours at Cards, the Rema[in]ing part of the Evening past at home in Conversation with Mrs. Shee about her Courtship."[25]

Horse racing, as well as dances and sports like discus throwing and wrestling were also part of the community fairs that were held every six months or so. Intended as an opportunity for merchants to sell their wares, these fairs also caused considerable controversy. Gambling, drunkenness, fights and riots were common.[26]

There were few schools in lower Delaware when Caesar Rodney was growing up, and those that did exist tended to be of low quality. Children were educated by itinerant teachers or their own parents. While it is thought that Caesar Rodney and his brothers and sisters were taught to read by their mother, as well-to-do Delaware Anglicans, they probably also had a private tutor.[27] When he was fourteen, Caesar Rodney went to Latin School in Philadelphia where, on July 16, 1743, his father sent him "two shirts, 3 stocks, a Cap and a prayer Book" and advised him to "use all posable means to git in favour with the Better Sort of people, for there is no greater advantage to youth than good Company. Nor No greater Disadvantage than ill."[28] There is no evidence that he had any formal legal training.

Caesar Rodney grew into an elegant, graceful young man of about five feet, ten inches. According to his brother, Thomas, he also had "a greate fund of wit & Humour of the pleasing kind, so that his conversation was always bright and strong & Conducted by Wisdom . . . He always lived a bachelor, was generally Esteemed, and indeed very popular."[29]

We don't know why Caesar never married, he certainly seemed to enjoy the company of women. In an early, undated letter to one Polly Davis, he tells her "With Miss Polly Vining . . . I had one night . . . at least five or six hours chatt. You was the chief subject of conversation." In the same letter, he refers to a Miss Lawrence as "a lady who from a short acquaintance I greatly esteam. I well know she has charms sufficient to conquer, and hope she is too good to be cruel."[30]

The persistent story that Caesar was in love with Mary (Polly) Vining, the daughter of the then deceased Captain Benjamin Vining and Mary Middleton is based on a single letter written from Dover on May 27, 1761 or 1764, when he was in his thirties.

Yesterday evening (by Mr. Chew's Tom) I had the unwelcome & unexpected news of your determining to go to Philadelphia, with Mr. and Mrs. Chew—If you Remember, as we were riding to Noxontown fair, you talked of taking this journey & mentioned my going with you: you know how readily . . . & how willing in this, as in every thing else, I was to oblige & serve you—When I was last down, you seemed to have given over all thoughts of going, this determined me, & accordingly, gave Mr. Chew, for answer, that he might not expect me with him; thereby I'm deprived of the greatest pleasure this World coul'd possibly afford me, The company of that lady in whom all my happiness is placed—Molly, I love you from my soul, in this believe me, I'm sincere, & honest: but when I think of the many amiable qualifications you are possessed of—all my hopes are at an end—nevertheless intended down this week, & as far as possible to have known my fate—you may expect to see me at your return, till then God bless you—"[31]

Caesar lost out. Mary Vining married a young English missionary named Charles Inglis who had been sent to the church at Dover. Incidentally, at the time Caesar wrote this letter, her widowed mother was married to Caesar's guardian, Nicholas Greenberry Ridgely. Their son, Dr. Charles Greenberry Ridgely, half brother to Caesar's lost love, would also figure prominently in Kent county politics during the Revolution.

2

Delaware Life Under the
Colonial Government

CAESAR RODNEY'S ENTRANCE INTO PUBLIC LIFE IS MARKED BY A HAND-written notice, dated 1755. Probably once nailed to a tree, it requested those living along the main road between Dover and Little Creek to meet at Griffith Gordon's house on April 12 for the purpose of forming a militia company. In it he exhorts those able to bear arms and "zealous to exert themselves in protection of country, liberties and property."[1] This was no call to revolution, however; the militia company was intended to fight for England in the French and Indian War. Nevertheless, the wording reflects the zeal of a young man eager to engage in the wider concerns of politics and country. Caesar, at that time, was twenty-seven years old.

The next year, in fact, he was one of twelve Delaware citizens to be commissioned a captain of "a Company of Foot Militia." His company was to be "raised in the Hundred of Dover in the said County of Kent" in a document dated April 9, 1756 and signed by Robert Hunter Morris, "Lieutenant Governor and Commander in Chief of the Province of Pennsylvania and Counties of New Castle Kent and Sussex on Delaware."[2] The company, as far as we know, never saw action.

In 1755, Caesar Rodney also conducted his first political campaign. It was successful. He was chosen high sheriff of Kent county; a post he would be reelected to for the next three years, the maximum number of consecutive terms permitted at the time. The method of choosing sheriffs and other officers in Pennsylvania and the Lower Counties was markedly different from that in Anglican Virginia, where the office was controlled by a clique of county gentry, or puritan New England, where constables were chosen by consensus of the local community. In the Lower Counties, a popular election was held in each county, after which the governor chose the winner from the two leading contenders.[3]

The office of county sheriff was a powerful one; he ran the

county elections and choose the grand jurors who, in turn, helped set the county tax rate. The sheriff was also charged with keeping peace and order within the community. The office was so popular, and apparently so lucrative, that after serving three consecutive terms a man must wait three years before he was eligible to run again.[4] Candidates for the office were prohibited from offering bribes of any sort, including liquor and entertainment. Any infraction of this rule carried a heavy fine of ten pounds, plus costs, for each offense. However, according to the Reverend Charles Inglis (the same who had stolen Polly Vining's heart away from Caesar) this ruling had little effect. In 1760, he reported, rather primly, that candidates held frequent public meetings before an election at which free liquor was the chief attraction, causing "Scenes of Drunkeness and Debauchery."[5]

One does get the impression that colonial political careers were pursued as much for social prominence as conviction. The rules governing the elections, while strict, were apparently flaunted with impunity. For instance, it was a common practice for residents of the county seat to "welcome" illiterate rural voters on the day of the election by filling out their ballots. The ballots, which were written but not secret, were then cast at the county courthouse. To be eligible to vote, a man had to be at least twenty-one and have resided in the Lower Counties at least two years. He also must own at least fifty acres of land (of which twelve must be cleared for farming), or equivalent property worth forty pounds. Voting was also mandatory; if a qualified man failed to do so, he was subject to a fine of twenty shillings.[6]

In 1758, when his third term as sheriff had expired, Caesar was made a justice of peace and judge in all lower courts. This was another powerful local office. Colonial justices not only presided over civil and criminal cases, they took depositions, issued warrants, and set the price of bread and beer. They also acted with the assessors and grand jurors to set the county tax rate. Their jurisdiction was all encompassing: in the course of a week, a single colonial judge might sit, in turn, on the orphan's court, the court of common pleas, the court of equity and the court of common sessions, despite the fact that few of them had any formal legal training. Usually, they read law with a mentor using whatever English law books were available in private libraries. An appeal of the decision of any lower court was handled by a supreme court of three judges (later four) who met twice a year in each county.[7] Technically, any decision of the colonial supreme court could be appealed in the privy court in England, but that was rarely done.

Ever since 1704, when Caesar's grandfather, William Rodeney, had served as its first speaker, Delaware had had its own legislature, a unicameral assembly that met in New Castle on October 20 and often for a second time in the spring. It was comprised of eighteen assemblymen, six from each county, elected annually on the first of October. The assemblymen were paid ten shillings a day and their legislative body was to have powers and privileges "according to the Rights of the free-born subjects of England." Interestingly, an assemblyman also had to swear that he believed in the Sacrament of the Lord's Supper, but that the "Adoration of the Virgin Mary or any other saint or the sacrifice of Mass, as they are now used in the Church of Rome are superstitious and idolatrous."[8]

A great deal of politicking went on before these elections between the "court" and "country" parties. According to Thomas McKean, an advocate of the country party, members of the "Court" party were "composed of the Governor, his officers, the expectants of office," while the "country" party was made up of "those who wished an independence of the judges and impartiality in the laws."[9]

This is admittedly a biased description, yet generally speaking, the "court" party was more closely connected with the proprietary government, whereas those in the "Country" party favored a more popular type of local government. However, individual membership shifted frequently and both parties often backed the same man. Philosophical differences were not nearly as important as local issues, family relationships, friendships, and ethnic or religious connections. Before the political climate began to heat up in the days before the Revolution, a man's primary purpose in joining a faction seemed to be to acquire a cohort of supporters.[10]

Caesar Rodney was first elected to this assembly in 1761, a week before his thirty-third birthday. Even then, he seems to have been respected by friends and opponents alike as a modest, thoughtful man, who strove to carry out his duties fairly and responsibly. He must have also had considerable political talent, for, with a few notable exceptions, he would be reelected every year thereafter.

In those days, the Three Lower Counties, like their mother colony Pennsylvania, were under the jurisdiction of a governor appointed by the Penn family. He governed with the help of an executive council, (made up of associates with close ties to the Penns) and the two provincial assemblies, one in Philadelphia and the other in New Castle, whose members were elected by the people. According to the Pennsylvania constitution of 1701, any bill passed by an assembly had to be approved by the governor before it could be enacted into law; in return, no governor or council could arbitrarily dissolve an assembly he didn't agree with. The Pennsylvania charter also required all laws to be sent to the Crown within five years of passage for approval; if declared invalid within six months they were considered annulled. This so-called "Royal Disallowance" was unpopular and usually ignored: there is no evidence that any laws from the Three Lower Counties were ever submitted to the Crown.

In Philadelphia, the governor and his council, primarily interested in protecting the financial interest of the Penn family, frequently clashed with the assembly over questions such as the proprietors' refusal to take proper measures for the defense of the colony, and what was seen as the unfair exemption of their lands from taxation.[11] In time, these disputes would become so bitter that Benjamin Franklin would go to England to try to persuade the Crown to do away with proprietary rule altogether. He wanted the king to rule Pennsylvania directly, arguing that the system of paying quitrents to the Penns was appropriating money that should have gone directly into the royal treasury.

The Delaware assembly showed little interest in such controversies. Their relations with the Penn government seems to have been so serene that some Pennsylvania assemblymen accused the governor of showing favoritism, particularly as he had not required Delaware to share in the burden of defense. "Their lands are rich" these assemblymen complained, ". . . many of their farmers [are] wealthy, and [they] have all the Advantages of our Market."[12]

With the exception of two who owned property there, Benjamin Chew and William Till, Pennsylvania's council members rarely came to Delaware. The governor, himself, traveled only as far as New Castle for the meetings of the Delaware Assembly, and lodged at a nearby inn to wait for bills to be submitted for his signature. He also met with individual assemblymen, made an occasional suggestion and approved the speaker of their choice. While he had the power to veto bills, he rarely did, possibly because the assembly also approved his annual stipend.[13]

The Penns' preoccupation with their own economic well-being reflected England's mercantile policy in general, which held that the principal role of a colony was to bolster Britain's economic and commercial supremacy.[14] From Delaware's point of view, this policy was a disaster, resulting in a continual drain of natural resources; a balance of trade that was always in Britain's favor; and a severe lack of hard currency. In fact, by the mid eighteenth century, much of the Peninsula's sandy soil had been depleted by tobacco farming and her majestic white oaks and Atlantic white cedars had been cut for Britain's shipbuilding industry. Delaware, a small colony without Pennsylvania's wide trading network, Virginia's tobacco or New England's furs, had little to sell to England directly. Farmers like the Rodneys had to sell wheat to the West Indies in order to acquire enough currency to import goods from England.[15] The general lack of currency was further complicated by the fact that eighteenth-century money was easily debased by counterfeiters who shaved off slivers of silver for their own enrichment resulting in coins whose weight rarely equaled the face value.

Money, in fact, was a very complicated affair in the eighteenth century. In 1761 one Henry Callister, a Chester Pennsylvania merchant, complained in a letter: "Our money . . . is imaginary, and will forever fluctuate with the course of exchange."[16] He had good reason to complain. Each American colony had its own currency, which was not only different from Britain's, but also different from that used in the trading ports of the West Indies. Delaware's so-called "New Castle money" was supposed to be on a par with Pennsylvania's, yet was apparently worth 5–10 percent less in the actual market place, since it cost a hundred and ten pounds of Delaware money to buy a hundred pounds of Pennsylvania currency.[17] At the same time, between 1758 and 1760 one needed 172 Delaware bills, versus 161 Pennsylvania bills to buy 100 pounds British sterling.[18] Although both Britain and the colonies counted their money as pounds, shillings and pence, the premier coin of the Atlantic trading world as a whole was the Spanish peso or piastra. It was also known as the "piece of eight" and later, the dollar.

On May 7, 1759, the Delaware Assembly voted to issue £27,000 in paper money and Caesar Rodney, Jacob Kollock and William Armstrong were appointed to oversee its preparation. Of this sum, £20,000 was for the use of the State while £7000 was to be set aside to "demonstrate [Delaware's] loyalty . . . to the best of Kings, and . . . exert ourselves with the utmost vigor, to the annoying [of] his Majesty's enemies, and restoring peace to America. . . ."[19] The act provided for 59,000 bills of varied denominations between one and twenty shillings, all bearing the arms of the King.

The £7000 earmarked for the use of the king was not sent to him directly but turned over to a group of commissioners that also included Caesar Rodney. They were to use the money to recruit and equip 180 men to fight in the French and Indian War. While these troops were raised and apparently left the colony, the extent of their service is not known.[20]

Britain, hoping to discourage the issuance of colonial paper money, had already passed a law forbidding it in 1752 and did so again in 1760. Neither action seems to have had any effect. By that time, colonial tradesmen had begun to prefer paper money to the old system of personal credit and barter. A paper bill had its value clearly printed on the face, thus circumventing the problem of debased and devalued coins.

In 1760, George II died and his grandson, George III ascended to the throne of England at the age of twenty-two, the first of the Hanovers to be born in England and the first to speak English without a German accent.

After Britain's triumph in the French and Indian War, the Whig statesman, William Pitt, decreed that it was in Britain's interest for Parliament to repay the colonies some of the money they had donated for the king's use, ". . . as the active vigour and strenuous efforts of the respective Provinces shall justly appear to merit."[21] Delaware's share of this was £3044 sterling, which translated to £5250 in Delaware currency. Pitts' action was symptomatic of ideas that had begun to surface in England. In reaction to George II's high-handedness and the pervasive corruption of his ministers, some men had begun to question the notion that traditional social heirarchies had been ordained by God; an idea that also began to cross the Atlantic on ships entering Philadelphia. Published in newspapers like "The Philadelphia Packet," these ideas were carried to the Lower Counties by the shallops that plied the Delaware coast. The "Philadelphia Packet" also regularly carried Delaware news and advertising.

Before 1765, life in Lower Counties seemed as pleasant, and generally uneventful, as it had always been, yet the seeds of change had already begun to sprout. Delaware's population, although less than forty-thousand, was growing and diversifying. While the town of Dover had only about fifty families, it became an important hub of activity, serving as the major port of St. Jones Creek, and the market town for all of the area's farmers and tradesmen. It was also the seat of Kent county and stood at the center of a major road system; two attributes that would draw it into the political activity of the coming years.[22]

The French observer, St. John de Crèvecoeur, writing on the eve of the revolution, described the English colonists and their descendents as "western pilgrims, who are carrying along with them that great mass of arts, sciences, vigor and industry" He saw the American as "a new man, who acts upon new principles; [and] must therefore entertain new ideas, and form new opinions. . . ."[23] Yet, until the momentous events of 1765 began to fray the ancestral ties with England, it is doubtful that such qualities were recognized by the Americans themselves. A man like Caesar Rodney still thought of himself as an Englishman, living in an essentially English society that was closely connected to the mother country by its culture, its history, its heritage and its language.

3

Sugar and Stamps

IN 1762, CAESAR RODNEY WAS THIRTY-FOUR YEARS OLD, LIVING AT Lebanon Farm with his brother Thomas and becoming ever more involved with the colonial government. He and a fellow member of the assembly, Thomas McKean, had been commissioned to collect, revise and publish the laws of the Three Lower Counties. In October of the following year, 1763, he was elected register of wills for Kent county; a post he would hold for five years, and was once again elected sheriff in 1764. At this point, he was also a judge, a trustee of the loan office, and recorder of deeds; all positions that would come to be known as ROW offices, presumably because they occupied a row of offices at the County Court House.[1]

As yet, there were no intimations of trouble with Britain. After several decades of occupation by family employees, the post of Governor of Pennsylvania had recently been given to John Penn, a member of the third generation of the proprietary family. John Penn seems to have been a cautious and somewhat passive man, primarily interested in increasing the prosperity of Philadelphia and protecting his own position. He was the son of Richard Penn, then junior proprietor and nephew of Thomas Penn, the senior proprietor. That these Penns were Anglican, not Quaker as their famous ancestor had been, may have smoothed their relations with the predominently Anglican Delaware assembly.[2]

Seventeen sixty-three was also the year in which the French finally surrendered their claims to territory in North America. Britain had won the French and Indian War, but her perennial conflicts with France and Spain had left her deeply in debt. Nevertheless, the new prime minister, George Grenville, was determined to keep a large British army in the colonies; to remind the Americans of their colonial status as much as to insure against further hostilities.

The cost of maintaining such a force, however, was far more than Britain was willing to pay. Grenville's seemingly simple, yet potentially explosive, solution was to enforce old tax acts, which he saw as both a lucrative source of income and a symbol of colonial obedience to the Crown. He began with the lapsed Molasses Act of 1733, which called for a tax of six pence on every imported gallon of molasses. It was a levy ignored by the American colonists; while technically conceding Britain's right to regulate foreign trade, they usually disregarded any tax that might inhibit business with the West Indies.[3] Now, as the Molasses Act became the Sugar Act of 1764, Grenville ordered formerly lax custom officials back to their posts and commissioned British Naval officers of the North American squadron to act as their deputies.

It has been said that the Sugar Act was the only successful tax Parliament ever imposed on the American colonies, raising more than enough revenue to support British customs operations while stirring surprisingly little reaction. Even those Massachusetts radicals who tried to make an issue of it had little success; apparently molasses was just too important to the New England economy.[4]

In Delaware, however, planters like the Rodneys were seriously affected, since so much of their corn and wheat were sold by Philadelphia merchants to the sugar-rich West Indies. The new tax slowed trade and caused prices to fall, hurting not only the farmers, but also the carters and shallopmen who transported the grain to market. Eventually, as the planters found themselves with less money to spend, seemingly unconnected trades like clockmaking and silversmithing suffered as well.[5]

Perhaps because of this, John Dickinson, a neighbor of the Rodneys' on Jones Neck, wrote a pamphlet in the fall of 1764, supporting the proprietors as a buffer between the colonies and the Crown. Subsequently, the Delaware Assembly voted unanimously to have Benjamin Chew, a member of John Penn's council, express to the king their satisfaction with the status quo. While these actions particularly galled Philadelphians like Benjamin Franklin and the members of his antiproprietary party, the Delawareans, apparently, feared the unpredictable power of the British Parliament far more than they did the Penns.

In 1764, Caesar was again appointed a justice of the peace to add to his other offices, and he and Tommy moved to Dover. Tommy, then twenty years old, was already running Caesar's personal affairs for he tells us that, "my brother . . . got the Offices moved to Dover, and I [moved] with him. . . ."[6] Tommy, apparently, also took to "his station as a young man about town and one of the ruling gentry. He frequently sought the ministrations of his barber, killed time about the taverns, and courted the girls. . . . If he had any paid employment, it was an occasional job as surveyor and a 'viewer' in land litigation."[7]

We do not know exactly where they were living, but it was probably somewhere on Courthouse Square, now known as the Green. At that time, Dover's official boundaries were North Street, South Steet, West Street and St. Jones Creek, but in the mid-eighteenth century, less than a quarter of this roughly one hundred acre site had been built upon. About twenty-five individuals owned the lots around the perimeter of the Square and on either side of King Street (now State street), that ran two blocks to the south and one to the north. The open center of the square was used as the site of public gatherings and celebrations, such as the annual spring and fall market fairs. In the meantime, it was grazed by wandering livestock. (People rarely penned their livestock in the eighteenth century, they simply nicked their ears as a means of identification and let them run free.)

With the exception of a scattering of small frame or log houses, most of the land outside the town was owned by the same people who lived on the square and rented to local farmers for crops or pasture land.[8]

Beside his official duties, Caesar, at this time, had many family worries and responsibilities. After his mother died in 1763, having survived all the Rodneys of her generation, Byfield was left to him. During the next two years, 1764 and 1765, both his brother Daniel, whose "idle" and "indolent" life had been much on Caesar's mind, and Elizabeth, the sister that was just two years Caesar's junior, would also die.

Their deaths must have imposed a heavy emotional burden on the young man in what would prove to be a time of riotous political upheaval. For 1765 was also the year in which, the British Parliament, heady with the success of the Sugar Act, passed the Stamp Act, setting off a virtual explosion in the colonies.

The Stamp Act was pervasive. It not only taxed business documents, such as newspapers, professional licenses, and ship clearances, but, by levying fees on diplomas, deeds, wills, and other personal legal documents, it adversely affected landholders, merchants, lawyers, judges and printers; men who had faithfully supported Britain in the French and Indian War. Even the Penns, Pennsylvania's powerful proprietary family, felt the impact. All these men saw this tax as having little to do with foreign trade. Rather, it was a serious impediment to business within the colonies themselves; matters they considered to be well outside of Britain's jurisdiction. As loyal Englishmen, they felt profoundly betrayed.[9]

The act was passed in March and set to go into effect in November. By May, the reaction had begun. Patrick Henry rose in the Virginia House of Burgesses in violent objection, even going so far as to suggest that the king should reflect seriously on the fate of Charles I and Julius Caesar. Virginians, he asserted, were entitled to all the rights of Englishmen, especially the right to be taxed only "by themselves, or by persons chosen by themselves to represent them."[10]

This, of course, would become the germ of the conflict. What was the proper role of Parliament vis-à-vis her American colonies? The English view was that Parliament had the right to legislate for the entire empire; they had little regard for the rights of colonial assemblies, treating them rather like the principals of chartered companies. The Americans, on the other hand, believed strongly that their assemblies superceded Parliament in all matters concerning their own internal affairs.[11]

Of Patrick Henry's seven specific objections, only four were actually approved by the house of burgesses. They rejected as too extreme his accusation that Parliament was deliberately trying to destroy American freedom; nor could they agree that Virginians were not bound to obey *any* tax act levied by Parliament. They also refused to endorse the notion that any man who failed to support Henry's objections was an enemy of "this, his majesty's colony." The newspapers of the time, however, printed all of Henry's statements as if they had been officially approved, adding further fuel to the flames.[12]

Other colonies soon followed Virginia's lead. Patrick Henry's heated call for no taxation without representation became a rallying cry, galvanizing ordinary Americans, and causing widespread uprisings. In Philadelphia at the end of May, when it became known that John Hughes, a member of the Pennsylvania Assembly and close associate of Benjamin Franklin had been appointed to distribute the official stamps, a mob surrounded his house and burned him in effigy. In Boston, on August 14, an ugly mob tore down the business office of the man designated to distribute stamps in Massachusetts, and ten days later, moved on to attack an officer of vice-admiralty court and the comptroller of customs. They even stormed the office of Thomas Hutchinson, the chief justice and lieutenant governor of Massachusetts.[13]

The fact that so many ordinary Americans took part in the rioting reflected the fundamental difference that had already arisen between British and colonial society. Here, ordinary men had become so used to running their own affairs that they saw little need to defer to their betters. The European who came to America, according to de Crèvecoeur, immediately began ". . . to forget his former servitude and dependence. His heart involuntarily swells and glows; this first swell inspires him with those new thoughts which constitute an American."[14] However, the Stamp Act riots soon became so fierce and unruly that some Americans who fundamentally opposed the act were actually frightened into siding with Britain.[15]

The Stamp Act rebellion was also important in that it was the first time the colonies had acted in concert in a dispute with Great Britain. Up to that time, as George Read, then a young Delaware lawyer practicing in New Castle, wrote to an acquaintance in England in July 1765, "political disputes were confined to parties formed in the respective colonies." He went on to warn: "They are now all resolved into one, and that with the mother-country."[16] In fact, George Read's ambivalent feelings as an American Englishman toward the conflict seems typical of many of his compatriots.

> The stamp-act you made on your side of the water hath raised such a ferment among us . . . that I know not when it will subside. . . . I sincerely wish the furious zeal of the populace may not be resented by your people in power as to prevent them from lending a candid ear to our just complaints. . . . If this law should stand unrepealed, or, indeed, any other enactment . . . imposing an internal tax . . . the colonists will entertain an opinion that they are to become the slaves of Great Britain. . . ."[17]

On September 17, an obviously nervous John Hughes wrote Governor John Penn that he had not yet received the necessary stamps or commissions to carry out his assignment. Two weeks later, on October 3, he confessed in a letter to John Dickinson that he was afraid to take charge for fear of being tarred and feathered. Protestors were even threatening to sink the ship that had brought the official documents to New Castle. Later that month, after his house was again surrounded by angry mobs, John Hughes publicly pledged not to exercise his duties as official stamp distributor.[18]

Not surprisingly, those who had consistently opposed Parliamentary taxing power were now eager to capitalize on the overheated political climate. One of these was John Dickinson, who had long mistrusted direct Parliamentary rule. He had a problem, however. When, in September 1765, Massachusetts' call to convene a Congress in New York to protest the Stamp Act reached Delaware, the scheduled fall meeting of the assembly was still a month away. Delegates would need to be chosen immediately, yet those eager to join the protest knew that, however much John Penn might want to curb Parliamentary power, he would never call a special session for such a purpose. Thus, Dickinson and others arranged to have the assemblymen from each county sign a letter nominating three men: Jacob Kollock of Sussex, speaker of the last assembly and a supporter of Benjamin Franklin's antiproprietary movement; Caesar Rodney of Kent; and Thomas McKean of New Castle. The wording of the "popular indignation" that was expressed in those three separate, "spontaneous" nominations was suspiciously similiar.[19]

The Stamp Act Congress opened in New York city on October 7. As it turned out, the seventy-three year old Jacob Kollock did not make the trip, pleading poor health and pressing duties in New Castle where he had once again been chosen speaker for the fall assembly. His absence left Delaware's participation in the congress in the hands of two relatively young men; Caesar Rodney, who would celebrate his thirty-seventh birthday on the day the Congress opened and his thirty-one year old associate, Thomas McKean.

McKean and Rodney would become close compatriots in the stormy years to come, even though they were from markedly different backgrounds. Rodney, as we have seen, was as close as one could get to being an American aristocrat. Thomas McKean, on the other hand, was the son of an Irish immigrant to Chester county, Pennsylvania. In a later portrait by Gilbert Stuart, he is depicted as a stern, rather austere Scotsman. He was certainly determined, as well as somewhat vain and ambitious, and his Scotch-Irish background had left him with precious little sympathy for the British.

After studying law in New Castle under his cousin, David Finney, McKean had been admitted to the Delaware bar at the age of twenty-one, and had served as a deputy prosecuting attorney in Sussex county. His connection to David Finney's father, John Finney, a member of the Delaware Assembly, helped him get elected to that body in 1762. He would serve until 1779, take a prominent part in the coming revolution and go on to become both chief justice and governor of Pennsylvania.

From the start, the more aristocratic Caesar seemed far more reluctant than than McKean to embark on a serious quarrel with Britain. He was a man who always combined strong principle with balanced judgement; qualities that would earn him the respect of Delawareans on all sides of the political spectrum. The people of Delaware repeatedly sent him to protest against what they saw as Britain's infringements of their rights, precisely because they knew him to be essentially conservative in his respect for tradition and authority.

Typically, while both Caesar and McKean entered into the work

Thomas McKean, Courtesy Delaware State Museums, Dover.

of the Congress boldly and with enthusiasm, taking an active part in drafting the final petition,[20] Caesar confided to his brother Tommy that writing the declaration of grievances was "one of the most Difficult Tasks I ever yet see Undertaken, as We had Carefully to avoid any Infringment of the prerogative of the Crown, and the Power of Parliament, and Yet in Duty bound fully to Assert the Rights & Privileges of the Colonies."[21] Nevertheless, both Caesar and McKean actively supported the radical James Otis for chairman of the congress, although Otis would lose out to his fellow delegate from Massachusetts; the conservative Timothy Ruggles.

The Stamp Act was scheduled to take effect on November 1, 1765. Long before that time, however, virtually all the men who had been appointed to distribute the hated stamps had been forced to resign or otherwise prevented from exercising their commissions. Everywhere merchants refused to import British goods. At first, all those whose business operations required stamps closed rather than use them. By the beginning of 1766, however, many had resumed operations without stamps in open defiance of the act. In fact, except for a brief period in Georgia, Britain did not collect a single penny in revenue under the Stamp Act.

In December 1765, Caesar wrote a Mr. Wilmer, a relation of his half sister, Sally, about the work of the Stamp Act Congress. He stressed once again that the "members took into consideration the British Constitution, and the Rights and priviledges of the colonists . . . as subjects of Great Britain."[22] The final petition sent to the Crown asking that the Stamp Act be repealed, "dutifully, yet most firmly," asserting the right of the colonies to be exempt from taxes imposed by Parliament. It also insisted on the "Privelege of trial by their peers," and threatened to suspend all orders of British goods, except only the most necessary articles, until the Stamp Act had been repealed.[23]

At the close of the congress, a curious thing happened. Chairman Timothy Ruggles and certain other delegates refused to sign the final petition. Thomas McKean was so incensed by this that he accused them of unfaithfulness and cowardice, causing an outraged Ruggles to challenge him to a duel. The fiery McKean promptly accepted, but when he turned up on the field of battle the following morning, he found that Ruggles had already left New York. (McKean's suspicions about Ruggles' true allegiance would prove correct; he later joined the British army as a brigadier general.)[24]

On his way home to Delaware, McKean boldly informed the people of New Jersey that their representative, one Robert Ogden, had not only refused to sign but had asked McKean's father-in-law, Joseph Borden, not to mention the fact. According to McKean, Ogden, the speaker of the New Jersey Assembly, had wanted Borden, who was also a New Jersey assemblyman, to keep McKean quiet. McKean said he only agreed to remain silent "unless the question was put to him," but having been asked in "two or three different towns, the names of the Gentlemen who had not signed . . . [he] gave them without hesitation." When Ogden was subsequently burned in effigy and replaced as speaker, he, too, challenged McKean to a duel. McKean responded by going to Burlington where "he tarried two nights without hearing any menaces whatsoever."[25]

The anti-Stamp Act ferment continued through the winter. The grand jury that was scheduled to sit in New Castle in February 1766, refused to do so unless the court agreed to let them proceed without using stamped paper, and, in March, a riotous crowd gathered in Lewes, demanding that both that county's officials and the collector of customs disregard the Stamp Act. Stamps were burned throughout the colonies, causing the captains assigned to carry them into American ports to refuse to do so for fear of attacks on themselves and their ships.[26]

On February 5th, Caesar's cousin John, the son of his father's half brother, William Rodney, wrote that he had seen "favourable Accounts from England in the last papers, with regard to American affairs. . . ." The "best piece of news . . ." however, would be the repeal of the Stamp Act. For "should the parliament resent the Misbehaviour of the Colonies & take it into their heads to Enforce the Act, . . . it would certainly terminate in Our Ruin for the Consequence I apprehend would be, Either to submit to that detestable Act, or to be Envolved in an open rebellion, both of which is Shocking even to think of. . . ."[27]

The rumors John Rodney had heard proved true; Parliament backed down and the Stamp Act was repealed in the spring of 1766, less than five months after it had become law. The king, under pressure from British merchants who had been hurt by colonial nonimportation acts, also replaced George Grenville as prime minister with the Marquis of Rockingham. Yet British power plays and tax schemes were still in the air. Immediately after repealing the Stamp Act, Parliament passed a "Declaratory Act" giving itself the right to "bind the colonies and People of America . . . in all cases whatsoever."[28] It was evidently designed to resolve the issue of American constitutional rights in Parliament's favor forever.

Meanwhile, the Delaware Assembly chose Caesar, George Read and Thomas McKean, a trio still in their thirties, to draft an address to the king, thanking him for the repeal and expressing their loyal sentiments. Their letter was based on a resolution drawn up by the assembly the previous fall and sent to London in June of 1766. It reminded the Crown that Delaware had contributed men and money to the French and Indian war and that her people were entitled to rights as loyal British subjects. It also insisted that the colonial legislature must give their consent before any new taxes could be levied, and objected to any extension of the powers of the admiralty court as subverting the peoples' right to be tried by a jury of their peers.[29]

This document was sent to the Three Lower Counties' agent in England, a man called Denys DeBerdt. In September 1766, he wrote to Rodney, McKean and Read that he had ". . . received your Packett . . . containing an address to his majesty which I put into the hands of Lord Shelburn our new Secretary of State who presented it to his Majesty & was very graciously received. I told His Lordship it appeared to me, wrote with the most honest symplicity of any I had seen, he said . . . the King was so well pleased with it that he read it over twice."[30] While it was hardly a revolutionary tirade, the lower counties had, nevertheless, put themselves on record as objecting to taxation without representation and supporting local trials by jury, a full ten years before the revolution.

4

More Troubles with Trade

In THE SPRING OF 1766, A TURNOVER IN GOVERNMENT GAVE ENGLAND both a new prime minister, the duke of Grafton, and a new chancellor of the exchequer, Charles Townshend. At that time, the earl of Shelburne, referred to in Denys DeBerdt's letter, was secretary of state for the "Southern Department," another name for colonial affairs. He was sympathetic to the American point of view, but, as a member of the House of Lords, had little influence in Parliament, particularly when it came to economic priorities.

Early in 1767, Townshend boasted he could easily raise enough revenue to support a British force in America by taxing imports, which he characterized as an "external" tax as opposed to an "internal" tax like the Stamp Act. Even George Grenville, now leader of the opposition, was dubious, but despite his warning that the Americans would "laugh at . . . your distinctions about regulations of trade," the "Townshend Acts" became law in July 1767.[1]

Triumphant at the defeat of the Stamp Act, the Americans were convinced that Britain had learned a lesson and would no longer attempt to impose any policy unpopular on their side of the water. They did not, however, realize how much that repeal was resented in England. Simply put, the English thought it the duty of the colonies to support a British force in America as their share of the defense of the Empire, and bitterly accused the Americans of protecting their own pockets by not doing so.[2]

The Townshend Acts levied a tax on all glass, paper, pasteboard, white and red lead (painter's colors), and tea imported to the colonies; establishing a customs board in Boston to collect the duties. Since, tea was the only item on the list that could not be made at home, the tax would not have been a serious burden for the colonies, nor would it have raised much money for Britain. The Americans, however, viewed it as an insidious first step of a fiscal policy that could make continuing and growing demands on their purse. At the same time, many hesitated to resist for fear of once again unleashing the sort of excesses that marked the Stamp Act riots.

Meanwhile, chancellor of the exchequer Townshend died and was replaced as by Lord North, a strong Tory who was fiercely loyal to the king. His appointment gave George III a powerful "royal block" in Parliament that immediately added two potentially explosive clauses on to the acts. The first suspended New York's assembly until they agreed to supply the British army as required under the Quartering Act of 1765, and the second decreed that all revenues collected through enforcement of the Townshend Acts would go toward the support of Britain's colonial officials. This last, of course, would have effectively freed John Penn from any reliance upon the good will of the Delaware Assembly. Little wonder that many viewed the Townshend Acts as a thinly disguised effort to reassert Parliament's constitutional power according to the hated "Declaratory Act."[3]

Nevertheless, the acts stirred little concern in Pennsylvania, possibly because Benjamin Franklin's antiproprietary party, in their zeal to do away with the Penns, were reluctant to find fault with Parliament. That Franklin's effort lacked support in the Lower Counties is evident from a letter Caesar received from his old friend John Vining on September 8, 1766: "I can tell you for a truth that B. Franklin has sounded the ministry & Council respecting a Change of Government & that he was informed by the President that if he should be hardy enough to offer the petition for that purpose again it would be taken notice of in a very Different way upon which he went to Spain for his health. . . ."[4] Even so, Franklin pressed on until firmly informed by Lord Shelburne in August of 1768 that there was no chance of a royal government for Pennsylvania and her Lower Counties.

That fall, a vigorous attack on the Townshend duties appeared in a Philadelphia newspaper. Although published anonymously under the title, "Letters from a Farmer in Pennsylvania to the Inhabitants of the British Colonies," it was common knowledge in Philadelphia, as well as in the Lower Counties, that the author was Caesar's friend and neighbor, John Dickinson.[5]

John Dickinson's characterization of himself as a "Pennsylvania Farmer" was a typical eighteenth-century conceit, apparently intended to project a gentlemanly detachment to worldly affairs. Yet Dickinson, at the time, was a prosperous Philadelphia lawyer and a member of the Pennsylvania Assembly; hardly a disinterested bystander.

When Dickinson's close friend, George Read, joined his protest, the influence of these two men was sufficient in the Lower Counties to convince the 1768 Delaware Assembly to reestablish the so-

John Dickinson, Courtesy Delaware State Museums, Dover.

called "Committee of Correspondence" that had written the king
to thank him for the repeal of the Stamp Act: Caesar Rodney,
George Read and Thomas McKean. Once again this triumvirate
sent a letter to Parliament, asserting their right to tax themselves
through their own assembly and objecting to the idea of sending
anyone caught smuggling in violation of the Townshend duties back
to England for trial. They also protested the dissolution of the New
York Assembly, correctly perceiving it as a potential attack on the
authority of all colonial assemblies.

Caesar, however, now forty years old, was having serious problems of his own. In June of 1768 he set out from his house in Dover on a journey to Philadelphia. On the seventh of the month, he wrote his brother Tommy that after arriving in New Castle, one of his horses had fallen ill, forcing him to borrow a saddle and bridle and continue his journey astride "the other horse." His coachman, John, was to follow with the carriage as soon as the first horse was able, although, Caesar added, he had "little reason to expect he will live. . . ."

Caesar had an urgent, not to say ominous, reason to make this trip.

> I got to Philadelphia on Saturday and on Munday applied to the Doctors Concerning the Sore on my Nose, who all upon Examination pronounce it a Cancer, and that it will be necessary I Should go through a Small Cource of Physick, and then to Extract it by a Costick or by Cutting it out, all which (to me) is a Dreadfull undertaking . . . it is impossible for me now to determine when you may . . . Expect to see me in Kent again, If ever,—as (no Doubt) it will be attended with Danger . . . Some advise me to [consult] one person, Some another, and some to go Imediately to England—however a day or two will determine me. . . ."[6]

The following week, he wrote again:

> The Governor [John Penn] Joyns with the Rest of my friends in pressing Me hard to go Immediately to England But has Assured me That I Shall have Liberty to appoint . . . Whom I please to Conduct My offices—upon Which I Informed him that I should appoint you.

Governor Penn, Mr. Allen and Benjamin Chew (all members of the proprietary government in Philadelphia) sent him to ex-governor James Hamilton, John Penn's predecessor, who apparently had also had skin cancer. Hamilton told Caesar that "it was a Cancer and in a Dangerous place—That he Thought the only Chance I had was to go to England." Nevertheless, he gave him some of his own medicines and pledged to visit Caesar every day to see if they were working "in the Same manner as . . . with him. . . ."

Caesar had put himself under the care of the eminent Philadelphia physician, Thomas Bond, telling Tommy that "If this fail in Making a cure and does not put me in a Worse Scituation than I now am I Shall go to England in two or three Weeks. . . . I am quite prepared for the Voige, Except that I must first Return to Kent to Settle a few Matters. . . ."[7]

On June 23, he described the operation, which after the custom of the day, was probably performed at Caesar's lodging. "The Doctr Extracted the hard Crusted Matter which had risen so high—And it has Left a hole I believe Quite to the Bone, and Extends for Length from the Corner of my Eye above half way down my Nose— Such a Sore must take some Considerable time to Cure up—if ever it does However Since it has been Extracted, I am perfectly easy as to any pain—And Mr Hamilton (Who continues to see me every day) is of Opinion as well as the Doctr that a Cure will be perfected."[8]

In view of Tommy's later reputation as a revolutionary hothead, his answer to his brother positively effuses admiration for the officials of Pennsylvania's proprietary government. Telling Caesar that the advice he has received "Seems to be the most prudent that coul'd have been Dictated to you in those Circumstances . . ." He is also grateful "to hear of Your being Treated with so much Kindness . . . in particular I am Charm'd with the Candid, Sincere and jenerous behaviour and advice of Mr. Penn and Mr. Hamilton . . . which Speaks Them worthy of more praise than My pen Dare Venture to Express. . . ."[9]

Possibly because of the growing controversy with Britain, Caesar did not go to England for further treatment. It would have made little difference if he had, although he probably did not know that at the time. Nevertheless, all of his subsequent actions, private and public, must be seen against the fact that he had a facial cancer that would continue to spread over one side of his face and ultimately kill him. Nor was it his only health problem. Around this same time, Tommy wrote in an entry in the Rodney geneology that Caesar's "spirits have abated of late years by having much sickness. He has had the astma [asthma] twelve years, but has been almost relieved lately by wearing amber beeds about his neck."[10]

Meanwhile, America's English ally, Lord Shelburne, had been eased out of office and his position, now called secretary for colonial affairs, filled by Lord Hillsborough. Hillsborough, instead of biding his time and letting the Townshend duties controversy evaporate naturally, as it now showed every sign of doing, immediately overreacted. After dismissing the Dickinson letters as "extremely wild," he dissolved the Massachusetts legislature for refusing to rescind a similar pamphlet, and ordered her to supply British troops and obey every letter of the laws of trade.

Of course, such actions merely strengthened the hand of the Massachusetts radicals. After simmering for several months, the conflict finally exploded on June 10, 1768, while Caesar was in Philadelphia consulting Dr. Bond. On that day, the British custom officers, backed by a fifty-gun warship called the *Romney*, suddenly seized John Hancock's sloop *Liberty* for loading goods without a permit. The citizens of Boston immediately rose up in protest, sacking the houses of the British commissioners and forcing them to flee to an island in Boston Harbor, where they vowed they would stay until British troops were assigned to Boston for their protection. By October, four additional regiments of British troops had landed in Boston, and the city placed under military occupation until 1770. Not surprisingly, the occupying British soldiers were constantly harassed by the citizenry, especially after it became known that Hillsborough had ordered the troops to Boston a full two days before the riot, validating the radical view that he had purposely instigated the confrontation.[11]

Furious, the Bostonians placed an embargo on the importation of British goods. Parliament once again reacted spitefully. They passed the so-called February Resolves of 1769 accusing Massachusetts of taking actions that were "illegal, unconstitutional, and derogatory of the rights of the Crown and Parliament of Great Britain." They also demanded, under an obscure statute dating back to the time of Henry VIII, that certain Massachusetts leaders be brought to England and tried for treason, further inciting colonial outrage.[12] Virginia and South Carolina immediately rallied to the support of Massachusetts by adopting nonimportation agreements of their own. By May, apparently under pressure from British merchants, Lord Hillsborough backed down and sent a letter to the colonial governors promising not to impose any new taxes. His concession had little effect on the colonial assemblies, however, because Hillsborough felt obliged to reiterate Parliament's assertion of power over America. The embargo continued to spread.

It reached Delaware in August 1769, a full year after the original boycott of Boston. A proposition was passed in the Delaware Assembly forbidding merchants to import British goods or have any dealings with British traders. Anyone caught in violation would have his name published in newspaper as a betrayer of the American cause.

John Vining, then speaker of the Delaware Assembly, also wrote Peyton Randolph, his counterpart in the Virginia House of Burgesses, promising that anyone caught selling embargoed goods would be reported to a newly formed "Committee of Inspection," with George Read as chairman. Violators would be required to apologize publicly, and give over their proceeds to the poor.

Philadelphia, however, proved reluctant to abide by the boycott, and the northern Delaware ports of Wilmington and New Castle even more so. All three towns, of course, were strongly dependent on British trade. When the merchants of the upper Chesapeake Bay adopted a more relaxed position, the assembly feared that Delaware merchants would abandon their usual trade routes through Philadelphia in favor of Maryland ports just across the Peninsula. Consequently, George Read, on August 17, 1769, wrote an open letter to the citizens of New Castle County. Some traders, he said, "tired of what they call virtuous attempts to restore freedom to America" were trying to dissolve the nonimportation agreements. He exhorted them to forgo "trifling inconvenience in hopes of greater advantage," arguing that the colonies' only hope to secure fair treatment was to support one another.[13]

Meanwhile, life in Kent county went on pretty much as usual. A year after his operation, Caesar was considering the order of a new carriage. A carriage maker in Philadelphia named William Tod wrote him in August of 1769, that a "Mrs. Magdaline Divine informed me . . . that you had seen her pheaton . . . [and] had some thoughts of having such a one built . . ." adding that "there is not a gentleman in all the Lower Counties, nor in this place that I woud chuse to do business with before you."[14]

Mr. Tod did build Caesar a phaeton, (a four wheel buggy with one or two seats facing forward and a folding top that could be raised in bad weather) but he could not recommend the horses Caesar had looked at "on account of there ages. . . ." In truth, he had already sold them to "a gentleman who with great impatience was waiting to hear your determination."[15]

Caesar had done business with Mr. Tod before. In November of 1767, he had suggested that Caesar's coat of arms would "make a very pretty figure upon your chariot. . . ." His book of heraldry had "been lent out" however, so he was not sure how it looked.[16] In fact, the ancient Rodney coat of arms, as described in the language of heraldry, was: "Or, three eagles displayed purpure."[17] Such aristocratic English symbols were evidently still important to Mr. Rodney and his compatriots.

By October, Caesar was in New Castle for the annual meeting of assembly where he was elected speaker. Tommy, meanwhile, had returned to Dover after a two-week trip to Philadelphia. On October 29, he wrote Caesar a letter that gives us a cryptic glimpse into Delaware politics of the time. "Willy Rodney" he writes, "has Declined sitting up for the Sherriff's office . . . and is for Setting up Crawford Rees Who is Very anctious about it and . . . weits to see the members before making a positive Diclaration—how he may Succeed I Know not—but the project appears Very absurd to me."[18]

(Willy Rodney was Caesar's cousin, the son of his father's older half brother.)

Around this time Caesar introduced a proposition to forbid the further importation of slaves into the province; it was defeated nine votes to seven.[19] The fact that all five delegates from Kent county supported the measure has been interpreted by some as indicating that this was merely an effort to control the supply, and therefore the price that Kent farmers received when they sold slaves to neighboring counties.[20] It is true that the farmers of Kent county had a surfeit of slaves. It is also true that owning slaves in Pennsylvania and Delaware was not always economically advantageous; they had to be fed and cared for during a winter of idleness that lasted at least two months longer than in the south. Nevertheless, the fact that the idea of curtailing slavery would resurface in 1775 and 1776, indicates that owning another human being was beginning to become a ticklish moral issue for political leaders who so fervently defended their own liberty.

It must be said, however, that neither Rodney ever suggested that slavery should be abolished altogether. Thomas was on record as believing that negroes were created by nature for slavery and the humbler tasks of life,[21] and in an early campaign speech, Caesar asked, sarcastically, if the people would vote for his opponent, a man who favored the emancipation of slaves, many of whom had been purchased at high prices.

This same speech fragment indicates a bit of his campaign style as well as his thinking in these years before the revolution. At a time when the idea of independence was far from his mind, he, nevertheless, stressed that "all freeholders under a British Government have that inestimable privilege of making the Laws by which they are to be governed. . . ." He then attacked his opponent: should not the people, he asked, be careful as to who they choose to govern them and not choose a man known to be a rogue in his private dealings? Would not such a person sell his country for a good living? Why vote for a man who would ruin another man's character by prosecuting him in court for only two or three hundred pounds, or favor construction of a new road in the county when taxes for the purposes were not available?[22]

Caesar evidently saw himself as a moderate, despite his support of the radicals in the Stamp Act Congress, and his participation as a member of the "Committee of Correspondance" that had informed Parliament of Delaware's unhappiness with the Townshend duties. He continued to be on close, cordial terms with Governor John Penn and the members of his proprietary government and, at this stage, there is no evidence that he was expecting, or indeed would support, an outright armed rebellion against Britain.

In the late eighteenth century, virtually all of Delaware's more prominent citizens looked to Philadelphia as the center of culture and political activity. Yet when at home in the Lower Counties, particularly in Kent and Sussex, they lived in relative isolation, cut off by bad roads and shallow creeks from coastal trade routes. Tommy, describing a trip to Philadelphia with Betsy, his intended wife, in September of 1769, gives a graphic account of the pitfalls one might encounter on the road.

> [We were] Very Safe Till We Came to Patersons Mill, who's Dam had been broke by the Storm. . . . Betsy got Down and walk'd behind the Chair, and I got out and Lead the Horse—about Midway [across] the Dam we had to go of[f] on one side, and as it was Very Steep . . . the Chair was Like to Over Set. I immediately Stopt the Horse to Run and Right it—but before I got to it . . . it Tiptd over Quite Topse Tirve and Scared the horse So that he took of[f] . . . the Spring Struck against a Large logg that Lay in the way which broke the Carriage all to Shatters Leaving Nothing Whole but the Wheels and Box.[23]

In spite of such hazards, both Tommy and Caesar, as well as many of their contemporaries made the three-day journey far more often than one might expect, staying at houses of friends and catching up with the latest news. As a consequence, the quiet rural town of Dover would be gradually but inexorably drawn into the coming conflict.

5

Clashes in the North

THAT CONFLICT WAS CONTINUALLY STOKED IN MASSACHUSETTS BY RADI-cals like Sam Adams, the leader of the controversial Sons of Liberty. Adams had been largely responsible for the Stamp Act riots in Boston and, like all successful revolutionaries, was skilled at manipulating public opinion. He continually wrote articles that kept the issues before the public, many of which were published in the *Boston Gazette* and the *Massachusetts Spy*. Adams was also skilled at persuading others to join his cause. His supporters included well respected men like the young lawyers John Adams and Josiah Quincy, Jr., the merchant John Hancock, and the silversmith, Paul Revere, as well as others of less savory reputation. Sam Adams was also responsible for establishing the Massachusetts Committees of Correspondance, the purpose of which was ostensibly to air the views of the citizens of each Massachusetts town, but in fact, became an effective propaganda machine for the dissemination of his own opinions.[1]

The more unruly members of the Sons of Liberty continually harassed the British troops sent to enforce the Townshend Acts. In January, 1770, there was an incident in New York, which was later dubbed the Battle of Golden Hill. The sons had lined a road with poles flying pennants bearing revolutionary slogans. When the British soldiers began to pull them down, some of the sons tried to stop them, while others advanced on the scene with clubs. An outright clash was avoided only because the British commanding officer quickly ordered his men back to quarters.

On March 5, 1770, there occurred a far more serious event in Boston. On that day, a crowd set out to "bait the Lobsterbacks," advancing on the soldiers with clubs and stones. Alarmed, the besieged soldiers fired into the mob, killing three outright, mortally wounding two more, and slightly injuring six others, in the incident that would come to be known as the Boston Massacre. Afterwards, in an effort to keep the warring sides safely apart, all British troops were quartered at Castle William in Boston harbor; the same island to which the customs officials had fled after the seizing of the sloop *Liberty*.[2]

While both the Boston Massacre and the Battle of Golden Hill were deliberately provoked by the Sons of Liberty, they were also a direct result of Parliament's uncompromising stance on the Townshend duties. On April 12, after much vacillation and indecision, North finally agreed to repeal all the Townshend duties except that on tea, which would be kept primarily as a symbol of Britain's imperial right over her colonial subjects.[3]

Frederick North was actually a commoner, called "Lord" only because he was the son and future heir of the earl of Guilford. North was man who instinctively tried to avoid trouble, but he was also beholden to the whims of George III, a king who never hesitated to remove any minister who displeased him.[4] Typically, North's capitulation on the Townshend duties was both ungracious and halfhearted, forced in the end, by England's own merchants, most of whom hated the Acts as much as their colonial counterparts.[5]

The remaining tax on tea was set at three pence a pound, a rate that actually made the price in the colonies nine pence less than it was in England. Most Americans, however, cared little about that; they were simply tired of the turmoil. The boycott collapsed as colonial merchants quickly abandoned nonimportation agreements they had never liked anyhow. The radicals, and their so-called "popular parties," lost much of their support, even though the fundamental question of Britain's constitutional relationship with her colonies was yet to be resolved.

By September, trade with England had been fully restored and the economy was thriving. Just how much the atmosphere had changed was evident when the British captain and his men who had fired into the crowd at the Boston Massacre came up for trial. They were successfully defended by two Sons of Liberty members, John Adams and Josiah Quincy, Jr., who convinced the jury that they had acted under extreme pressure. It appeared that the American Revolutionary movement had collapsed.[6]

Things were so settled that year, that Caesar, in New Castle for the spring session of the assembly, could shift his attention to more local matters. One of these concerned an idea to move the Sussex County courthouse from Lewes to Cross Roads, (Milton) the limit of navigation on the Broadkill River. On March 3, 1770, Caesar's cousin John Rodney wrote him a long, indignant letter strongly protesting the idea and asking Caesar to use his influence to prevent it. His language is a clue to the temper of the people in Delaware at the time: "[W]hat disturbances a few ambitious Men may Effect" he said, "—they seem Determined at all Events, to *oppose* whatever is *Proposed* by some other, who are not of their party, [and] . . . will immediately cry out their Liberties are sinking . . . so they make some people belive that Ruin is even at the door. . . ." John Rodney wanted the courthouse to stay in Lewes, which he defended as more central and practical than the proposed site. The Broadkill, he claimed, was so shallow "that Shallops often lay from Change to full, and from full to Change again before they can get out." His real concern, however, was all too familiar; he was worried about the value of his property. "If the Publick buildings should be Removed the Consequence would be very bad . . . [the people's] Lands & Improvements would be Reduced to less that half their present value, nay some will not sell for more than ¼ part. . . ."[7] (The bill was defeated, but the courthouse was ultimately moved to Georgetown in 1781)

On March 14, Caesar wrote Tommy about the doings of what he humorously referred to as the "Regislative Body now at New Castle," (a term he called an "expression frequently used by Some members, for want of Something better to say") complaining that he must do so with "as bad Pen, Ink and paper, as any private Gentleman would Ever Wish to Write with. . . ." Among the concerns taken up by the assembly that spring was a bill "for the better regulation of the poor," a move to build a hospital in Kent, which failed, even though there was "much argument for, and Verry Little against" the idea, as well as a tax bill to finance the improvement of the King's Highway and roads to the creek landings. He had also bought a "very fine Riding Chair, and if Sally Armitage Chuses to Go down will offer her a Seat. . . ."[8]

Dr. Charles Ridgely, the son of Nicholas Ridgely, Caesar's guardian after his father died, sent his concerns from Dover. In his opinion, voters should only be allowed to vote in the county where they lived and the term "freehold" should apply only to real estate producing five pounds a year. "No monied estate should do it, because in that there is too much uncertainty." He also protested that the present manner of trying slaves was unconstitutional.[9]

All these concerns were dealt with. The sheriff was given the power to oversee elections and require voters to be recorded in the hundred where they lived. Relief for the poor was to be managed by the justices of peace and taxes were levied for the purpose, although parents and grandparents were required to support their children, and vice versa. In addition, Wilmington's boundaries were finally delineated, and surveyors appointed to lay out the streets.

Two other matters occupied Caesar's personal attention, however. One was the possibility of his inheriting an estate on the island of Antigua. He wrote a man named Henry Bonin, telling him that "a friend of mine being in Philadelphia dined at Mrs. Willcocks's (I believe a native of that island.) One Dr. Gordon . . . told my friend (upon Mrs. Willcocks's mentioning my name) that he should be glad to see me, for that he knew a verry considerable estate in the Island of Antigua which belonged to some one of that name in North America. . . ."

Caesar's claim was based on the will of an earlier Caesar Rodney, the first cousin of his grandfather, William. This Caesar, who had had "several daughters but no sons," had written William Rodeney "requesting his next son might be named after him, and that he would leave that son half his fortune. Not long after the receit of this letter my father was born and was named Caesar." Caesar's essential decency, however, is apparent in the penultimate paragraph of this letter:

"Sir, I believe there can be no doubt that Caesar Rodney of Antigua left issue; therefore if there be any such estate it cannot come to me by de[s]cent, but by will to father, and then de[s]cent from him . . . if there [is] no foundation for any pretentions to such an estate [I] should be glad you'd let me know that and you shall be honourably paid [for] your trouble and expenses."[10]

That Caesar's health is still not satisfactory is all too evident from a letter he receives from Dr. Thomas Bond dated April 26, 1770:

I am greatly concerned at the Return of your Cancer, especially so near the Eye. The method of using Guy's powder is to make a thick Mucilage of Gum Arabic and form it into the consistance of a Plaster with a proper Quantity of the Powder, then spread it of the thickness of two common wafers on a Piece of Black Silk of such Dimension as may extend the Breadth of a Barley Corn beyond the Cancer, this Plaster must be continued on 5 or 6 Days, then softened with a Pultice of Bread and Milk and then taken off. Instead of Mr. Hamiltons green ointment I dress at first with the SpermaCali Ointment and then with dry Lint. When the Eschar is formed tis usually covered for a few Days with the Emp. Mercuvial. I heartily wish you a happy Recovery and am

Yours most respectfully
Th. Bond[11]

Meanwhile life in Dover went on. On June 16, while Caesar was still in New Castle, Tommy brought him up-to-date about the doings at the farm. "The clover was cut last Wednesday and seems to amount to a full crop of very fine hay, all of which I hope we shall git in the stable today without the least damage by rain. The hay down in the meadow . . . will not be fit to cut before you return home. It being too wet to draw out the ditch-banks, I have set Charles & Ezekiel at work in the piece of stumpy ground. . . . The corn is ploughed out and looks very well and the oats promiss fair to produce a very fine crop."[12]

The following spring, on April 8, 1771, Tommy married Elizabeth Fisher of Jones Neck, the "Betsy" that was with him on his eventful carriage trip to Philadelphia. Probably he had known her all his life. With Caesar's encouragement and presumably financial backing, the young couple moved to Philadelphia where Tommy opened a store. Apparently it was deemed time for him to stop merely enjoying his life as a man about town and go to work.[13]

In the fall of 1771, Caesar failed to be elected to the Delaware Assembly; the only year out of fourteen that he would not serve. Tommy, suspecting foul play, wrote from Philadelphia of a conversation he had with a visitor from Dover. "Matthew Manlove inform'd me that you Lost you[r] Election in Murderkill Hundred, and that there is Some Reason, for Suspicion of fraud at the General Election . . . the best thing you Can Do (to have a fair Election) is to . . . have all the Votes of Each Hundred in a Box by itself—And as they are Re[a]d out, not Tare them, but string them or put them into another Box . . . And this is the practice here in Philadelphia, and no Doubt must insure a fair Election, or at Least if any fraud is Commited you'l find the author. . . ."[14]

While fraud was not uncommon in eighteenth-century elections, something else may have been at work here. Caesar's participation in the Stamp Act Congress and in subsequent protestations against the Townshend duties may have branded him in some people's eyes as a dangerous radical. His firey compatriot, Thomas McKean, was also left out of the assembly that year. It seems evident that few citizens of Kent and Sussex were interested in quarreling with Britain.

As it happened, the assembly that met that fall without Caesar also dealt with a new proprietary governor. Caesar's friend and advisor, John Penn, had returned to England and was replaced by his brother, Richard.

6

Personal Plans

ON APRIL 14, 1772, CAESAR SPENT A LONELY NIGHT AT AN INN IN CHESter, Pennsylvania, while returning to Dover after a visit to Tommy's mercantile business in Philadelphia. Tommy, at that time, had a garrulous servant named Betsey Sims and Caesar writes that, with no one to speak to except "Irish Ned the waiter," he would even "be happy in hearing her limber tongue employed in giving a history of the new fassion in caps . . . and the better ordering and securing them, from vulgar eyes & hands," adding, rather apologetically, that he had been so distracted by her incessant chatter that he had "entirely forgot to pay the man for mending my carriage and to pay my barber, both of whom I hope you will take care to see and pay. . . ."[1]

Caesar had recently been appointed second justice of the supreme court of the Lower Counties and, in his answer, Tommy teased that "Betsey Sims is pleased to hear that one of the Supreme Judges of the Lower Counties would condescend to make her the subject of his thoughts." In this same letter he asked, in the callous manner of the eighteenth century, if Caesar had "any little useless negroe boy, that you'l be please to, lett [little Caesar] have one to rock his cradle."[2]

Apparently there had been an outbreak of small pox in Philadelphia. Caesar wrote that he "shall be uneasy till I hear that Betsey and the child are settled and well recovered of the small pox . . ." but adds that he hopes Betsey will take it "for her's and the child's security. . . ." (This Betsey is Tommy's wife, Elizabeth Fisher Rodney and the child is Tommy's son, Caesar A. Rodney, born January 4, 1772.)[3]

Caesar was referring to the eighteenth-century practice of "inoculation." Although Edward Jenner's discovery that infection with the relatively mild disease of cow pox also conferred immunity to small pox was still twenty-six years in the future, it was well known that one bout with the disease protected you from future infection.

Therefore, people were often "inoculated" with a small bit of "matter" from someone with a mild case, in hopes that it would induce a similarly mild case. Obviously, it was a risky practice, since the recipient could become dangerously ill and even die. Tommy assured his brother that "Betsey and the child are both very well and intend to be inoculated next week . . ." but asked him not to mention this for fear that "people should grumble at the shallopmen for coming to my shop in which there is no other danger."[4] As a matter of fact, there was considerable danger; anyone inoculated in this manner was quite contagious.

Caesar had also been ill. On May 16, he complained to Tommy that he has had the most severe pleurisy that he has ever had. "I was taken last Tuesday fortnight in so violent a manner that the Doctor took near 60 oz of blood before he could make the least alteration in the disorder, besides several strong vomits."[5] This was the common, but debilitating, practice of "bleeding" a patient, under the mistaken idea that it would drain disease from their system.

These are but a few of the affectionate letters that traveled back and forth between the two brothers during the spring and summer of 1772. They are full of gossip about Dover people, notably about one Nicholas Vining and his, "Lady," as well as various requests for supplies to be sent on the shallops from Philadelphia to Dover. These included whalebone stays for Sally (Caesar's half sister, Sally Wilson, who kept house for him), an umbrella, a pump, new shoes and "the best cut tobacco in an ozenbrigs bag."[6] Tommy also sent frequent news of baby Caesar, reporting that he was "as fatt as a little bare and as frolicsome as a lamb. . . .[7]" In August, he reported that, at seven months, he "has cut one of his teeth and being about the rest keeps him sometimes poorly."[8] Both brothers expressed the hope that Caesar will be able to visit Tommy and Betsey between the end of the court session and haying time on the farm.

Tommy's business, however, was not going well, even though he insisted that he was not discouraged "from anything that has heretofore happened, nor doubt but our care and industry will be crowned with success."[9] Nevertheless, he found it necessary to move his young family into the house next door, "which is not quite so roomy, but is £16 a year less rent." He also worried that Caesar will not be able to "dispose of the marsh," suggesting if it didn't sell quickly, he might be able to raise £300 by taking out a mortgage, as sum which "may enlarge my trade to great avantage."[10]

By late summer, the brothers were once again preoccupied with politics, hoping to reinstate Caesar as a member of the assembly in the October elections. Tommy reported on August 17 that he had "informed the Doctor [Dr. Charles Ridgely, then Kent county treasurer, and a leader in the "court" party] that "all the political papers will be distributed this week," thus forcing the opposition in Dover to "erect some engine against their powers, which no doubt will very much perplex them." He adds that Caesar should have his "Other piece ready to attack them in the rear, which perhaps may bring on a total rout."[11] Tommy had little respect for the current members of the assembly, calling them "sinister sighted prags" that are "like the froth or scum which rides upon the ocean when it is agitated and disturbed by a terrible tempest. . . ."

Nevertheless, he worried that Caesar was not up to the continual drinking and socializing that went with an active campaign, telling his brother that his health was not worth ruining for the "previlege of puting on again the same old coat you have been used to ware. . . ."[12] There was ample reason for his concern. While Caesar did succeed in regaining his seat in the assembly in the fall of 1772, his health was not strong. In December he was once again bled by Dr. Ridgely after suffering a bad pain in his side, a chill and fever. Betsey Rodney had also been very ill with "a most dangerous malady, which had reduced her (from all appearance) to the last ebb of life,. . . ."[13] possibly as a result of her small pox "inoculation."

Ever thoughtful, Caesar sent her a "flaxseed cask of turnips," an item he deemed "necessary in a family" yet expensive to buy in Philadelphia, whereas he had so many that "a hundred bushels would hardly be missed." Asking if young Caesar could walk yet, he joked that he was "apprehensive the fellow has too much beaf about him to be found guilty of any such piece of activity."[14] Tommy replied to this letter with an endearing description of the baby, then about eleven months old: "Caesar is very hearty & can box like a corsair, but is not man enough to walk alone, though he can walk all around the house by the wall and can make his [commands] known. . . . [He] can say Mama very well & I believe will talk (as well as walk) very soon, for he seems to understand any thing that is said to him & is very apt at immitating."[15]

During this time, Caesar and Dr. Charles Ridgely, his physician and the son of his one time guardian, Nicholas Ridgely, had important plans for some property in Kent county. Their idea was to create a new landing, to be called "Rodney's Burgh" on Jones Creek between Isaac's Branch (now Moore's Lake) on the south and Walker's Branch (now Puncheon Run) on the north. Caesar and Dr. Ridgely planned to buy a farm known as Shoemaker's Hall for £3 10s an acre. Twenty acres would be set aside for the mill and the

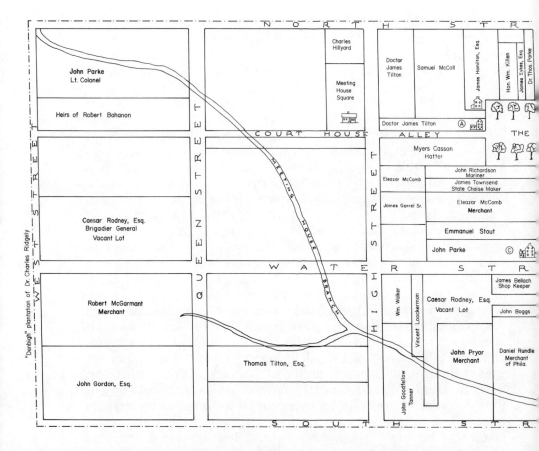

Map of "Dover, Delaware in Revolutionary Times" 1776: Drawn by Jeroen van den Hurk from the original by Leon deValinger, Jr. 1936, with additional information about Caesar Rodney's properties supplied by James B. Jackson.

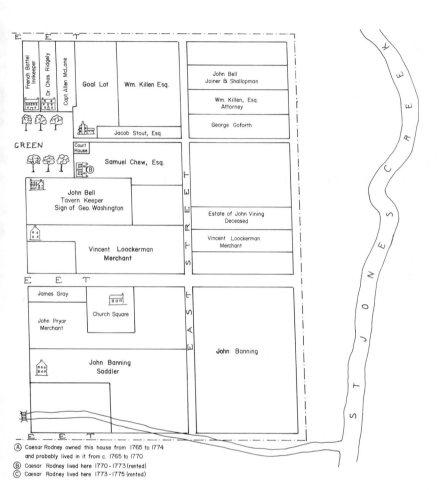

French Bottel
Innkeeper

Dr. Chas. Ridgely

Capt. Allen McLane

Goal Lot

Wm. Killen Esq.

John Bell
Joiner & Shallopman

Wm. Killen, Esq.
Attorney

George Goforth

Jacob Stout, Esq.

GREEN

Court House

Samuel Chew, Esq.

Ⓑ

John Bell
Tavern Keeper
Sign of Geo. Washington

Estate of John Vining
Deceased

Vincent Loockerman
Merchant

Vincent Loockerman
Merchant

James Gray

Church Square

John Pryor
Merchant

John Banning

John Banning
Saddler

ST JONES CREEK

Ⓐ Caesar Rodney owned this house from 1765 to 1774
and probably lived in it from c. 1765 to 1770

Ⓑ Caesar Rodney lived here 1770-1773 (rented)

Ⓒ Caesar Rodney lived here 1773-1775 (rented)

rest developed. Caesar assured Tommy that the people in the vicinity are so "taken with the plan that they are determined to have a road across the cripple and a bridge across the Creek, cost what it will, saying there is no trouble and expence equal to the advantage of the making the mills so covenient to them."

There was concern, however, that the water was not deep enough to be navigable. Caesar, himself, admitted that if this proved to be the case, he would be "fairly well taken in." However, he had been assured by Vincent Loockerman, a large Kent county landowner, that "there is water plenty and that as soon as the warfe is built, he will be dam'd if [the property] won't be worth ten pounds per acre. . . ."[16]

Caesar was also trying to buy the house he was currently living in; an elegant three-story brick house belonging to Phoebe Vining, the widow of John Vining. It stood on the southeast corner of the Green, next door to the present statehouse. At the time, there was a small brick courthouse and jail on the statehouse site, although, Caesar and James Sykes had been given the reponsibility of overseeing the building of "new public offices" in April 1772.[17] On his other side stood the King George Tavern, (later renamed the George Washington), owned by John Bell. The Golden Fleece Tavern was across on the northeast corner of King Street and the Green next to the Ridgely house.

Oddly enough, Caesar already owned a house on the west side of the Green, at the corner of Court House Alley. He had bought it in 1765 and probably lived there until 1770 when, for reasons known only to himself, he chose to lease it "for a term of years." He also owned two vacant lots on Water Street: the first, two blocks west of the Green on the corner of Queen Street, and the other, one block south between King and High Streets.[18]

Caesar had leased the Vining house from Phoebe Vining after her husband's death, when she and her daughter Polly moved to Philadelphia to be near her son. (Nicholas?) Tommy had reported to Caesar in August 1772, that "poor Polley never liked Philadelphia [and that Mrs. Vining] . . . is just as undetermined as ever" about staying or moving back to Dover. Nevertheless, he predicted that as "she will soon go to housekeeping, and I imagine she will not think much of moving afterwards. So that it is probable this fall you'l git a favourable answer about the house."[19]

In March 1773, however, Caesar complained that "contrary to solemn contract" Mrs. Vining was now asking £1200 for her house in Dover, which he considered "such an imposition, I cannot think of doing it." (He had previously contracted for £1000). He told

Tommy that he would actually prefer to rent the house for two years at £50 a year, even if he could buy it for as little as £800, since he hoped to build himself a new house on the Rodney's Burgh site. He wanted Tommy to arrange a lease that Mrs. Vining and her agent "cannot refuse on condition that I release them from the contract."[20]

In the meantime, however, Judge Samuel Chew offered Mrs. Vining the full £1200 on condition that he could have the house immediately. An interesting scene then took place between Tommy and Mrs. Vining. As reported to Caesar, Tommy "spoke as tenderly as the case would admit" yet could not deny his resentment at what he saw as the unfair treatment of his brother. The widow though "much destrest," claimed that Caesar told her he "would not prevent her getting 2 or £300 more for the house . . . considering her circumstances. . . ."[21]

Caesar and Tommy both lost out in that spring of 1773. Judge Chew bought the house in Dover, Rodney's Burgh was never built, either because the creek proved too shallow or the war intervened, and Tommy's Philadelphia business went bankrupt.

On June 7, Caesar moved into a house owned by young John Parke, heir to Thomas Parke, who was currently studying at the Newark Academy (now the University of Delaware). The house stood on the corner of King and Water Streets, one block south of the Green. It was "very well maintained" and had a newly built stable and smokehouse.[22] A few days later, on June 10, Tommy wrote that he expected to sell all his store's stock by the following week, surrender the property to his landlord, and return to Dover to "git the house and store in order there."[23]

Tommy opened a store in Dover on July 17. He sold nails, gunpowder and shot; cooking pots, china and glassware; clothes and shoes; and coffee, tea, spices and rum from the West Indies. He also shipped Kent county wheat, corn, and bacon, as well as Sussex county lumber and shingles, for sale in Philadelphia.

One more upsetting event occurred that year. Betsey gave birth to another son, named Petolama (?) on October 12. He was, according to a note in Thomas' hand in the Rodney Geneology; "begot in Philadelphia and born at Dover, but died eight days old."[24]

7
Tea

ALTHOUGH MANY PEOPLE, INCLUDING THE RODNEYS, SEEMED TO THINK the problems with Britain had been solved, Sam Adams and his more ardent followers continued to fan the flames in Boston. Each year, they celebrated the March 5 anniversary of the Boston Massacre with graphic reenactments, memorial services, and rousing speeches. Adams himself, continued to write articles for radical papers and worked to widen the membership of what he called "local associations to promote American liberty" far beyond the boundaries of Boston.[1]

On June 9, 1772, an incident occurred that gave him a new "cause celebre." The Royal Navy schooner *Gaspee*, notorious for her captain's zealous enforcement of revenue laws, ran aground in Narragansett Bay and was set afire by persons unknown. There was even talk that she had been deliberately lured into shoal waters.

The British response was to establish a "commission of inquiry," a relatively mild reaction probably designed to exonerate the captain from any responsibility for the loss of his ship. Nevertheless, it was denounced as an "Inquisition more horrid than that of Spain" by those who saw it as one more infringement of their local jurisdiction.[2] Sam Adams, quick to take advantage of the uproar, created further committees of correspondance, and eventually set up what amounted to an underground network throughout the colonies.

Although the British commission failed to find the culprit responsible for the burning of the *Gaspee*, it remained in place, ready to deal with any future crisis. Indeed, such a crisis now seemed inevitable; George III was in firm control of both houses of Parliament and his ministers appeared increasingly reluctant to challenge the royal will.

Meanwhile, a number of things were happening in Delaware that would begin to disturb the hitherto serene relationship between the Delaware Assembly and the Penns' proprietary government. The first of these occurred in the spring of 1773, when Governor Richard Penn rejected a bill to elect, rather than appoint, the officers of the levy court. Few Delaware bills had ever been questioned and this one had wide support because it was seen as a brake on higher taxes.

During this same period, Delaware's boundaries and those of the counties were permanently set according to surveys conducted between 1750 and 1768. Delaware was becoming a colony in her own right and would no longer be seen just as a subsidiary of the more economically powerful Pennsylvania.[3]

A third development was the emergence of a strong, Presbyterian faction in Delaware politics. The Presbyterians, in fact, were now the largest religious group in Delaware with twenty-nine established congregations, more than all other groups combined. Led by Caesar's friend and compatriot, Thomas McKean, among others, it reflected the new strength of the Scotch-Irish population, particularly in New Castle county where they had no less that seventeen established churches as against four in Kent and eight in Sussex.[4] The members had so little love for the British that Thomas Rodney would later remark that the revolution in Delaware was made by a "handful of men and the Presbyterians."[5]

Then, on May 10, 1773, the British Parliament made another tactical blunder: they passed the Tea Act. Actually, the act had nothing to do with the American colonies; its purpose was to rescue Britain's economic arm in Asia, the East India Company, from bankruptcy. According to the revised Townshend Act, tea sent through Britain to America was already exempt from English duties, but subject to a charge of threepence a pound when it entered America. In hopes of finally solving the company's financial difficulties, Parliament would now allow the tea ships to bypass England altogether and sail directly from the Far East to America.

No doubt the British saw this as a reasonable solution. After all, even with the threepence duty, tea was cheaper in America that it was in England. By now, however, the Americans were so deeply suspicious of Parliament that they perceived the change as another attempt to seduce them into paying what they saw as an unfair and unconstitutional tax.[6]

The Tea Act was passed about a month before Tommy closed his business in Philadelphia, although it took several more weeks for the news to cross the Atlantic. As so many of his goods, including tea, came in on trading vessels, Tommy was usually well up on the latest news, yet he never mentions the act in his letters to Caesar that spring. We can only conclude that he hadn't heard the news or didn't realize its significance. Just before he left in June 1773, a

full month after the act was passed, he wrote only of "warlike preparations in England, France and Spain, but for what purpose is unknown to the public" and reported that a gentleman had arrived
from New York with news that England was "enlisting and pressing
men" and fitting out her fleet.[7] Tommy, always ready for a fight,
boasted that a "defensive fort" was being built near "one of Mr.
Galloway's islands near red bank. . . . So that if any hostile invaders
shou'd attempt the navigation of the Delaware . . . we shall (barring
high tides inundations & storms) be able to give them a warm reception."[8] (The "Mr. Galloway" here mentioned is the Philadelphia
Tory Joseph Galloway and "red bank" is a site on the New Jersey
side of the Delaware River across from Philadelphia.)

By the autumn of 1773, resentment against the Tea Act was
sweeping through the colonies, sending the revolutionary movement once again into high gear. Unlike the Stamp Act rebellion,
the opposition this time was carefully orchestrated. Well aware that
there were many smugglers of tea who were determined to continue business as usual the radicals focused their attention on the
four great colonial seaports: Boston, New York, Philadelphia, and
Charleston.[9]

On September 27, 1773, news reached Philadelphia that the
ship *Polly* had left London with a cargo of East Indian tea and was
due to arrive in that city around the third week in November. On
October 16, a mass protest took place, attended by more that seven
hundred people. Declaring the the Tea Act had "a direct tendency
to render assemblies useless and to introduce arbitrary government
and slavery" they demanded that anyone caught selling tea be
branded a traitor.[10]

Caesar, Thomas McKean and George Read, together with Presbyterian party member, John McKinly, and a Sussex landowner
named Thomas Robinson, were appointed to another "Committee
of Correspondence" at the October meeting of the Delaware Assembly; in effect joining the radical network. With Thomas Mc-
Kean as chairman, their mission was to contact like committees in
other colonies, informing them about the actions of their own assembly, and passing on news about the activities of Parliament.

It must be said that the strength of their revolutionary fervor was
decidely mixed. Thomas McKean, of course, had always been a radical, and, by this time, even the more balanced Caesar must have
been seen as one, too. Both, after all, were seasoned veterans of the
Stamp Act Congress of 1765. George Read, however, was decidedly
moderate. While he supported the American cause in principle, he
was deeply reluctant to sever ties with Britain. John McKinly, al-

though a member of the Presbyterian faction and destined to become Delaware's first president, was generally perceived as lacking resolve. The last member of the committee, Thomas Robinson, would become Delaware's most combative Loyalist.[11]

The Philadelphia Assembly was similarly ambivalent. The pacifist Quaker members, generally reluctant to resist British authority, occupied the largest block, eighteen out of forty seats. The other twenty-two seats were generally divided between Anglicans, Presbyterians, Baptists and others, most of whom were more inclined to support radical, or at least, moderate positions.[12]

As it happened, John Penn returned to the post of governor of Pennsylvania in the fall of 1773, replacing Richard. He was warmly welcomed by both the New Castle and Philadelpia Assemblies, who saw him as a buffer against the mercurial actions of Parliament.[13] Their confidence in him subsequently was justified; John Penn refused to lend his protection to the only Philadelphia firm of tea importers that declined to join the October boycott.[14]

On November 27, just as the *Polly* was due to arrive in Delaware Bay, two handbills, signed by "The Committee for Tarring and Feathering," appeared on the streets of Philadelphia The first promised to "attend to" any river pilot who guided the *Polly* up Delaware Bay's narrow channel into the harbor, while the second, addressed to the ship's captain, Captain Ayres, charged that the tea under his care was "sent . . . as a trial of American virtue and resolution." "What think you Captain," it went on, "of a halter around your neck—ten gallons of liquid tar decanted on your pate—with the feathers of a dozen wild geese laid over that to enliven your appearance?"[15]

Captain Ayres, having brought the *Polly* up the Bay without a pilot, arrived off Philadelphia on Christmas Day, 1773. Met by more than eight thousand determined citizens, he did not unload his cargo. The city had just received the news that, nine days before, a group of Americans dressed as Indians had dumped 340 chests containing tea into Boston Harbor.

8

Britain Acts: The Colonies React

On JANUARY 20, 1774, WHEN JOHN HANCOCK'S TRADING SHIP *HAYLEY* arrived in London with news of the tea party, the British were outraged. According to the earl of Buckinghamshire, the question was now "whether *we* are to be free or slaves to our colonies."[1] Those in the higher reaches of the government agreed. Furious at the incessant needling of the radicals, they were now ready to act.

As it happened, a petition calling for the replacement of Governor Thomas Hutchinson of Massachusetts and his deputy, Andrew Oliver, came up for consideration in Parliament on January 29. It had been originally submitted the previous August by Benjamin Franklin. Now in his late sixties, Franklin was acting as the London agent for Massachusetts, Pennsylvania, New Jersey and Georgia. He had secretly acquired some private letters of Hutchinson's and Oliver's, highly critical of Massachusetts, which he had sent to the speaker of the Massachusetts Assembly. Upon reading them, the men of that body rose up in fury, demanding that both men immediately be replaced.

Franklin's caustic wit and able advocacy had already ruffled English political feathers. In the fall of 1773, he had published two essays critical of British colonial policy: "Rules by Which a Great Empire may be Reduced to a Small one," a sardonic list of all their misguided moves since 1763, and "An Edict by the King of Prussia," which satirically cast England in the role of a colony subject to the whims of a foreign king.[2]

That Massachusetts' petition for the removal of Hutchinson and Oliver came up for consideration immediately after news of the Boston Tea Party reached London was unfortunate. The privy council's hearing on the case quickly turned into a bitter indictment of Massachusetts and a scathing personal attack on Franklin.[3] Immediately afterward, the king's cabinet (all members of the House of Lords, except "Lord" North, the prime minister), formally resolved that "effectual steps [be] taken to secure the Dependence of the Colonies on the Mother Country."[4]

A week later, on February 4, the king met with General Thomas Gage, commander of British troops in North America. Despite his reputation in England as a prudent and conservative soldier, Gage had little sympathy for the people of Massachusetts; he considered them either mad or wickedly corrupt.[5] On this occasion, he played to the king's petulance by requesting that four additional regiments (fourteen hundred men) be sent to America immediately, stoutly declaring that "They will be Lyons, whilst we are Lambs, but if we take the resolute part they will undoubtedly prove very meek."[6]

That evening the king's cabinet gathered to decide how to punish the city of Boston and the individuals responsible for the tea party. After a heated discussion, their resolve faltered; they decided only to move the seat of government and the customs house out of the city, leaving further steps to the discretion of Alexander Wedderburn, solicitor general of Great Britain: the same man who had previously savaged Franklin before the privy council.

Wedderburn branded the tea party an "act of high treason," equivalent to a declaration of war against the King, and called for the indictment of virtually everyone involved. His list of traitors included all those who guarded the tea ships; members of the Committee of Correspondence; the Boston selectmen; the town clerk; and the members of the Massachusetts Assembly, demanding that all be brought to England for trial. The idea collapsed only when it became evident that the captain of the *Hayley* was the only man in London who could possibly testify against them.[7]

Bitterly frustrated, the British cabinet then demanded that the port of Boston be closed, and a bill to that effect was passed by Parliament in March and signed into law by the king on April 1. Known as the Boston Port Bill, it closed the city to all vessels except those of the British navy as of June 1, 1774. After that date, only ships carrying food and firewood, with a customs officer aboard, could enter the harbor and no cargo at all could be carried out. Only when the East India Company was fully reimbursed would the king consider reopening it.

This was bad enough, but it was immediately followed by a bill to "alter the Government of Massachusetts." Prime Minister North had apparently convinced the members of Parliament that Massachusetts' real problem was too much democracy. The government, he said, was in the hands of rioters; therefore, the governor should have more power and the members of his Council less. Henceforth, the governor would appoint all justices of the peace, county judges, sheriffs and other magistrates while the members of his council, as well as all superior court judges, would be chosen directly by the king. Town meetings could be held only once a year and would no longer have the power to choose jury panels; they would be selected by the governor-appointed sheriff. Finally, Governor Hutchinson would be replaced by General Thomas Gage who would act as both governor and commander of the British troops in Boston.

Nor was this the end of the so-called "Coercive Acts." Claiming that no British soldier could get a fair trial in Massachusetts, Parliament also passed a "Bill for the Impartial Administration of Justice," and a "Quartering Bill." The first was immediately dubbed the "murder bill" in the colonies since it allowed the Massachusetts governor to shift any trial for a capital crime to England or another colony: an idea that was angrily perceived as a license to execute Americans. The second gave General Gage the use of any uninhabited building in Boston, allowing him to billet his soldiers in the heart of the city instead of isolating them at Castle William in Boston harbor. While the alarmed colonists denounced these ideas as a blatant invasion of private property, there was little opposition to them in Parliament. When all three bills were signed into law in May, the king was said to be "infinitely pleased."[8]

The Boston Port Bill, "printed, like a funeral notice, on black-bordered paper . . . [was] hawked through her streets, and sent with great expedition to the sister colonies of Massachusetts."[9] It arrived in Philadelphia on May 14 and the full text was printed in the weekly newspaper, the *Pennsylvania Gazette,* on the eighteenth. The *Gazette,* originally founded by Benjamin Franklin, probably had about fifteen hundred subscribers, yet each issue was read by many times that number, as it was passed from hand to hand in taverns and coffeehouses. It was also widely read throughout the Lower Counties.

On the nineteenth, none other than Paul Revere rode into town with Boston's plea that Pennsylvania join in a nonimportation movement. The reaction of Philadelphia's citizens was mixed. While they had been quick to denounce the Tea Act, the lawlessness of the Boston Tea Party had shocked and horrified many, particularly the conservatives who dominated Pennsylvania's assembly. The Quakers still had considerable influence there, and their pacifism made them reluctant to support any measure, including nonimportation, that might lead to violence. Philadelphia's thriving trade with Britain had also made many Quakers too prosperous to want to disturb the status quo. Thus, it fell to the hitherto moderate John Dickinson to make the first move.[10]

Dickinson and three others; Joseph Reed, Thomas Mifflin, and Charles Thomson, arranged for a mass meeting to be held at City

Tavern on May 20. Of these, only Thomson could be called a radical. Reed was a close friend of Lord Dartmouth, and Mifflin was a rich Quaker merchant only slightly more radical than most members of the Society of Friends. It is known that these four men met at John Dickinson's house before the meeting, and, since all were canny politicians, it is assumed that they planned their stategy very carefully. Three hundred people, mostly conservative Philadelphia merchants, came to the tavern on May 20. Reed led off the program with a moderate plea for John Penn to convene a special session of the assembly in order to ask Parliament for a redress of grievances. This was followed by a highly emotional speech by Mifflin in support of Boston's nonimportation agreement. Thomson came next and was in the midst of a dramatic speech seconding Mifflin when he suddenly fainted. Whether the faint was real or assumed is uncertain, but it effectively set the stage for Dickinson to step in with a cool and reasoned compromise. Endorsing Reed's idea for a special meeting of the assembly (later turned down by John Penn), Dickinson also called for the creation of a nineteen member Committee of Correspondance.

It is symptomatic of Philadelphia's conservative political climate that they did not already have such a committee, and the message they eventually sent to Boston was hardly inflammatory. They hinted that Boston ought to pay for the tea, and emphasized that such a step as nonimportation should only be taken after "mature deliberation." So lukewarm was the committee's support that it was scorned as a "stroke of insulting pity" by Daniel Dulany of Maryland.[11] When the same committee met to decide how Philadelphia should observe June 1, the day the Boston Port Bill was to go into effect, they called only for a day of mourning, an idea that was subsequently derided by both Quakers and Anglicans as unsupported by Scripture.[12] Nevertheless, when a similar day of "fasting, humiliation and prayer" was held in Virginia, "the effect," according to Thomas Jefferson, "was like a shock of electricity, arousing every man, and placing him erect and solidly on his centre."[13]

However, when a mass protest meeting of some eight thousand people marched on the State House on June 18, John Penn attempted to quiet their fury by allowing an extra session of the assembly under the pretext that they must address the indian troubles in the western counties. In mid-July, seventy-five delegates, representing all of Pennsylvania's eleven counties met in Philadelphia. Because each county had one vote, regardless of the number of delegates present, Philadelphia and the eastern counties were no longer able to dominate the discussion. The result was

far more radical than expected. The delegates endorsed the forming of a Continental Congress, choosing John Dickinson, James
Wilson and Thomas Willing as their delegates. They also agreed to
support an non-import/export agreement, as well as any other measures the new Congress thought necessary.[14]

Things moved even faster in Delaware. When the Port Bill was
passed, Caesar was speaker of the assembly and George Read was
attorney general. Although Thomas McKean was now practicing
law in Philadelphia, he had kept his Delaware residence and was
also a member and former speaker of the assembly.[15] Under the
firm leadership of this seasoned triumvirate, the Delaware Assembly immediately denounced all four Coercive Acts, as well as most
aspects of British policy since 1763. On May 25, Caesar, George
Read and John McKinly, as members of the Committee of Correspondence, wrote their Virginia counterparts, pledging Delaware's
support of both the "Boston resolve" for a non-import/export agreement and the idea of a Continental Congress. They also assured
Virginia that they considered "each Colony on this Continent as
parts of the same Body, and an Attack on one to affect all."[16]

On June 17 a flyer appeared on the streets of New Castle addressed to all "Gentlemen, Freeholders and others" inviting them
to a meeting to be held at the courthouse on Wednesday, June 29
at 2:00 P.M. to consider the "most proper mode of procuring relief"
for Boston and redressing grievances. Besides the shutting down of
Boston harbor with a "formidable fleet and army," they listed
among their grievances property seizures; odious excise taxes; trials without jury; the limiting of free debate; and the altering of the
Massachusetts charter, all of which were declared to be facts, not
"phantoms from a heated brain." Signed, "A Freeman," the pamphlet was probably written by either Read or McKean.[17]

Five hundred people crowded into the courthouse on the appointed day, with Thomas McKean presiding. (Caesar, although
deeply involved in all these actions, never appears as a principal
speaker, perhaps because his health was not strong and his facial
cancer made him a less than a prepossessing figure.) Under Mc-
Kean's leadership, the meeting took up donations for the citizens
of Boston and denounced the Boston Port Bill as "unconstitutional,
oppressive to the inhabitants of that town, [and] dangerous to the
liberties of the British colonies. . . ." They further resolved that a
"Congress of deputies from the several colonies" was the "most
proper mode of . . . obtaining redress of American grievances . . .
and re-establishing peace and harmony between Great Britain and
these colonies."[18] Delegates were summoned from all three Dela-

ware counties to New Castle on August 1 to select the men who would represent them. They also promised to support any suspension of trade with Britain agreed to by the congress.

Kent county held a similar meeting in Dover on July 20, attended by more than seven hundred people. Although miffed that New Castle county had acted without first consulting them, Kent nevertheless endorsed most of their resolutions. Whereupon, Caesar, as speaker, formally called for an extra session of the assembly to be held in New Castle on August 1. In so doing, he illegally usurped the power of Governor Penn.

The citizens of Kent were annoyed once again; they thought Dover a far more central and appropriate location for such a meeting than New Castle. In a letter to George Read, dated July 21, Caesar admitted that "some people were much displeased with your having appointed New Castle as the place of meeting, and it was not without some difficulty that [we] reconciled the people to the place." Things were even worse in Sussex county; there, the people were "so offended at your fixing the mode and place, but more especially the place, that they are determined not to fall in with your plan." Instead, Sussex planned to pick their own delegate and bypass the meeting altogether. Caesar told Read he would write Thomas Robinson a "very pressing letter from the Committee here, to adopt your measures, [for] if they should not, they will defeat the whole business."[19]

Sussex fell into line only after Thomas McKean travelled to Lewes on July 23 to give a lengthy and impassioned speech at the largest public meeting ever held in the Low Counties. While indignantly listing all the British offenses since 1763, McKean was, nevertheless, careful to blame their present troubles on "base" colonial officials, which he called the real enemies of both Britain and America. While boldly asserting that "no Englishman [is] bound by any law to which he has not consented by himself or his own chosen representatives," he was also careful to declare his desire to continue the union with "the land of our fathers." As to the idea of a Continental Congress, McKean reminded his listeners that Americans now numbered nearly five million people and would soon "double that number . . . If we were now united," he said, "we need not dread . . . any single prince or empire upon earth. . . ." (It's of interest that McKean also wanted the new Congress to end African slavery on the ground that it was both "dishonorable to us and . . . provoking to the most benevolent parent of the universe.")[20]

McKean was well aware that very few citizens of Delaware, especially in Kent and Sussex counties, were ready to entertain the thought of a permanent break with Britain. Nevertheless, the resolves of each of these county meetings contained more than a hint of rebellion. On the one hand, both Kent and New Castle counties reaffirmed their allegiance to king; on the other, they pledged to cease all trade with any individual or colony that withheld support of the decisions of the impending Congress. Sussex went even further, declaring that "every act of the British Parliament respecting the internal police of North America is . . . an invasion of our just rights and liberties."[21]

When the county delegates met in New Castle on August 1, 1774, they chose the same three men who had represented them at the Stamp Act Congress of nearly ten years before: Caesar Rodney, Thomas McKean and George Read.

There is little doubt that the year 1774 was a pivotal one. At its beginning, there seemed no reason to believe that the constitutional difficulties between Britain and America could not be resolved. Yet tempers rose by midsummer, widening the breach, and by year's end war seemed inevitable.[22] The forming of the Continental Congress was, in fact, symptomatic of a profound change in the way the colonists saw themselves. At the beginning of 1774, no colonial would have called himself an American; he was a Virginian or a Pennsylvanian, or whatever the case may be.[23] Now such men as Thomas McKean and Caesar Rodney were beginning to realize how much power a unified voice could wield.

9

The First Continental Congress

On SEPTEMBER 9, 1774, CAESAR WROTE TOMMY FROM PHILDELPHIA:

On Thursday the 1st of this month after a verry warm disagreable Ride I arrived in Town together with some of the Virginia Gentlemen—by Sunday evening last the delegates from all the different Colonies (Except North Carolina and Georgia) Came to Town and on Munday they met at Carpenter's Hall, when the Hon Peyton Randolph was unanimously Elected to the Chair. . . . The Congress then proceeded to business and have set every day since—I doubt their Rising before some time in October. . . .[1]

Because the First Continental Congress was held outside the laws of England, it was inherently revolutionary. Yet it was far from a radical gathering. Despite the presence of Sam Adams of Massachusetts, Patrick Henry of Virginia and Thomas Lynch of South Carolina, most of those who gathered in Carpenters' Hall in the fall of 1774 represented colonies that had been comfortably British for over a century. John Adams described them as "one third Tories, one third Whigs and the rest mongrels."[2] They were also "strangers, not acquainted with each other's language, ideas, views, designs [and] . . . therefore jealous of each other—fearful, timid, skittish."[3] These "strangers" included tobacco and rice planters from the south, wheat farmers from Delaware and the other Atlantic colonies, as well as New England "yankees," the least prosperous but most politically radical of the lot.

The delegates considered their quarrel to be with Parliament and continued to pledge allegiance to the king. For some, however, his majesty's championing of Parliamentary actions had begun to blur that distinction. All the delegates were opposed to Parliamentary powers of taxation, and feared that if Massachusetts was forced to obey the Coercive Acts their own colonies would suffer, yet many still clung to the idea of reconciliation.[4]

The people of Philadelphia opened wide their houses and wine cellars for the delegates' entertainment. We have had "the greatest respect paid [us] by all the first people here," Caesar told Tommy with satisfaction, obviously enjoying the hospitality of eminent men. He was particularly impressed with the Virginia delegation: "All seven members are here, & more sensible fine fellows you'd never wish to see. . . ." He also found "the Bostonians who (we know) have been condemned by many for their Violence, [to be] moderate men when compared to Virginia, Rhode Island and South Carolina. . . ."[5]

As is common in delicate negotiations, there was early disagreement over the meeting place. Joseph Galloway, the conservative leader of the Pennsylvania delegation, wanted the State House, a choice that, according to Silas Deane of Connecticut, was immediately opposed by the "other party" merely because he had suggested it. Thomas Lynch, a radical from South Carolina, declared firmly for Carpenters' Hall. Lynch also suggested Peyton Randolph as president, to no one's objection, but then insisted that Charles Thomson, a man that John Adams called "the Sam Adams of Philadelphia" be named permanent secretary. The radicals won these two skirmishes, whereupon Sam Adams, no churchman himself, tactfully suggested that the Reverend Jacob Duche, an Anglican clergyman, lead the opening prayer.[6]

When it came to the important issue of voting procedure, these radical and conservative factions immediately gave way to more regional concerns. The question as to whether property, as advocated by South Carolina, or population as called for by Virginia, Massachusetts, and Pennsylvania, should determine the weight given to each colony's vote was won, in the end, by Delaware. When she and the other small colonies protested that they had as much to lose as any, it was decided that "each colony or Province shall have one Vote."[7]

On September 6, just as the delegates were settling down to business, they received the disturbing news that Boston had been shelled by "the King's ships" and six Americans killed. "When that News came to this City, the Bells were Muffled, and kept Ringing all that day," wrote Caesar.[8]

The following morning, Congress opened their session with the reading of the thirty-fifth psalm: "Plead my cause, O Lord, with them that strive with me; fight against them that fight against me. . . ." The aptness was accidental, since the choice was dictated by the Anglican cycle of morning service, yet it was immediately seized upon by the delegates as an auspicious sign.[9]

Two main committees were formed. Caesar reported to Tommy

that he was on the first one, consisting of twenty-four members "Who are to report the Rights of the Colonies, the infringments of those Rights and the means of Relief. . . ."[10] Thomas McKean was also a member of the first committee, while George Read was assigned to the second: twelve members who would study how Parliamentary statutes affected colonial trade and manufacture. Each committee was to meet for ten days and then make a report. The proceedings, Caesar wrote Tommy, were to be kept strictly secret "until the Whole business is done . . . to avoid needless disputations out of Doors . . . much to the disappointment of the curious."[11]

The next morning the news arrived that Boston had not been shelled after all and no one has been killed. Again bells were tolled all over the city, this time for joy and relief. Caesar reported to Tommy, that "When the Expresses [secret messengers] Went to Contradict this false Report they found in [Massachusetts and Connecticut] . . . upward of fifty thousand men Well armed, Actually on their March to Boston for the Relief of the inhabitants: and That every farmer Who had a Cart or Waggon . . . were with them loaded with Provisions, Amunition and Baggage."

They all returned home peacefully when it was found the news was false. Nevertheless, "It is Supposed by Some of the friends of Liberty at Boston that the alarm was set on foot by some of the friends to the Ministerial plan [Coercive Acts], in order to try Whether there was that True Vallour in the people—if this was the Case, I suppose you will think with me That by this time they Can have no doubts remaining."[12]

In fact, the incident was caused by General Gage's preemptive seizure of a large stock of stored gunpowder to prevent its falling into the hands of the radicals; the first skirmish in a series of confrontations that would come to be known as "the Powder Wars." In Gage's view, his action had safeguarded the "King's powder" and prevented the outbreak of violence. The people of Massachusetts, on the other hand, rose up in fury, accusing him of an underhanded assault on their "right to bear arms." Boston's Whig leaders took frantic steps to avert bloodshed, but were secretly delighted with the people's reaction, bragging to their compatriots that "the Spirit of Liberty never was higher. . . ."[13]

Caesar, meanwhile, was not feeling well. He had first admitted to Tommy on September 9, that he had been feeling "Verry poorly ever since I Came to town"[14] and wrote again on the twelfth, that he continued "in a Verry poor State of health not so bad but that I have given my constant attendance in the Congress."[15] It was tedious work. Caesar's committee on rights had reached an impasse between the Whigs, who thought Parliamentary power should always yield to the will of the colonial assemblies, and the conservatives, who defended Parliament's right to set trade regulations for the empire. As the delegates engaged in heated discussions as to whether a man is ruled by "Natural Law," that is, his own conscience and morals, or by established tradition and the English constitution, little practical action was taken in support of Boston.[16]

The committee's hand was forced, however, on September 16, when a leading Boston radical named Paul Revere rode into town with the so-called Suffolk Resolves, having covered some three hundred and fifty miles over rough roads in roughly five days. In early September, the towns of Suffolk County in Massachusetts, which included Boston, had met to decide the best way to resist the Coercive Acts. Although "cheerfully acknowledg[ing]" George III as their rightful sovereign, their recommendations were clearly rebellious. They declared the "Intolerable Acts" to be unconstitutional and decreed that no courts should sit, no taxes paid nor goods imported from Britain until they were rescinded. They also called for the organization of a militia "to defend their inherent rights—Even with Loss of Blood and Treasure" as well as a provincial congress to protest General Gage's fortification of Boston Neck; described by Caesar as "a narrow neck of land about 120 Yards wide at which [Gage] has placed a number of Troops and 28 Canon" and where "Country people passing and Repassing this place are . . . insulted by the Soldiery. . . ."[17]

Although the decision to support such an inflamatory document must have presented a painful dilemma for the moderate and conservative delegates in Congress, Caesar seemed unconcerned. He remarked only that "The Congress mett on that business this day and have Resolved thereon—which you will see in the Packet of Munday being ordered immediately to be printed [so that] the General [and] the people might know what they thought of the matter. . . ."[18]

In Delaware, these events would gradually splinter the class loyalties and communities of the traditional "Court" and "country" parties. While serving in the Continental Congress, Caesar was also a "court" party candidate for the Delaware Assembly from Kent county. Led by his old friend and Rodney's Burgh partner, Dr. Charles Ridgely, the party included at least three men who would actively oppose independence, John Cook, Jacob Stout and John Clarke, as well as one who would later serve as a lieutenant colonel in the Kent county militia; John Cook's brother-in-law, Thomas Collins.

Thomas Rodney, on the other hand, was now a member of the opposition "country" party, which, in 1774, was led by William Killen, and John Haslet. Killen was a prominent Presbyterian and a known radical, while Haslet would become Caesar's firm friend and ally during the revolution.[19]

This confusion of political sympathies and alliances is also evident in the members of the Kent county Committee of Correspondence. They represented the full gamut of political opinion including both Rodney brothers, the loyalists Clarke and Stout, the moderate Ridgley and the radicals Killen and Haslet. With the exception of the Presbyterian Killen and Richard Bassett, a Methodist layman said to be the richest man on the peninsula, most were also Anglicans.[20] While there were fewer Anglican churches in Delaware than Presbyterian, more than half of the population in Kent county and two thirds of Sussex was thought to be Anglican. Not surprisingly, the clergy, as well as many of their members, were reluctant to sever ties with Britain.[21]

Meanwhile, the impetuous Tommy waded deep into political intrigue. On September 11, he scornfully wrote Caesar that that "our Vicars [a reference to the Anglican Tories] . . . seem put to silence by the . . . hostile invasion of Boston, perhaps judging it impolitic longer to oppose the popular opinion against such unhear'd of oppression." In reference to his brother's candidacy, he assured Caesar that although "their junto of domestic police, had [tried] to exclude you from their political favour & ticket, [they] were defeated in this by your warm friends in their council . . . together with the popular warmth for you out of doors. . . ."[22]

These increasingly bitter conflicts soon threatened Caesar's old friendships. Tommy reported that: "Your good friend Doctor R[idgely] has layed a trap with his Old Machine L[oockerma]n, which he no doubt thinks may gain his purpose of throwing you off the assembly—but your friends are apprized of this and will not omit to lower his Turban at this election; and the voice of the people is increasing greatly against him."[23] Caesar's reply is characteristically calm: "Your account of Polltick's in Kent . . . places them in that State I Expected they would be—However do not Doubt but a great Majority of the people will Shew Such a firm Attachment to the Cause in which I am embarked as (with the assistance of my Real friends) [we] Will defeat their little Low Ungreatefull Schemes. . . ."[24]

By September 20, Tommy reported that "matters seem some[what] changed. . . ." He has had a long conversation with the conservative court party member, John Cook, about Dr. Ridgely, making it clear to Cook that the doctor's conduct in public "had deprived him of my assistance." Tommy's idea was to form a third party, made up of what he considered right thinking men from both traditional parties. Cook presses him to include Ridgely but Tommy refuses, telling Cook his "sentiments were fixt." He tells Caesar that Loockerman, on the other hand, has seen "the rapid progress of our third party scheme [and] has . . . tackt about and is [now] violently against the Doctor." Tommy enclosed a list of his new alliances. Caesar was listed on both the old court and the new "middle" party, which was now unabashedly Whig and consisted of Caesar, John Haslet, Thomas Collins, William Killen, John Baning and the vacillating Vincent Loockerman.[25]

However, when Tommy registered this list with the Sheriff, he had to admit that it caused "great commotion among some of your [court] party." Dr. Ridgely, in particular, has reacted "with great rage and fury [and] . . . determined to send express to you . . . to know if you were not concerned in my conduct."[26] The hotheaded Tommy, now seriously worried that Caesar's opponents may get hold of "something . . . that may be turned to your disadvantage" begs his brother to "write a few words . . . that you have not advised anything to me, and are not acquainted with what I may do. . . ."[27]

Caesar was not pleased with Tommy's political maneuvering. While he was a man who invariably stood up for his principles, he also respected the views of his less radical colleagues, and was careful never to allow political differences to affect long standing friendships. It was a quality that would serve him well in the coming conflict. Now, he rebuked Tommy for his impetuousness, scolding that "some people with you are mistaken in their Politics, and you may also take for granted every Body here are not well pleased with the coalition of the two Brothers. . . ."[28] Caesar spurned Tommy's new party, and again won a seat on the assembly as a member of the court party ticket.

One example of Caesar's inherent tolerance is his continued friendship with the Penns, despite the fact that he had usurped John Penn's power by calling an illegal session of the Delaware Assembly to elect delegates to the illegal Continental Congress. "Mr R. Penn," he wrote Tommy from Philadelphia, "is a great friend to the Cause of Liberty and has Treated the Gentlemen delegates with the greatest Respect . . . his brother [Governor John Penn] wishes his Station would admit of his acting the same part. . . ."[29]

In fact, John Penn, like many colonial governors, was in a painfully ambiguous position. As an appointee of the proprietary family, he was a servant of the Crown. Yet he had lived in Pennsylvania most of his life and was as fully American as any of the people he governed. While only one colonial governor, Jonathan Trumbull of Connecticut, would actively choose the American side, Caesar knew that John Penn, like many others, had a great deal of sympathy with the American view of Parliament. Indeed, all during the time that the Continental Congress was in session, Governor Penn continued to work with the Delaware Assembly, endorsing, among other things, their nominations for important offices.[30]

By the end of September, Caesar is exhausted by the long hours of work and constant round of visiting. "Tell Betsey [Tommy's wife] and Sally [Wilson, his half sister who keeps house for him] that I have not got well Yet," he wrote Tommy, "and that I have verry little Expectation that I Shall while I am under the necessaty of Spending all those that ought to be my Leisure Hours, in Feasting or be thought to neglect those who kindly invite. . . ."[31]

In a final effort to reconcile British/American differences, the conservative, Joseph Galloway, had proposed a new plan to the Congress. It called for the American government to be administered by a "President/General," appointed by the king, and a "Grand Council," the members of which would be chosen every three years by the colonial assemblies.[32] In return, Parliament would renounce the Declaratory Act and allow each colony to control its own internal affairs. In a different climate, it was an idea that might well have been approved. Now, it was defeated by six votes to five.[33]

Meanwhile, General Gage tried to pour oil on troubled waters by assuring the people of Suffolk county that he had no intention of stopping people from passing "between the Town and the Country," nor to "disturb the peace and Quiet of the inhabitants of the Town. . . ." At the same time, he vowed: "[As] the people of the Massachusetts Bay are determined not to Submit to the Several Acts of Parliament, [I] Shall Write to his Majesty for further instructions. . . ." Caesar relayed this message to Tommy with the comment: "from this you Will readily Suppose the General is about to Act a prudent part—Query, was he not friten'd into that prudence by the many prudent opposition of the inhabitants of that Government?"[34]

In fact, Congress' support of the Suffolk Resolves had put them on a collision course with Britain. At the end of September, they agreed on a resolution forbidding merchants to import any further goods after the first of December, including those already contracted for, pending "the sense of Congress, on the means to be taken for the preservation of the liberties of America. . . ."[35] Debate on the stickier problem of prohibiting exports was begun on October 15. After five days of heated debate, during which they agreed to put off implementation of the agreement until September 1775, so as to accommodate Virginia's tobacco crop and allow South Carolina to continue to sell rice to Europe, Congress passed the resolution that came to be known as the "Association Agreement" on October 20, 1774. All three Delaware delegates signed this document, which also called for the creation of the Committees of Inspection who were given the power to publish the names of violators. The Association Agreement also included a pledge to "neither import nor purchase any slave imported after the first day of December next, after which time we will wholly discontinue the slave trade. . . ."[36] At the very time they were so resolutely calling for liberty and justice, there is no question that the slave question preyed on at least some Congressional sensibilities.

In November, when the news that the Continental Congress had endorsed the Suffolk Resolves reached King George, he declared that he was "not sorry that the line of conduct now seems chalked out; the New England colonies are in a state of rebellion; blows must decide whether they are to be subject to this country or independent."[37] Two weeks later he opened Parliament with a rousing speech declaring that "fresh violences of very criminal nature" in Massachusetts called for vigorous enforcement of Coercive Acts. It was received in the House of Commons with overwhelming acclaim.[38]

Meanwhile, meetings were held in Delaware's counties to appoint the new committees of inspection. Unlike the assembly's various committees of correspondence, the inspection committees tended to attract only the most zealous supporters of the boycott and it wasn't long before they would wield extraordinary political and economic power in the colonies.

One of them, the newly fledged New Castle Committee of Inspection formally endorsed the acts of the Congress in a resolution on November 28, 1774. Like the Association Agreement, itself, it also discouraged "every species of extravagance and dissipation, especially all horse racing and all sorts of gaming, cock-fighting, exhibitions of plays . . . and other expensive diversions and entertainments" as well as any show of mourning other "than a black crepe or ribbon on the arm or hat. . . ." The committee also warned all vendors "not to take advantage of scarcity" by raising their prices and called for a public boycott of any merchant who failed to comply.[39]

In December, this committee went one step further, calling on "inhabitants from the age of sixteen to fifty years . . . to assemble on the second Tuesday in January . . . and organize themselves into companies of not less than fifty or more than seventy-five men. Each company is to choose a captain, two lieutenants, an ensign, four sergeants, to corporals and one drummer. . . ."[40] Preparations for armed resistance had begun.

10

The Breach Widens

Tommy's daughter Lavinia was born in Dover on January 16, 1775; a time full of uncertainty and tension. Across the Atlantic, King George III had abruptly dissolved Parliament, boasting that he had foiled "the nabobs, planters and other volunteers who would not be ready for the electoral battle." The king then took steps to acquire the sort of members he wanted: the new Parliament's high number of more "desirable" country gentlemen was the direct result of bargains made with the owners and patrons of certain boroughs. For instance, Lord North paid Lord Chatham 2500 guineas from the royal treasury to secure three "safe" seats in Cornwall.[1] Even so, America's friend, Edmund Burke, was once again returned to Parliament by Caesar's ancestral city of Bristol, now an important tobacco trading port. For economic reasons alone, Burke's merchant constituents wanted the crisis with America resolved as quickly as possible.

Despite Burke's best efforts, however, every proposal to repeal the offensive acts went down in defeat. In a frantic effort to avert the violence that now seemed inevitable, Lord North made one last offer: Parliament would agree to exempt any colony from all taxes except those needed to regulate trade, if, in return, the colony would agree to fund a "fair proportion towards its own common defense and expense of civil administration." It was an idea that pleased no one: the royal bloc saw it as a betrayal of principle; the colonies as a thinly disguised demand for their surrender.[2]

In February, Parliament declared Massachusetts in rebellion and passed a number of bills "to Restrain the Trade and Commerce" of all New England." These "Restraining Acts," as they were called, were Britain's answer to the Continental Congress' boycott. They increased the British force in Boston by ten thousand men and closed the North Atlantic fisheries to ships from New England. Henceforth, New England was only allowed to trade with Britain or the West Indies. By the end of March this restriction had been expanded to include New Jersey, Pennsylvania, Maryland, Virginia and South Carolina with special mention of the "ports within the government of the counties of New Castle, Kent and Sussex on the Delaware."[3] It was said in the House of Commons that any gentleman who doubted that the inhabitants of these counties deserved to be singled out need only to peruse certain papers to be convinced.[4]

It's possible that they had seen a letter from the Kent Committee of Correspondance to their compatriots in Philadelphia, a letter that Tommy told Caesar, "breathed tar and feathers." Written by William Killen, it was apparently sent over Dr. Ridgely's objections and was, according to Tommy's informants, "ill received" in Philadelphia. They scorned it as a "mixt medley of nonsense" and did "not hesitate to call the Kent Committee very harsh names. . . ."[5]

Tommy seemed unaware of the king's growing determination to punish the Americans, not to mention the boiling antagonism in Parliament. In this same letter, he naively informed Caesar that he had "received the good Tidings of the favourable reception the Congress Petition has met with at the Throne" news that he thought would "work the same effect on those factious discontented spirits here, [that] it is said to have done on those of the same stamp in England." Caesar, at this point, is in New Castle for the Assembly and suffering so painfully from "gout in both feet" that he had to ride the few blocks to the meetings in his carriage "for five days past."[6]

In stark contrast to the zealous committees, the Delaware Assembly was indecisive. In March 1775, after Caesar, Read and McKean were reappointed to the Second Continental Congress scheduled for May in Philadelphia, they were instructed on the one hand, to "studiously avoid . . . every thing disrespectful or offensive to our most gracious Sovereign, or in any measure invasive of his just rights and prerogative," and on the other, to adhere to all "claims and resolutions" agreed on at the last meeting of Congress. . . ." Also, while Delaware's delegates were urged to insist on an equal vote with all other colonies, they were also told to break ranks, if necessary, and deal directly with anyone appointed by king.[7] It was a document that bore the unmistakable stamp of its ambivalent authors: John McKinly and Charles Ridgely, among others.

Such dithering was common the early months of 1775; a time when many Delawareans fretted over the strong stance taken by the First Continental Congress. In fact, Thomas McKean, writing to John Adams many years later, claimed that a majority of the population were against the idea of armed resistance.[8] At the beginning of February the following unsigned letter from Kent County appeared in the Pennsylvania "Ledger:"

> the people here begin to change their sentiments, concluding, in their more deliberate moments, that such violent measure as have been pursued will not heal, but . . . widen the breach; . . . I believe, if the King's standard were now erected, nine out of ten would repair to it. The people have not, till lately, considered the consequences of a civil war with so . . . powerful a nation as . . . Great Britain . . . Who could think that a three penny duty on tea could have occasioned all these difficulties when only a refusal to purchase the article would have kept us free?"[9]

When the Philadelphia Committee of Correspondence inquired after the truth of such claims, the Kent county Committee of Inspection rose up in outrage, calling the letter "very injurious to spirit of the inhabitants of this County. . . ." Claiming that the people "have not in the least changed their opinions and are well disposed to make a virtuous stand against tyranny and oppression," they accused the "wicked and insidious author" of trying to "excite mutual suspicions and distrust . . . weaken our hands, and prepare the way for an easy victory for the enemies of America."[10]

Robert Holliday, a Kent county Quaker, finally admitted writing the letter, but protested that the original text had been altered and that he had neve meant it to be published. "I am sincerely sorry I ever wrote it," he declared, "and hope I may be excused for this my first breach . . . I intend it shall be the last."[11]

The committee, however, did not let him off easily. Holliday was summoned to appear before them and sign a full recantation of his "weakness and folly." He was also required to promise to "never again oppose those laudable measures necessarily adopted by [his] countrymen for the preservation of American freedom. . . ."[12] When Tommy wrote Caesar about the incident in May, he mentioned that a certain Richard Smith had also written a letter to the Committee protesting that "he had never had any thing in view but a reconciliation between England and the colonies . . . but the Com[mittee] . . . has not said any thing on that head. . . ."[13]

Smith and Holliday were not the only ones. As revolutionary emotions heated to the boiling point, more and more of Delaware's Tory sympathizers were forced to recant and at least one was actually tarred and feathered. According to a contemporary account, when a certain Captain Byrne, late from England, tried to capture two wagons for the king, he was overpowered and taken to a nearby mill where a grapevine was put around his neck. After being coated with varnish and sprinkled with feathers from a pillow, he was led into town, drenched with rum and thrown into a duck hole.[14]

Nor was the practice of tarring and feathering confined to the Americans; Sam Adams wrote Richard Henry Lee that when the "polite Gentlemen of the British Army" had paraded a tarred victim by General Gage's house in Boston, the general had pretended that he didn't see it.[15]

The Boston Whigs continued to publish polemics against British rule, causing Parliament to grow ever more scornful of Gage's apparent inability to control them. Arrogantly dismissing the Whigs as a "rude Rabble without plan, without concert, and without conduct," Parliament also ignored Gage's pleas for more men.[16] Gage had told the British secretary of war, Lord Barrington that, "If you think ten thousand men sufficient, send Twenty, if one Million is thought enough, give two; you will save both Blood and Treasure in the end. A large force will terrify, and engage many to join you, a middling one will encourage Resistance, and gain no friends."[17]

In fact, the British soldiers already in Boston were so poorly equipped and their morale so dismally low, that the general was having trouble keeping them from deserting. When some who tried were shot, the Americans were horrified. While they were not against executing a man for disobeying the commandments of God, they did not think it a just punishment for disobeying a general.[18] Meanwhile, the city buzzed with talk: Gage was about to arrest the Whig leaders; the leaders had fled Boston; more British troops were on their way. The Whigs seemed to know everything the British planned to do as soon as they did themselves. It is now widely believed that their information came directly from General Gage's own wife; the American-born Margaret Kemble Gage.[19]

Both sides now openly planned for war. On April 14, Gage received word that seven hundred Royal marines were on their way to Boston, along with instructions to raise additional forces from "sympathetic" New Englanders.[20] In a continuation of the so-called "powder alarms," Gage had determined to destroy a supply of munitions stored in the town of Concord. After his scouts reported that the shorter route through Weston would be dangerous for a marching army, being "woody in most places and commanded by hills," he decided on the longer route through Lexington despite the danger of hostile "bushmen." To his credit, he also instructed his commander, Colonel Smith to ". . . take care that the soldiers do not plunder the inhabitants, or hurt private property."[21]

Caesar, writing after the fact, said he believed:

from the best accounts, . . . [that] General Gage was forced upon the plan of Sending Troops to Concord by the other officers of note, together with ye tory party in Boston . . .—The purpose of the Expidition was to destroy the ammunition, arms, provisions and Bridges, and some say to take Hancock and the other delegates who they know to be in that part of the Country. Mr. Hancock told me he had been to see that Small Company [in] a Lexington Exercise, and had not left them more ten minutes when the [British] Troops Came up. . . .[22]

The Whigs, as usual, already knew of Gage's plans. Paul Revere's famous midnight ride, actually one of many he took across the Massachusetts countryside, was as much to warn Sam Adams and John Hancock in Lexington as to protect the store of arms in Concord.[23]

A few hours before dawn on April 19, the British troops crossed the frigid waters of the Charles River. They landed at Cambridge and marched toward Lexington, meeting a group of American militia on the Lexington Green at 4:30 A.M. It is not certain who fired first, but all was soon smoke and confusion. The green British regulars panicked and broke ranks, charging forward, firing wildly and lunging with their long bayonets at anyone in their way. When it was over, eight Americans were dead and nine wounded, most of whom had been shot while trying to escape. The British had but one wounded infantryman although a Major Pitcairn was said to have sustained "a bloody finger."[24] Subsequently, the American minister Jonas Clark claimed, that after "the most careful enquiry . . . far from firing first upon the King's troops; . . . it appears that but very few of our people fired at all."[25]

Caesar described what happened next in a hurried, emotional letter to Tommy dated May 11, 1775.

Last Evening I S[aw] a verry intelligent man from Massachusetts Government who was in the engagement, and got him to relate the Story- He says they fired on the people at Lexington . . . and killed seven on the Spot, they dispersed without returning the fire, that the Troops went on to Concord distroyed much flower & pork, threw a Quantaty of Ball in the River, Broke two cannon and did other damage, That by this time one hundred and fifty Provincials had Collected near the Bridge, that the Troops fired on them and killed three, that the provincials for the first time Returned the fire, which they Continued and [i]ncreasing in . . . number drove the Toops back as far as Lexington—where, when Joined by the second Brigade they made some Stand but Soon Retired again . . . without making any Stop till they got to Charles-Town. He says they retreated at the rate of near six miles an Hour—That there never was more than four hundred Provincials . . . till they got to Buncar's Hill at the Edge of Charles-Town, that there were better than two

Thousand provincials who . . . were on the wrong Road, and about two thousand more who followed verry fast but Could not Come up till at Buncar's Hill—That the Provincials had thirty Six Killed, That he Cannot tell how many Regulars were Killed, but that the provincials buried one hundred and three of them which they found dead on the Road from Concord to Charles-Town."[26]

The American Revolution had begun.

11
News of War

CAESAR WROTE THIS LETTER FROM PHILADELPHIA ON MAY 11 AS THE second Continental Congress was getting under way. A few days earlier, while travelling up from Dover, he had sent Tommy the following note from New Castle:

> I arrived here yesterday afternoon and [visited] Col. Bland, one of the delegates from Virginia, who is since gone up to town in the stage & says the other delegates from his colony . . . might have got as far as Chester last night. Mr. Hall, Mr. Johnson & Mr. Tilghman of Maryland set out from here this day soon after dinner & about the same time a brig from South Carolina passed by [on the Delaware River] with the delegates from that colony. Mr. Chaise of Maryland went through yesterday. Mr. Read & I are to set out tomorrow morning attended by the Militia of this town at the ins[istance] and request of the Company."[1]

Later, Caesar described the Boston delegation's "public entry . . . into this City . . . [It was] verry grand and Intended to Shew their approbation of the Conduct of the good people of that Government in the distressing Situation of affairs there. . . ."[2] He also adds that "BFrank attended PA assembly now sitting."[3] Upon Benjamin Franklin's return from his long sojourn in London, the Pennsylvania Assembly had immediately appointed him to the Second Continental Congress where he joined forces with the Presbyterians in an effort to shift Pennsylvania from the Toryism of Joseph Galloway to the more radical position of the Pennsylvania committees. Galloway, himself, had now refused to participate at all.[4]

The mood of all of these men must have been both somber and resolute. The first news of the battles of Lexington and Concord had arrived in the city about two weeks earlier, having been brought down the east coast by mounted messengers in an astonishingly short time, each rider contacting the next according to a system set up by the Massachusetts Committee of Safety.[5] One of them had galloped into Philadelphia on April 26, ridden on to Chester, and

arrived in New Castle about nine o'clock in the evening. By midnight, the message was in the hands of Lieutenant Colonel Patterson at Cooch's Bridge who sent it on to Tobias Rudolph at Head of
the Elk. It then went on to Baltimore and points south.[6]

Tommy was mustering troops in Dover, bragging that the people
assembled at the courthouse had unanimously appointed him captain. "I drew up the military rules," he claimed, "which being
adopted later by all the county, made the first militia of the revolution."[7] On May 10, he reported to Caesar that ten companies had
been enrolled and "we expect all the rest will be inrolled this week.
. . . The people go so fully into it that I expect we shall form twenty
companies." If Caesar could spare the money, he wanted "a drum,
colors, etc. by this vessel."[8]

In this he was disappointed. "Such a martial Spirit prevails" Caesar wrote, "That I can't get you a Drum & Colours in less than two
weeks. . . ."[9] Martial spirit, indeed; at this point, the militias were
little more than armed vigilante bands, and with feelings running
so high between the radicals and conservatives, as much a danger
to each other as they were to the British.[10]

In an effort to impose order on what was fast becoming a dangerously unruly movement, the officers of some twenty companies of
the Kent county militia met in Dover on May, 25, 1775, with John
Haslet as chairman. A hint of the precariousness of the situation
was contained in their promise to "subject themselves to such . . .
penalties, military punishments and disgrace as courts-martial" if
they should offend "against the rules of military discipline, or in
contravening in word or deed the true interest of America. . . ."
Kent was divided into two sections, each to contain one regiment.
Caesar Rodney was elected colonel of the upper regiment, with
Thomas Collins lieutenant colonel and French Batell as major.
John Haslet was to be colonel of the lower regiment with William
Rhoads and Robert Hodgson as lieutenant colonel and major. All
signed a solemn oath to defend liberties and privileges of America
at risk of their own lives and fortunes.[11]

To fund such activities, the New Castle Committee resolved to
collect 1s. 6d from each taxable inhabitant, over and above that
needed for current expenses; a tax, Caesar declared, that "the people pay . . . with more cheerfulness that they have been known to
pay any tax heretofore."[12]

In the same way, the Continental Congress took control of the
military on the national front, informing the Delaware Assembly on
June 7, that they thought it necessary for "the twelve united colonies and parish of St. John, in Georgia, to have an armed force at

their general expense sufficient for repelling and defeating all hostile attempts by arms. . . ."[13] Upon receiving this message, the Delaware Assembly voted, without dissent, to bear their share of military expenses and asked Caesar, as speaker, to authorize an immediate loan of £500.[14]

Caesar informed Tommy on June 20, that the Congress had ordered 2,000,000 dollars to be "Struck here as a Continental paper Currency . . . to defend our Constitution Rights and priviledges. . . ." The money was to be underwritten by all twelve colonies within seven years, each portion to be meted out according to "the number of Inhabitants in Each Colony."[15] Delaware's share would be about $37,000 or £30,000.

He also reported that Colonel George Washington had been appointed general and commander in chief of all the colony forces and would set out for Boston within the next two days, adding that he "will have a large Escort from this City as far as Trentontown at least. . . ."[16] Caesar also recommended his young landlord, John Parke, to Washington for a position in the army. Parke, who had just come of age and was "resolved to draw his sword in support of the American cause," was later ordered to Boston as deputy quartermaster general.[17]

Upon receiving his appointment, the forty-three year old General Washington described his feelings to a friend: "Unhappy it is . . . that the once-happy and peaceful plains of America are either to be drenched with blood or inhabited by a race of slaves. Sad alternative! But can a virtuous man hesitate in his choice?"[18]

The new general faced a daunting task. It had been decided that the core of the new Continental army would be drawn from the New England militia plus ten companies of expert riflemen, six from Pennsylvania and two each from Maryland and Virginia. (As time went on, of course, this nucleus grew. Although the number of men in each unit of the Continental army would vary considerably, a company, which consisted of about seventy-five officers and men, was the smallest unit; a regiment, composed of eight companies, was next and a brigade, made up of several regiments, the largest.)

From the start, Washington had trouble keeping his best men. His original army was made up of 16,667 New England militia, so far the only soldiers who had had any experience in battle. However, he soon discovered that, not only were they reluctant to serve with troops from "foreign" colonies, but, like all militia, they had volunteered for a specific time and, when that time was up, they simply left for home.[19]

In his additional capacity as commander of the navy, Washington ordered a number of armed vessels to be fitted out on the Delaware River. These included the *Lexington* under Captain John Barry, and the *Alfred*, with First Lieutenant John Paul Jones aboard, said to be the first vessel to fly the American flag. Meanwhile a permanent lookout was stationed at Lewes, and Delaware river pilots forbidden to conduct armed British vessels up the Delaware Bay.[20]

Inevitably, all these preparations for war had an economic impact at home. Tommy managed to sell one of the "sloops" that had been used to transport grain from the farm. Caesar, while glad of the sale, worried about the upkeep of the remaining vessels. "As times have but a verry Gloomy appearance I wish both the other Veshells were Sold, provided they were *well* sold. . . ." He also worried about the sale of their crops: "the Hay we know how to dispose of, but God knows what we shall do with the Wheat. . . ."[21]

Also, with no time to devote to business, they planned to rent the farms. Tommy reported to Caesar that a certain Richard Turly wanted them by August. He thought "the whole of the farms including the meadow to be worth £500 per annum divided thus: for the old place £230, with permission to clear what you intended to add to it; homeplace & Hartsfield £230, with permission as aforesaid; wares(?) & meadow 60, on seven year leases." Tommy thought this a fair price, (it adds up to £520, not £500) "though wheat has fell, every other article has risen . . . they would lett for more if wheat was still at 7/6." With the farms rented the brothers had little need for farm workers: "some applycations have been made for negroes—all the men except old Charles I believe will bring £100 each when it is convenient to sell."[22] There is no doubt that Old Charles and Caesar's coachman John, two Rodney slaves that have been mentioned by name, were to find their lives profoundly affected by the momentous events now on the horizon.

The thirty-one year old Tommy, however, was excited by the prospect of war and childishly eager to receive his military accoutrements. Caesar could now report that his drum was on the way but it would take about two more weeks for "the colors." In fact, they would not arrive until the middle of September.[23] Tommy's coat was "for the Light Infantry of the first Battalion . . . [of which] the Lieutenant Colonel . . . is to have an Epelet on the Right Shoulder and a Strap on the left, the Major an Epelet on the Left, and a Strap on the Right, of Gold Lace." The uniform for the "Second Battalion is to be Brown, & White facings, and their infantry Blue, & white faceings."[24] Caesar did not describe his own uniform as Colonel, but knowing how important they were to his younger brother, told Tommy he could "assure Mr. Loockerman they will be ellegant and cleaver."[25]

Caesar, unlike his brother, did not relish the prospect of war. The news was ominous. Part of the British troops expected from Ireland, he wrote, had already "landed at Boston and the remainder are looked for Every day . . . We may Expect warm work, and warm it will be I dare say, for we Just had an Express from our provintial Camp . . . that we have there Eighteen Thousand men ready to Receive the [British] Regulars and indeed wishing they may Come out . . . I wish our new Generals were at the Camp."[26]

The "Battle of Bunker Hill" took place on June 17. The British, having occupied a narrow neck of land overlooking Boston harbor, had positioned themselves to bombard the city while the Americans had gathered on adjacent Breed's Hill. During the night of June 16, the British attacked, marching up Breed's Hill in close military order, wave after wave, while the Americans fired until they ran out of ammunition. The British succeeded in capturing the hill, but only after nearly half their force of twenty-four hundred men had been killed or wounded. It would be a long time before they would attempt another frontal assault on the American "rabble."[27]

On July 3, Caesar reported to Tommy that nine companies of Pennsylvania riflemen were nearly complete and would march to a camp near Boston by the end of the week.[28] He also enclosed an account of the battle at Bunker Hill from a Philadelphia newspaper. It reported, falsely, that the British general William Howe had died of his wounds three days after the engagement. (The brother of Admiral Lord Richard Howe, and the son of a mistress of George I, General Howe was said to be a "left handed" cousin of the king. He was one of three generals sent to serve under Gage after the battle of Lexington.)

Meanwhile the Boston Committee of Safety rushed to get their report on the battle to London in advance of General Gage's, sending nearly one hundred depositions and a letter, written by Dr. Joseph Warren, to the "Inhabitants of Great Britain" on the American schooner *Quero*. The *Quero* proved to be so fast that it reached London a full two weeks before General Gage's report of the battle arrived on the brig *Sukey*. The American story caused a sensation, particularly since the depositions included one from a wounded British officer that supported the American version and praised the humanity of his captors. One member of the British government, frustrated that he could neither confirm or deny the reports, complained that the American's "saint-like account of the skirmish . . . has been read with avidity and believed."[29]

Caesar wrote Tommy from Philadelphia on July 27 that "we have had a London paper informing us of the arrival of the Vessel that went Express from the people of Boston . . . giving them an account of the Battle at Lexington—upon the spreading of this news there, the Ministry [said] . . . they had received no accounts from America, [and] . . . many people were led to discredit the accounts brought by the Massachusetts Express." However, when it was advertised that "all those who doubted the truth of the news—Might Repair to the Mansion House, Where the Depositions . . . were deposited . . . the news was generally Credited." A ship had already left Bristol and a weary Caesar thought the Congress would not rise until "the news is generally credited . . . I do know that they are heartily tired—and so am I."[30] He was, in fact, "verry little if any better than when I wrote you last. Yet able to attend the Congress."[31]

At home, the revolutionary committees continued to root out suspected Tories in their midst. On July, 18, 1775, a witness testified that Thomas Robinson, the Sussex landowner who had been a member of the October 1773 Committee of Correspondence, had sold tea to two customers from his store at the head of the Indian River, having "taken it out of a canister that held twelve to fifteen pounds." A second witness then claimed that when Robinson was told that the people were forming militia in order to defend their liberties, he called them "a pack of fools, for it was taking up arms against the King . . . and we ought to obey the King and those put in authority under him . . . and that the great people were only leading the poor into a premunire, and after they had done it would not help them out of it."

Robinson had also dismissed "the present Congress an unconstitutional body . . . pushing the common people between them and all danger." However, when the Committee summoned Robinson to appear, he effectively snubbed his nose at them, saying he "would not think of coming before them unless he could bring forty or fifty armed men with him." The essentially powerless committee could do nothing except brand Robinson an enemy of his country and call for a boycott of his store. Whereupon Robinson trumped them again. When a notice to that effect appeared in a Philadelphia newspaper, he produced a certificate signed by five members of the committee asking the public to suspend judgement until his case could be heard by the full committee![32]

12

Spies, Storms, and Tories

AFTER THE BLOODY CONFLICTS AT LEXINGTON, CONCORD AND BUNKER hill, the Continental Congress made one more try at reconciliation. In a move calculated to circumvent the hated power of Parliament, they sent what is now known as the Olive Branch Petition directly to the king urging him to intervene on their behalf. All three Delaware delegates signed this document; surely a difficult move for men who so passionately supported representative government. It was also an impossible request, however much the king wanted to hold on to his colonies. To do as they asked, George III would have had to overrule his own ministers and summarily negate the decisions of an elected Parliament. While the king, himself, may have cared little about such things, he lacked the strength to resist the charges of tyranny that would surely have erupted from America's remaining supporters in Parliament: the Whigs.[1]

As a matter of fact, at the very time the Congress was drafting the Olive Branch Petition in May of 1775, the king's ministers were busy negotiating with the German prince of Hesse for seventeen thousand men to bolster their British Regulars in Boston, and, just two days after Richard Penn delivered the petition to London, George III issued a proclamation declaring the colonies in rebellion.[2] Lord Dartmouth was replaced by Lord George Germaine, who would henceforth direct the British military strategy from London. Germaine, a strong advocate of Parliamentary power, was convinced that this was a war that would be easily won.

Back in Boston, General Gage was still trying to convince the king and his ministers that it would take a strong army to put down the rebellion and that the Americans were not the disorderly rabble that they imagined. Despite Parliamentary doubts as to his competence, Gage managed to be reappointed in August, even though he had been so damaged by recent events that even his own officers now questioned his authority. Three new generals, William Howe, Henry Clinton and John Burgoyne, were sent to serve under him, and by October, Howe had taken over the command.[3]

Meanwhile, an election was held in Kent county to form a new revolutionary committee. On August 14, thirty-five members, including both Rodney brothers, were chosen, with Caesar as chairman. Three days later, a new Committee of Correspondence was also chosen, consisting of Thomas Rodney, chairman, James Tilton, William Killen, John Baning and Vincent Loockerman. It is unclear whether this was the same Vincent Loockerman whom Tommy had earlier accused of vacillation, or his son. In any case, all were now considered radicals.

The duties and interrelationships of these committees are complex. The Committees of Correspondance that first arose in response to the Stamp Act, and gained new strength after the Tea Act of 1774, had been subordinated to the Committees of Inspection at the beginning of 1775. Now, in September of that year, a new larger body called the Council of Safety came into being. By claiming the right to act in lieu of Governor John Penn when the assembly was not in session, it further undercut the power of the colonial governors.

Delaware's Council of Safety took over military matters from the Committee of Inspection, and reorganized the militia into three county brigades. At a six day meeting in September, John McKinly was placed in command of New Castle county's brigade and John Dagworthy in charge of the one from Sussex. Kent's two battalions, formerly commanded by colonels Caesar Rodney and John Haslet, were consolidated into one brigade with Caesar in command. He, McKinly and Dagworthy, were now given the rank of brigadier general. Caesar was not present at this meeting; Tommy wrote him of the outcome from Dover.

The Council of Safety, however, was not without its own political controversy. Tommy told Caesar that Dr. Ridgely had been made a member, despite being accused of defeatism and undue criticism of Congress, and the "resentment of the people is high against him." Tommy also ran for the assembly in the fall of 1775, having been "prevailed on to be mention[ed] as the sixth man" even though "much against my own Interests and inclynation. . . ."[4]

The old Committee of Inspection was then concerned only with "civil matters," which is to say the implacable rooting out of Tory sympathizers.[5] Much later, Thomas Rodney denied that he ever took part in the more blatant persecution of suspected Tories, insisting that, as a member of the Council of Safety, he had opened himself up to "hard words from such violent patriots as Killen and Parson John Miller" when he tried to restrain them. Nevertheless, whenever anti-Tory action occurred in Kent county, the ebullient

Tommy or his Dover light infantry company usually were in the midst of it.[6]

Caesar was disgusted with such petty bickering. He feared, he told Tommy, that "there will be much disturbance at Your Election, and perhaps events brought about in Consequence . . . that neither you nor I would wish. . . ." Once again, he scolded his brother for acting in a partisan and imprudent manner and for not standing up for "men who both you and I would wish to be in friendship with. . . ."[7] Thomas was elected, but Caesar, well aware of his patriotic fervor, had little confidence that his brother would discharge his duties in a statesmanlike manner. He begged him to be "Careful to deserve as much of the [honor] your Station affords . . . [and to be] puctual in the discharge of every public trust."[8]

Caesar, meanwhile, was working harder than ever. On September third, he wrote Tommy's wife what he teasingly called "the first epistle of Caesar to Elizabeth" from New Castle where he was serving in the assembly. Tommy had visited him there a day of so before on his way to Philadelphia to sell the crops. He had no sooner left than a violent storm, possibly a hurricane, had swept up the Atlantic coast. Caesar was worried about their load of grain on its way to market.

> [Tommy] told me that the schooner has left the creeks mouth the day before he left Dover and that he imagined she must have passed New-castle before he came. Whether she has passed here or not, I cannot say, but am apt to think she has not, and if that be the case, the chances are much against her, for we had here last night one of the most dreadful storms I ever [knew].
>
> I thought poor Newcastle would have been carried away, part of it is gone, some [persons] were obliged to stay up stairs till breakfast time, the tide heavily covered the lower portions . . . [I am] extreamly anctious to know . . . how much I may have suffered by the storm, wither in my banks, meadows, seeding wheat or in any other way. Therefore shall be oblidged to you immediately on the rec[eip]t of this letter to send for my overseer and inquire particularly of him into these matters. . . .[9]

As it happened, the schooner survived without damage and Caesar was able to sail in her from New Castle to Philadelphia for the next session of the Continental Congress. "I have undertaken the work," he wrote Betsey, "and am determined to go through with it if possible, though much jaded in the service." Tommy, meanwhile, cut short his visit and returned home to check on damage done to the farm.[10]

Philadelphia was preparing for war. Fire-rafts and a floating battery were built to protect the port and, on September 9, the channel buoys were removed and underwater obstructions called "chevaux-de-frise" installed to prevent enemy vessels from coming up the river. (These were large boxes filled with rocks on which iron spikes were attached at a forty-five-degree angle.) Two river pilots were instructed how to navigate the unmarked channel in order to bring in vessels carrying stores and ammunition; all others were ordered to lay up their craft and stay in port.[11]

Of course, local shipping was now vulnerable as well. In November 1775, Caesar told Tommy to be very careful with their new schooner, as a brig belonging to a local man had run up on the Chevaux-de-frise while loaded with sugar, molasses and coffee and "immediately sunk in five-fatham water,—no part insured. . . ."[12]

Meanwhile, Delaware authorized the issue of £30,000 in paper money, the largest to date. The notes, which still bore the arms of the king, were to be dated January 1, 1776. They consisted of ninety-six thousand separate bills, ranging in value from one to twenty shillings and were to be signed by John McKinly of New Castle, Thomas Collins of Kent, and Boaz Manlove of Sussex. Caesar was appointed to serve as trustee for Kent county, his cousin John Rodney for Sussex, and Richard McWilliam for New Castle.

The third signer of the bills, Boaz Manlove, subsequently fled to the British army. His defection would come as a bitter shock for the assembly. Manlove had not only been a member of the 1774 Committee of Correspondence, he had also taken part in the Lewes meeting to protest the Boston Port Bill, and had been a member of the extraordinary session of the assembly called in August 1774 to elect delelgates to the First Continental Congress.[13]

Manlove was not Delaware's only clandestine Tory, however. Around the same time, Daniel Varnum had complained to a friend that "He as lief be under a tyrannical king as a tyrannical commonwealth, especially if the d——d Presbyterians had control of it." Also, a citizen of Sussex county wrote James Tilton that a certain "JC" had stated that Congress and its "damn set would ruin the country."[14]

"JC" was subsequently called up before the Committee of Inspection. He did not, however, back down as readily as Robert Holliday and Richard Smith. When some in the audience said his statement "sounded like a death warrant," he, in "an insulting and swearing way said put it into execution." Even after he reluctantly agreed to sign a recantation, there were some who wanted to "proceed in the new mode of making converts by bestowing upon C. a

Back and front views of a Two Shilling & Sixpence note dated 1 June 1776 signed by John McKinly, Thomas Collins, and Boaz Manlove. Courtesy of the Historical Society of Delaware.

coat of tar and feathers." In the end, however, cooler heads prevailed. There was no violence beyond the "beating the drum a few rods and two boys throwing an egg apiece."[15]

While Varnum and "JC" may have been merely imprudent in their statements, some Tories posed a much more serious danger. When, in October 1775, a Philadelphian named Dr. Bearsly was jailed for writing letters to England "injurious & distructive to us in the American Cont[ine]nt," Caesar reported that he had been "marked out as a thorough-power Torry" for some time and was once carted through the streets for having "insulted the people."

Caesar told Tommy the story of his capture in a letter dated October 9. A certain Mr. Carter was known to have booked passage from Philadelphia to London. A few days before the ship was due to sail, the son of the local sheriff had gone to Dr. Bearsly's house to settle a debt and surprised him with this same Mr. Carter. Both men were huddled over a batch of papers which they immediately gathered up in "seeming confusion." Suspecting foul play, the sheriff's son reported the incident to the revolutionary committee. On October 4, the ship left Philadelphia on schedule and put in at Chester to pick up her passengers (a common arrangment at the time because it shortened the voyage). The passengers who had journeyed overland to Chester, however, now included a small group of committeemen travelling incognito. Immediately upon boarding the ship, they seized Mr. Carter and questioned him about the mysterious papers. Panicking, he confessed that several letters from Dr. Bearsly and a Mr. Brooks were hidden in the "shifty-tails" of a woman passenger. After securing the packet from the woman, the committeemen left Mr. Carter on the ship, while they hurried back to town to "seize the authors" of the letters.

The packet, ostensibly addressed to a Mrs. MacCawley, was found to contain letters to Lord Dartmouth and other ministers of state. They promised if five thousand Regulars (British troops) were sent to Philadelphia, five thousand locals would be found to join them, and boasted that "Great numbers of those who now wear Cockades and Uniforms were hearty in the [British] Cause." Dr. Bearsly, claiming that the Americans were such cowards that he could make "five thousand of them run by snapping a single pistol at them," had also included a satirical cartoon of himself being carted through the streets of Philadelphia surrounded by a savage mob.

Far more ominous than these idle boasts, however, was the fact that the packet contained detailed plans showing the positions of the chevaux-de-frise in the Delaware River. After examining them, the Committee of Safety immediately sent a pilot boat down the river to seize Carter off the ship.[16]

In November, Caesar was back in Philadelphia "after a very cold and disagreeable ride." He had also had "a smart fit of the astma." He was staying "with a certain Widow Dewer opposite John Cadwallader's in Second St." whom he described as a "very genteel, well behaved kind Body . . . who keeps a good Table." Caesar has "a good lodgeing Room and Parlour. . . ." for which he is to "pay her 30/ a week for my self, and 10/ a week for my Servant, and am to find my own Wine, Spirits and fire-wood. . . ." Caesar, like all eighteenth-century gentlemen, never travelled without a servant to tend to his domestic needs.[17]

In the same letter he enclosed a newspaper "account of the surrender of Montreal to General Montgomery on the thirteenth instant. . . ." The previous May, Congress had sent an expedition to Canada in an effort to persuade the French Canadians to join in the revolt against England. After initial easy victories against British forts along the shore of Lake Champlain, Brigadier General Richard Montgomery had invaded the province of Quebec, and successfully taken Montreal after the British commander fled the city.

However, by December, the American campaign had foundered. Early in the month, a separate force under Benedict Arnold had crossed the St. Lawrence river to join Montgomery, arriving seriously weakened by cold and lack of food after an arduous advance through the Maine wilderness. Arnold and Montgomery attempted to storm the city of Quebec through heavy snow on New Year's Eve, 1775, but failed when their plan was betrayed by a deserter.[18] In the ensuing fight, Montgomery was killed, Arnold wounded, and four hundred Americans forced to surrender. This event led George Read, in a letter to Caesar dated January 19, 1776, to exclaim that ". . . there are great doubts whether we shall retain our Situation in Canada. . . ."[19]

13

Battles in Delaware Bay

THE BRITISH CONTINUED TO DISMISS THE AMERICAN REBELLION AS little more than a large scale riot led by a group of irresponsible rabble rousers. The new director of military operations in London, Lord George Germaine, was convinced that if the British army managed to subdue New England, the radicals would disperse; allowing loyalist majorities in the middle colonies and the south to rise in support of the mother country. His plan was for General Henry Clinton to secure the south, still seen as a British stronghold, while General John Burgoyne cleared the Americans out of Quebec. Burgoyne would then advance down Lake Champlain to the Hudson River to join General William Howe in New York; effectively isolating New England. Once that was accomplished, Howe could advance through New Jersey into Pennsylvania and Delaware.[1]

In Canada, as we have seen, things began badly for the Americans. Yet, despite the death of General Richard Montgomery and the fall of the city of Quebec, the colonists could claim a few minor victories closer to home. The first occurred on February 5, when the American major general, Charles Henry Lee, arrived in New York with several thousand men to inspect the city's defenses. Lee immediately challenged a British agreement with New York's governor that would have allowed the ships carrying General Clinton's army to North Carolina to take on provisions in New York harbor. The British, with too few men to take on Lee, gave way; in any case, they had promised not to attack the heavily Tory city.

The British fleet left New York on February 13, but encountering strong gales, did not arrive at Cape Fear, North Carolina until the middle of May; too late for Clinton's men to help a Tory uprising that was supposed to augment his southern campaign. By that time, the loyalists had already been soundly defeated by the North Carolina militia at Moore's Bridge on February 27.[2]

Meanwhile, General Howe's ships in Boston harbor were vulnerable to attack from American positions. Indeed, some Americans were so eager for Washington to launch such an attack, that they hotly accused him of delaying in order to prolong the war and thus his own position as commander in chief. Washington, however, was having trouble persuading his men, used to serving short stints in the militia, to stay in the army long enough to be effectively trained; a situation he dared not publicize for fear of alerting the British. "To maintain a post," he wrote in his own defense, "within musket-shot of the enemy, for six months together, *without ammunition*, and . . . to disband one army and recruit another within [the] distance of twenty British regiments, is more than probably ever was attempted."[3]

The British, meanwhile, were well aware of the precariousness of their position. On March 11, after a violent storm prevented him from attacking the American fortifications, Howe decided to evacuate the city. On the seventeenth, an American lookout reported: "The men of war and transports were hove short to their anchors, their sails were let fall, and, soon after, boats were lowered and manned, and, impelled by the steady man-of-war's stroke, neared the quays, and received company after company of British soldiers, the sun glancing on their scarlet uniforms and burnished muskets."[4] Howe sailed to Halifax, Nova Scotia, with seventy-six hundred British troops and a thousand loyalists, to await the reenforcements that would allow him to attack New York City.

The sight of the British leaving both New York and Boston was widely seen as a triumph of "raw troops over veteran soldiers," and greatly buoyed the Americans' confidence.[5] Talk of reconciliation began to fade, even in the cautious Delaware Assembly. On March 22, they instructed Caesar, McKean, and Read to pursue it only "on such Principles as may secure to your Constituents . . . their just Rights and Privileges." Stressing the need to preserve unity among the colonies, the assembly also gave them leave to "join . . . in all such Military Operations as may be judged proper and necessary for the common Defence. . . ."[6]

Delaware soon had her own taste of war. On March 27, the Philadelphia Committee of Safety, in charge of all the river fortifications above Wilmington, was informed by Henry Fisher of Lewes that the British man-of-war *Roebuck* had entered the mouth of Delaware Bay with a tender. The committee immediately ordered four "row-gallies" to report to the American ship *Lexington* under the command of Captain Barry, and "to exert their utmost endeavors to take or destroy all such vessels of the enemy as they might find in the Delaware."[7] (A row-galley was a large open boat, propelled by up to twenty oarsmen, with a ten pound cannon mounted on the bow.)

At the time, Colonel John Haslet was under orders to send his Sussex militia to the continental army for training. Instead, he deployed two companies of his battalion to Lewes. In a letter to George Read explaining his decision, Haslet reported that he had the *Roebuck's* third lieutenant and three soldiers in custody. They had been taken from the tender about four in the morning after "the helmsman fell asleep [and] Providence steered the boat ashore." The British officer told the Americans that the *Roebuck* had left England the previous September, and had spent the winter in Halifax. "She carried forty-four eighteen and nine pounders and can mount ten more," Haslet told Read, adding that he would keep the men in custody until Congress "directs what to do."

On Easter Sunday (April 7, 1776), the officer Haslet had put in command of the Delaware battalion at Lewes sent some troops to help unload provisions from a schooner sent by the Sussex Council of Safety. They arrived to find the *Roebuck's* tender off shore, firing her "swivels and musketry. . . ." The Sussex troops immediately pulled the schooner up on the beach and marched along the strand to return fire.

According to the Delaware commander, the troops kept up "a constant fire . . . until we perceived the distance too great. We then left off firing and unloaded the schooner, though several hundred shots were fired at us to prevent it. Our people picked up many of their balls rolling on the sand." When the tender sent to the *Roebuck* for assistance, the man-of-war raised sail and rounded the cape, but "was soon obliged to come to anchor for fear of running on the Hen and Chickens [reef]." The tender, meanwhile, was anchored within musket shot of the schooner and kept up "a continual fire with her swivels." By this time, the schooner's guns had also been loaded and "a constant fire for two hours was kept up on both sides. We undoubtedly wounded their men, for we perceived some to fall and others run to their assistance. They made several efforts to [raise] their anchor [but] were prevented by our fire, but at last they succeeded. Fortunately, however, one of our swivels cut their halyards and down came their mainsail, which compelled them to anchor once more." In the end, after a wind shift threatened to blow the crippled tender ashore, the British sent a boat from the mother ship to tow them away.

Once again the Americans were jubilant. It was said that: "This spirited little skirmish . . . [removed] from the minds of the patriots the exaggerated impression of the invincibility of the British ships

"A View of the Lighthouse on Cape Henlopen, taken at sea, August 1780." Courtesy of the Biggs Museum of American Art, Dover.

and sailors, and they flocked to the shores of the bay in readiness for another encounter." On April 17, James Tilton wrote to a friend in Philadelphia that the *Roebuck* was still near Lewes but had moved south of the cape. The British sailors, surprisingly, had asked permission to fish on the beach; an idea that was met with understandable scorn. "If they should attempt [it]," Tilton wrote, "We are determined to show them Yankee play as we did on Easter Sunday. . . ."[8]

During the first week of May, the *Roebuck* was joined by a second British ship, a sloop-of-war called the *Liverpool* carrying twenty-eight guns. Colonel Haslet wrote Caesar from Cantwell's Bridge (Odessa) on May 7 that he had received a message that they were off Port Penn and that the *Roebuck* was "fixt on one of the Thorowfare Shoals" but when he sent Captain Thomas Rodney and a Lieutenant Learmonth to check, they found she had "gone off" and was moving up toward New Castle and the chevaux-de-frise. Both ships then established a position in the upper bay, where they continually patrolled between Chester, Pennsylvania and the mouth of the Christiana River.[9]

At about three in the afternoon, May 8, thirteen row-gallies, under the command of a young Philadelphia sailor named Houston, attacked the British ships, aided by a six-gun schooner called the *Wasp* which came out from Christiana Creek to join in the battle. According to an account that was later published in a Philadelphia newspaper, a heavy exchange of fire continued for three to four hours while thousands crowded the riverbank to watch. At just about nightfall, the *Roebuck* ran aground in shallow water and the *Liverpool* was forced to anchor nearby to protect her until darkness finally brought the firing to an end.

The *Roebuck* managed to float off the bar during the night and the row-gallies renewed their attack about five the next afternoon. Firing constantly, they chased the British ships six miles down the river to New Castle where they finally moored for the night. In a letter written on May 10 pleading for more powder and lead for the troops at Lewes, George Read told Caesar that he thought the British were afraid the row-gallies would get below them and cut off their retreat. He reported that the gallies had again come out of Christiana Creek "about two hours ago" but he was afraid that "the high wind now blowing would prevent their acting to advantage. . . ." He told Caesar that while "it will be thought that too much powder and shot have been expended by the gallies on these attacks," he was "well satisfied they have produced a very happy effect on the multitudes of spectators on each side of the river. . . ."[10] Indeed, while several of the row-gallies were slightly damaged in the engagement, the British had fared far worse. It was reported that the damage to their ships' hulls was enough to keep carpenters busy patching for two days. The battle was not without American casualties, however: one man was killed and two wounded.[11]

The frustrated British retaliated by running a trading schooner aground near the Christiana Creek and plundering her cargo. They also burned an abandoned shallop. Nevertheless, on being told that the *Roebuck* was a particular favorite of Lord Sandwich, the Americans crowed, "What must his Lordship say of his ship when he hears she was beaten by 'cowardly Americans' with rusty guns and broomsticks?"[12]

Tommy was so buoyed up by "the great success of our Gallies" that he was sure "our River will soon be cleared of the British Pirates [so] that [our] shallop may git up again."[13] He was busy overseeing the spring planting, despite his military duties, and had written Caesar a week or so previously, that the wheat was in the ground and the corn due to be planted the following week. They also had nearly a thousand bushels of wheat in the granary of which he was sending a sample so that Caesar could negotiate a sale. "I never saw better wheat," he boasted, "It is quite clear of the fly & and has very few onions, so that I am persuaded it is fit for the best super fine flower." The cattle, however, were still "thin but beginning to thrive, as the grass on the marsh is prety good & and old Charles & one of the boys is constantly with them." (The "fly" refers to the so-called Hessian fly, a European pest that attacked the stalks of wheat. It was thought to have arrived with bedding for the Hessians' horses and would soon become a serious problem for Delaware farmers.)

Tommy and Caesar were still trying to rent the farms. Old Charles was presumably among the slaves who, Tommy reports, have "been pleading with [Billy Rodney] & are so averse to being sold that he does not know how you will part with them, & seems to think you had better . . . rent them with the places . . . [as] they have been all raised in your own home. . . ."[14] It was hardly surprising that the Rodneys' slaves were upset. They had, after all, belonged to Caesar all their lives and were uncertain how another master might treat them.

Again, neither Rodney brother questioned the *idea* of slavery, although Caesar would ultimately free his slaves in his will. He was also on record as opposing the further import of slaves even though his motives for doing so may have been mixed.[15] Now, as a bloody war loomed, he had apparently sided with those who chose not to make an issue of it for fear of fracturing colonial unity. At the same time, engulfed by political and military duties, he evidently wanted to be free of the economic burden of supporting slaves who would henceforth be working for a tenant.

Caesar wanted all the farms rented by the end of the year. However, since he was "seldom there, and when I am, [have] very little time to attend to it," he had to rely on the often unreliable Tommy to get it done. Now, his reaction to Tommy's letter was testy and defensive.

> You say the negroes are much aversed to being sold, which I don't doubt and agree with you and Billey that it will be a verry disagreable task, though from their past vile misbehaviour they have no right to expect any favour or partiallity . . . at my hands. They have done me so much damage and behaved so wickedly that I have lost all confidence in, and almost all affection or feeling for them, and am apprehensive that the plantations will not procure such additional rent with negroes on them [to offset] the risque of their lives and the certain expence of Doctor's bills, etc.[16]

In Delaware, the lines between Tory and Whig were now clear. Caesar wrote Tommy in early May that they were about to have "as warm if not the warmest Election that was ever held in this city—The terms for the party are Whigg & Tory—dependence and Independence."[17] In fact, many in the overwhelmingly Anglican counties of Kent and Sussex were still very ambivalent. It would take a firm commitment, as well as a good deal of political skill, on the part of Whigs such as the Rodney brothers, John Haslet, James Tilton and others, to induce respected moderates such as John Dickinson and George Read, to follow their lead. Read and Dickinson were among the large number of Delawareans who still hoped for reconciliation with Britain. They were not, as some of their enemies claimed, outright loyalists, but rather cautious, conservative men, reluctant to abandon known customs for an unknown and precarious future.[18]

That George Read was uncomfortable with the more radical, revolutionary fervor had become evident during a conflict concerning Thomas Rodney's company of light infantry in March. At that time, two assembly delegates from Sussex county; the notorious Thomas Robinson and his colleague, Colonel Jacob Moore, (a man Caesar had appointed as attorney general in 1774), were on their way to New Castle to take their seats. As they passed through Dover, they were seized by certain zealous members of the infantry and thrown into jail. Thomas' account of the incident claimed that he, as captain of the infantry, "would not submit to such proceedings; That it was unbecoming the caractor of Gentlemen. . . ." However, when he sent a written request to Robinson that he not take his seat "Till the charge against him was heard by the Assembly . . . the messenger mett Jacob Moore at the door, who drew his sword . . . whereupon a scuffle Ensued . . . the sword was broke to pieces & Robisson & Moore both seized and Confined. . . ."[19]

In an attempt to forestall further controversy, Tommy and the other Kent county Whigs, petitioned the militia to release Robinson and Moore on condition that the assembly investigate their fitness to serve. George Read, however, went one step further, charging the officers of the light infantry with breach of privilege and summoning them to appear for disciplinary action.[20] In so doing, he opened himself up to angry accusations of tyranny and Toryism from James Tilton and others of the more fervent Whigs.

While Thomas Rodney may have tried to forestall the reckless seizure of Robinson and Moore, he was, nevertheless, firmly on the side of independence. On May 12, he wrote Caesar that "I trust that this Subject will not be disputed much longer—the worst of the Tories must now Confess the black design of Administration— And that Independance is the only Guardian of freedom in America."[21] Nor was he above humiliating those who were reluctant to go along. Loockerman, he told Caesar "is frightened almost out of his wits & seems half at least on the other side of the question—his late conduct has been so particularly penurious that he is abused by almost every body—There was much fun with him last night but it is too long to tell . . ."[22]

Caesar, as he worked to bring Delaware in line behind the decisions of the Continental Congress, was also moving toward the idea of outright independence, although without the arrogance and emotion of his impetuous brother. As he slowly approached the fateful crossroads, he would increasingly find himself in opposition to most of his own Anglican communion as well as their "country cousins," the Methodists.[23] (The Methodists, at this time, had no churches of their own. They were followers of a group of itinerant preachers who, under the influence of the teachings of John Wesley, traveled around the country attempting to infuse new fire and enthusiasm into the Anglican church. They were widely suspected of having Tory sympathies because of statements made in England by Wesley.)[24]

14

Further Troubles with Tories

THE PIVOTAL EVENT THAT FINALLY PUSHED CAESAR TO OPENLY ADVOCATE independence from Britain, occurred during the week of May 10: Congress passed a resolution "recommending . . . to the Assemblys . . . of all those Colonies (who have not already done it) to Assume regular government. . . ."[1] A wary Caesar told Tommy that: "Most of those here who are *termed the Cool Considerate men*, think it amounts to a declaration of Independence. It certainly savours of it. . . ."[2]

Caesar, who surely counted himself among those "cool, considerate men," nevertheless, went to work immediately to secure the adoption of Congress' resolution in Delaware. He was well aware of the profound significance of such a move; establishing her own government would finally sever all Delaware's ties to Pennsylvania as well as to the British Crown. Nevertheless, as he wrote John Haslet: "the Absurdity of Governor and Magistrates holding their Authority under our principal Enemy, must be Evident to every one. . . . The Reason, if duly weighed, must inforce the Necessaty of immediately laying the foundation of a new Government . . . similar at present to the one we now have, Except as to the derivation of authority."[3]

Caesar knew that the Whig's hold on power in the Assembly was precarious, and that a new election not only "Could not mend the ticket, but might make it worse."[4] Therefore, he wanted to avoid an open debate in order to forestall those who "would be apt to say at their next meeting, We ought to know the Sence of our Constituents. . . ."[5] He also rejected Pennsylvania's plan to have representatives from each county "lay the plan of Government," on the grounds that it would cause dangerous delays at a time when "a very powerful force is Expected from England against us."[6] Instead, he suggested to John Haslet that he and the Whig members for Kent county, that is Haslet, Tommy, William Killen and Dr. James Tilton hold a meeting of their own to prepare their arguments.

In the end, these men simply instructed themselves, as Kent county delegates, to comply with the recommendation of Congress; a special convention to consider the question would only be called if the rest of the assembly refused to go along. If the idea of a meeting was also rejected, the Kent members planned to simply withdraw, in effect dissolving the assembly. It was a bold plan, politically risky and fraught with uncertainty, yet Tommy wrote Caesar on May 26 that when he circulated the idea to the members of his Light Infantry, twenty-six signed immediately. The rest took it under consideration "Till next muster day, but many of them now say they are ready to sign."[7]

Tommy was wrong, however, in thinking the Congressional resolution would "meet with no opposition in [Kent] county."[8] The Tories immediately began issuing petitions and counter propaganda in both Kent and Sussex counties, begging the people to consider the overwhelming strength of Britain. They also implied that the resolution was a Presbyterian attack on the Anglican church.[9] So determined was this effort that John Haslet wrote Caesar that "A vast majority in Sussex are against . . . [I] fear Congress must either disarm a large Part of Kent & Sussex, or see their Recommendation treated with Contempt. . . ."[10]

On Saturday, June 1, John Clarke, a Methodist member of the Committee of Inspection opposed to the resolution, circulated "certain printed Petitions from Philadelphia against Independence" at the Mispillion muster, causing the militia to "break up in disorder." A clearly worried John Haslet warned Caesar that the Whigs should be very careful to "conduct this whole business in a manner as little Offensive to the Inhabitants as possible . . . The Congress," he wrote, was cursed in southern Kent as a "Nest of Hornets." Also, people believed that "the source of corruption & Direction is at Dover; a hint from thence pervades the Lower Part of the County in a trice. . . ."[11] Fearful of the "Poisonous Example of Maryland"[12] Haslet dispatched some of his men to guard the militia's supply of ammunition in Lewes with instructions that "if the matter assumes a still more serious appearance, to seize the most suspected of the Ring Leaders as Hostages for the good Behaviour of their Dependents."[13]

The strain soon caused dissension among Whigs as well. Haslet accused William Killen of doing nothing about circulating a petition in favor of the resolution, telling Caesar that Killen had told him that it "was not his business to Collect the Sense of the People, etc. [Afterwards as] you will Imagine, I left him with Looks of Indignation."[14]

On June 8, when Kent's Committee of Inspection met in Dover to discuss the resolution, some of their supporters seized John Clarke, the bearer of the Tory petition, put him in the pillory and pelted him with eggs. Afterwards, Thomas Rodney claimed that John Haslet stood watching the scene from the door of Bell's Tavern and refused to act. As a result, he, Thomas, "had to face the mob alone and release the victim from the pillory."[15]

After this incident John Clarke and Thomas White, another

Richard Bassett, Courtesy Delaware State Museums, Dover.

Methodist member of the Committee of Inspection, went off to enlist the help of Richard Bassett, now a captain of a company of the light horse. According to Thomas Rodney, Bassett sent some of his troops to "stir up the countryside" and was, therefore, to blame for the first large scale insurrection in Delaware against the revolution. Thomas never forgave Bassett, a man he said was "bred up in low life" and therefore capable of "the most odious villainy."[16] (Basset was later one of the first US senators from Delaware and served as Governor of the state 1799–1801.)

When Thomas Rodney heard of Bassett's plotting, he ordered the light infantry to seize Bassett and his store of arms at daybreak the following morning. By nine on the same morning, however, a Tory mob had gathered at Walker's Branch, about a mile outside of Dover, to protest the treatment of Clarke and demand that the four members of the light infantry who were responsible be handed over to be hanged. Thomas ordered his troops to march against them if they did not disperse immediately, whereupon they all "rose like a flock of Sea fowl from the Shore and fled home."[17]

This incident was followed by an even larger and more serious insurrection in Sussex county. On June 13, the assembly was informed that thousands of loyalists had assembled near Cedar Creek, eighteen miles from Lewes, and were reportedly in contact with the *Roebuck* and *Liverpool*, which were rumored ready to supply them with arms and a detachment of British troops. Colonel John Haslet immediately ordered his battalion down from Wilmington together with a company of militia from New Castle county. Meanwhile, Thomas McKean, aware that they were woefully short of ammunition, sent an urgent request to Congress to send "a ton of powder and lead . . . down by land immediately, as it is uncertain to what height this mad affair may be carried."[18]

Thomas Collins, now colonel of the first battalion of the Kent county militia, reported to Caesar in New Castle, that at eleven in the morning of Wednesday, June 12, his battalion and a company of light infantry had marched toward Lewes from Dover. They were joined at three that afternoon by a company of light horse and by still more troops at dawn on Thursday. When they arrived at Mispillion Church, however, they were informed that the dispute had been settled.[19]

According to James Tilton, "many of the most zealous tories had rode and laboured whole nights in their secret machinations to accomplish this grand insurrection" causing bitter prejudices to rise in "the ignorant multitude." Afterward "many of the deluded wretches, terrified [by] the . . . appearance of the military force now in their county, confessed their guilt, and . . . promised . . . faithful submission in future, to all the regulations of Congress." Others, however, having "gone on board the ships of war, . . . absconded and could not be taken."[20]

Order was restored, at least temporarily. Yet Tilton's reference to "the appearance of the military force" seems greatly exaggerated. Haslet's army was in serious need. Since early May he had been agitating for more provisions, complaining to Caesar as his commanding officer that his troops had not been paid, that the quartermaster had "furnished almost nothing but flower," and that a "large tract of the County is now unguarded & . . . Open to the Depredations of the Enemy!"[21] He had been ordered to send two companies of his battalion to Cape May, New Jersey, but confided to Caesar that "this Order is to me extremely embarrassing; it appears to me very probable the Commissary, now absent, will not supply those two Companies with Provisions at such a Distance; you also know, that we have no arms fit to be depended on but the Militia Arms of Kent. . . ." He begged Caesar to "furnish us with Arms . . . To send Over two Companies of unarmed men wou'd by no means answer the Intentions of Congress."[22]

15

Independence Is Declared

DELAWARE WAS NOT THE ONLY COLONY WITH CONFLICTS BETWEEN THE Whigs and the Tories; the Maryland militia had also been called out to disarm the "non-enrollers," as they were called. At the same time, the Congress's call for the colonies to establish their own governments had left the royal and proprietary governors virtually powerless. One, Virginia's governor, Lord Dunmore, became so frustrated that he left his seat in Williamsburg for a British man-of-war with the intention of leading pirate-like raids on his former province. He not only burned the city of Norfolk on New Year's Day, 1776, but further alarmed the citizens of Virginia by offering to free any slave who agreed to join him.[1]

Dunmore's antics stiffened the resolve of the Virginia House of Burgesses. Caesar had written Tommy at the end of May that "The Colonies of North-Carolina and Virginia have both by their Conventions declared for Independence by an unanimus Vote and have Instructed their members to move and Vote for it in Congress . . ." adding that "South Carolina and all the New-England Colonies have [already] declared [for it]. . . ." An excited Caesar was convinced that "When these things are known to the people [of Delaware] they will no doubt have great weight with them. . . ."[2]

Meanwhile, to bring the issue squarely before the Congress and force each delegation to take a stand, those committed to separation had called on Virginia's Richard Henry Lee to introduce a resolution that would express in principle the philosophy of independence. It was to be the first stage of a political strategy they hoped would eventually commit all the colonies to a formal declaration. The passage of Lee's document was far from certain, however, and its supporters knew well that a defeat would be a serious setback for their cause.[3]

Lee's resolution was first offered on June 7, 1776, the day before John Clarke circulated his Tory petition in Dover. While carefully avoiding the language of a formal declaration, it, nevertheless, stated that: "These United Colonies are and of right to be, free and independent states, that they are absolved from all allegiance to the British Crown, and that all political connections between them and the State of Great Britain is and ought to be totally dissolved."[4]

The New England delegates, along with those from Georgia, Virginia and North Carolina, immediately called for a unanimous vote in favor. Was Caesar ready to move that fast? We don't know. Neither he nor George Read were present for this first reading of Lee's resolution. Caesar had left Congress the previous week to prepare for the upcoming meeting of the Delaware Assembly. Read, also in New Castle, would not return to Philadelphia until sometime after June 25. Thus, while Thomas McKean surely supported the move, he could not speak for the entire Delaware delegation.[5]

The resolution was debated for two days, from the eighth to the tenth of June, in "committee of the whole."[6] Afterwards, Thomas Jefferson remarked that it appeared "that New York, Pennsylvania, Delaware, and Maryland were not yet matured for falling from the parent stem. . . ."[7] Since Thomas McKean was the only Delaware delegate that took part, one can't help wondering why Delaware was included on this list. Perhaps Jefferson was referring to the turmoil in Kent and Sussex counties, or perhaps he was aware of George Read's reputation as a moderate. Read was also known to be a close friend of Pennsylvania's John Dickinson, who openly opposed the resolution.

When it was clear that there was no chance of Lee's language being unanimously approved, his supporters shrewdly called for a recess. The vote was postponed for three weeks to give the delegates time to go home to consult their own assemblies. The hope was that the rising tide of public opinion, which had been stimulated by the recent publication of Thomas Paine's "Common Sense," would serve to stiffen their resolve.

In fact, when Lee's resolution was first presented, Delaware's delegation, like that of many colonies, was still under orders to seek reconciliation. Appointed the previous March, Caesar, Read and McKean had been given their instructions before there had been any military clashes with Britain. Now, on June 15, this requirement was officially lifted. With Caesar presiding as speaker, Thomas McKean read Lee's proposal to the assemblymen in New Castle and informed them of the action of Congress. Afterward, the assembly unanimously resolved that, henceforth, "all persons holding any office, civil or military, [shall] execute the same, in the name of the government of the counties of New Castle, Kent, and Sussex, upon Delaware, as they used legally to exercise it in the name of the King, until a new government shall be formed. . . ."[8] A certified copy of this resolution was given to Thomas McKean to take to the Congress.[9] Delaware had, in effect, removed John Penn from the office of governor and declared its own independence. While the charter of the new government would not be completed until September, Caesar, as the speaker of the assembly, was now Delaware's highest ranking officer.

As such, he immediately left New Castle for Sussex county to address the Tory uprisings. Still there ten days later, he received a message from George Read urging him to return to New Castle as soon as possible so that the assembly could act on the "Quota of Militia demanded by Congress from this Government . . . before we return to Congress."[10] Caesar, however, must have thought the situation in Sussex too precarious to leave, despite the fact that he was due in Philadelphia on July 1 to debate Lee's resolution.

Meanwhile in Congress, the supporters of independence had appointed two important committees. The first, headed by John Dickinson and including Thomas McKean, was to prepare a tentative frame of government for a future colonial confederation.[11] (The result would come to be known as the Articles of Confederation.) The other was to prepare a formal Declaration of Independence that Congress could endorse immediately if Lee's resolution was approved.

To prepare the preliminary draft, they chose the thirty-three year old Thomas Jefferson, already well known for his scientific and literary acumen. He would be assisted by, among others, the veteran statesman, Benjamin Franklin; the stern, intellectual John Adams, Connecticut's Roger Sherman and New York's Robert Livingston. Jefferson originally suggested that Adams write the draft, but Adams demurred, claiming he was "obnoxious, suspected and unpopular . . . [whereas] You are very much otherwise."[12]

Thomas Jefferson closeted himself in the second-floor parlor of his rented house and sweated over the manuscript for two weeks in Philadelphia's summer heat. Afterward, to refute claims that he had lifted ideas from a pamphlet published in Boston by James Otis, as well as from John Locke's treatises on government, he claimed he had "turned to neither book nor pamphlet while writing it." His objective, he said, was not "to find new principles or new arguments, never before thought of, not merely to say things which had never been said before, but to place before mankind the common sense of the subject, in terms so plain and firm as to command their assent, and justify ourselves in the independent stand we are compelled to take."[13] His paper, with a few small corrections made by other members of committee, was completed by June 28.

When the members of Congress reconvened at Philadelphia's State House (Independence Hall), on Monday, July 1, Caesar was not among them. The first order of business, Lee's resolution, was debated for nine hours. John Adams, backed by Jefferson, Lee, George Wythe and others, argued in favor; John Dickinson argued against. While Dickinson was not a loyalist (he already held a commission in the Pennsylvania regulars), he was an extremely cautious man, wary of war and fearful that Lee's language would drive many Americans to side with the king.[14] John Adams had little use for such timidity. He dismissed Dickinson's conservatives as "the cold party" and ridiculed one of its supporters, Harrison of Virginia, as "an indolent, luxurious, heavy gentleman, of no use in Congress or committees . . . a great embarrassment . . . a corner-stone in which the walls of both parties in Virgina met."[15]

Then, finally, it was time to act. The first vote, held on the afternoon of July 1, showed nine colonies in favor and two, Pennsylvania and South Carolina, against. New York abstained; her delegates were still under orders to seek reconciliation. Delaware's vote was deadlocked in a tie, Thomas McKean, voting for, and George Read against.

McKean was shocked. Apparently, George Read had not interpreted the Delaware Assembly's instructions to "concur with other delegates in Congress in . . . all measures necessary to insure liberty, safety and interests of people" as requiring his vote for independence. Perhaps because of the painful split between Delaware's Whigs and Tories, Read thought it premature, not to say foolish, to ask for such a vote before Congress had even considered Dickinson's proposed Articles of Confederation.[16] In his view, Lee's language would only antagonize England and might even put America at the mercy of Britain's historic enemies, Spain and France.[17]

The majority of nine to two could, of course, have carried the motion, but it was thought that the vote must be unanimous in order to avoid any appearance of weakness and indecision. Therefore, a second and final vote would be taken the following day. Meanwhile, Thomas McKean, furious at George Read, was determined that Delaware should not fail in her support. He immediately "sent an Express (at my private expense) for . . . Caesar Rodney, Esq. the remaining member for Delaware."[18]

Caesar, however, was in Dover, eighty miles away. Fresh from the continuing turmoil of Sussex county, he had depended on both Read and McKean to vote in the affirmative, leaving him, as both

George Read, Courtesy Delaware State Museums, Dover.

the chief executive of Delaware and a brigadier general in the Delaware militia, free to confront the loyalist rebellion. George Read had also led him to believe that no vote would be taken for several days; "the several parts of the business referred by Congress to ye 1st of July may take up a length of time. . . ."[19]

The militia's presence in Sussex had temporarily suppressed the rebellion, but the Tories had by no means dispersed. Not only were they supplying the British warships still hovering off Henlopen with "cattle and stock, etc." from the Indian River, but, according to John Haslet, they were now in open communication "with Lord Dunmore, [who] daily recruits his shattered Bands among them."[20] Dunmore was holed up on the Nanticoke River aboard the British warship *Fowey*, and, according to patriots from the area, the "large majority of disaffected" in Sussex, as well as from Somerset and Dorset (Dorchester) counties in Maryland, were supplying his ships with cattle and provisions. The patriots had already asked Congress for assistance.[21]

We know that Caesar, in poor health and presumably exhausted, had left Sussex county sometime between the twenty-fifth and thirtieth of June, stopping in lower Kent county to confer about military matters with Colonel Haslet. Apparently thinking he had plenty of time, he had then gone home to rest before continuing his journey north. McKean's message reached him in Dover, sometime around midnight on Monday, July 1.[22]

Caesar was forty-seven years old and seriously ill. By now, the cancer had so disfigured his face, that he often hid it behind a silk scarf, and persistent bouts with asthma had left him chronically short of breath. He was so thin that John Adams described him as being "slender as a reed, pale; his face is not bigger than a large apple"; adding, however, that there was "sense and fire, spirit, wit and humor in his countenance."[23]

An entry in the diary of Christopher Marshall for the night of July 1 reads: "before 10 came on a heavy rain. Continued till past 2, cleared up by 5."[24] Would a man in Caesar's condition have set off on horseback in such weather? Thomas Rodney, in fact, boasted to McKean many years afterward, that he, Thomas, had put the case for independence so cogently that Caesar had immediately "called for his Carriage" and set off for Philadelphia.[25]

However he made the journey, it was a tired and ill Caesar who arrived at the State House on the afternoon of Tuesday, July 2, where McKean met him "at the state house door, in his boots and spurs, as the members were assembling."[26] He wrote Tommy that he had travelled all night, arriving "(tho detained by Thunder and Rain) in time Enough to give my Voice in the matter of Independence. . . ."[27] Indeed, in something less than fourteen hours, he had traveled eighty miles over muddy rutted roads, and crossed about fifteen streams by ford, bridge or ferry.

Delaware was the thirteenth colony to vote. McKean described the moment some thirty years later: Caesar, he said, rose to his feet and declared that, "As I believe the voice of my constituents and of all sensible and honest men is in favor of Independence and my own judgment concurs with them, I vote for Independence."[28] John Hancock, as president of Congress, marked Delaware's vote in the affirmative on a tally he was keeping on the back of Lee's original resolution.[29]

Caesar erred, however, when he wrote Tommy that "It is determined by the Thirteen United Colonies with out even one decenting Colony. . . ." The New York delegation, still under orders to seek reconciliation, once again abstained and did not, in fact, endorse the declaration until some ten days later.[30] The South Carolina delegation only changed their vote to the affirmative after being pressured throughout the night by their delegate, John Rutledge, and Pennsylvania was able to do likewise solely because John Dickinson and another delegate purposely stayed away.[31]

With Lee's resolution approved, the Congress turned their attention to Jefferson's draft; the document that would formally declare their action to the world. They debated it, paragraph by paragraph, for two long days. In a letter to Tommy, written on July 4, 1776, the day that Congress would declare the birthday of the nation, Caesar reported that "We have now Got through with the Whole of the declaration and Ordered it to be printed, so that you will soon have the pleasure of seeing it—Handbills of it will be printed and sent to the Armies, Cities, County Towns, etc. To be published or rather proclamed in form. . . ."[32]

At first, the Declaration of Independence was only signed by the president and secretary of the Congress. Not until July 19 was a resolution passed that called for the signatures of every member of Congress so that all should risk lives and property equally. Accordingly, on August 2, the document, now inscribed on parchment, was signed by all the members then present in Congress. Eventually there were fifty-five signatures, including those of all three Delaware delegates: Caesar, Thomas McKean and George Read.

George Read signed the final copy, despite his earlier objections, so as not to give aid and comfort to Britain. His initial hesitation was typical of many conservative minded Delawareans; reluctant to break old connections yet anxious to play a part in future events.[33] Read also knew that if he did not sign, he could not continue to be a Congressional delegate, nor indeed hold any public office, and would thus "be deprived of all power to serve his country." Such was the fate of his friend and colleague, John Dickinson. Even while insisting that he supported a "just war," Dickinson refused to sign and subsequently fell "from his exalted place in the esteem and confidence of his countrymen."[34]

There is little evidence, however, that Caesar, or indeed many

Congressional delegates, wholeheartedly subscribed to Jefferson's passionate belief in the equality of men and their endowment with natural rights. Even that passionate revolutionary, Thomas Rodney, writing many years later, sneered at Jefferson's "puerile continance on charges against King."[35]

Nevertheless, even though it could be said that it was a document conceived in contention, composed in a context of political expedience, and adopted only after a series of crafty maneuvers, Jefferson's declaration stirred the hearts of the people. It would ultimately unite a small group of diverse colonies into a great nation.

16

Reaction

IMMEDIATELY AFTER THE DECLARATION WAS APPROVED ON JULY 4, Caesar returned to New Castle. It was his duty as speaker to call for the election of ten deputies from each county to meet on August 27 "to order and declare the future form of government for this state."[1] After the decision was made to hold an election on August 19, Caesar, his business in New Castle finished, returned to Philadelphia, leaving Tommy to manage the Whig party's campaign.

Tommy was more than eager. After taking part in the assembly, convened on July 22, that officially adopted the Declaration of Independence and called for the election of a constitutional convention, he went to Dover to report to the Committee of Inspection.[2] After hearing his report, the committee members staged a public reading of both documents at the courthouse, receiving, according to Tommy, the "highest approbation of people in three huzzas."[3]

Cheered on by the crowd, the committee sent for a portrait of George III and paraded it around the square accompanied by Tommy's company of light infantry. Finally, to the slow beat of the infantry drummer, the soldiers lit a bonfire, formed a circle around it, and burned the portrait in effigy. Tommy reported triumphantly to Caesar that "Compelled by strong necessity, thus we destroy even the Shadow of the King who refused to reign over a free people."[4]

Tommy was pressing for an investigation by the Committee of Inspection of the incidents surrounding the circulation of John Clarke's petition in early June. Caesar strongly opposed this idea, and in an attempt to dissuade his impetuous brother, asked a number of cogent questions. "Are there a Considerable majority of [the Committee] that wish the Enquiry . . . ? Will they (if matters turn out as you Expect) publish their opinions to the County so that the friends to Liberty may benefit by it? . . . It is an Enquiry that ought to be made by men of understanding only—Do such make a Majority of the Committee . . . ? By what authority do they take it up? . . .

These things I submit to the Good Sence and prudence of You and Your friends—Tho you Seem to have determined on the measure . . . before my opinion was asked."

Caesar was also concerned about the manner in which Tommy planned to promote the Whig ticket in Kent county. In a further attempt to curb his brother's folly, he advised him to stress that the people's "rights and priviledges as freemen depends on . . . true Whiggism, True patriotism." Such an approach, he argued, should "Carry . . . persuasion and Conviction . . . with all [who are] not Governed by a party Spirit." He also advised Tommy that "If any person . . . be proposed in oposition to Your Ticket who have heretofore been unfriendly to the Cause—point out . . . their former Conduct and [warn of] Trusting . . . such men at such an Important Crisis." Finally, he begged him to "hold out to the people more of the Patriot, than of party-man. . . . For if they are lead to believe that you and your friends are Governed more by party Spirit than by the True Interest of America, they will hold you in the Light of all other party-men and deal with you accordingly."[5]

Tommy ignored this advice. Grumbling bitterly that the "Tories here are exerting them selves to git in[to the] convention," he persuaded the Committee of Inspection to send out summonses for an investigation of the Tory insurrection. The move was not well received. After putting forth several tickets, some of which included Caesar, the conservatives settled on many of the very people the committee would investigate. Led by Caesar's old friend, Charles Ridgely, it included Tommy's nemesis, Richard Bassett, as well as Thomas Collins, John Cook, Samuel West, John Clarke, Jacob Stout, Thomas White, James Sykes and Richard Lockwood. Lockwood, however, engendered disapproval by "saying he will not push [for one] Ticket but will vote for part of both. . . ."[6]

Caesar was not surprised that his old friends among the moderates did not include him on their ticket, remarking wryly that some who are listed now "are too far gone in personal prejudice . . . to do justice to merit."[7] Indeed, after his dramatic vote for independence, the fact that they considered him at all is surprising. Despite his brother's foolishness, Caesar's good sense and balanced voice were apparently still respected among all factions of Delaware politics.

The Whig ticket, Tommy wrote Caesar, would be "C. Rodney, W. Killen, Thos Rodney, J. Carty, S. Snow, J. Baning, V. Lockerman, Powell, Cox, Francis Many—J. Revell. . . ." Gloating that the "Tories" were "much Out of Heart at present," he bragged that "from the present disposition of the Whigs it appears we shall carry the Ellection. . . ."[8]

He was wrong. Caesar's doubts about his brother's conduct were well founded. Tommy's poor judgement and hot head were effectively exploited by the moderates; the Whig ticket went down in defeat. Complaining that he "is very Porely with the yellow Jaundice" Tommy reported the dismal outcome to Caesar: "their lowest man at this time is 150 votes ahead of you who are the highest [on] our side. . . ."[9]

Caesar was furious. He blamed Tommy for being too "sanguine in your expectations without taking the necessary steps to carry a point of that sort; added to all the rest of your bad policy. . . ." Nor was he pleased about the burning of the King's portrait: "Parke tells me the conduct of your Light Infantry heretofore had drawn down the resentment of the people."[10]

Kent county was not alone, however. Sussex county, as well as several seats in the New Castle delegation, were also carried by the conservatives in what appeared to be a general reaction to the precipitous actions of the Continental Congress. However, it is important to differentiate between the moderates who won this election and the loyalists who were causing so much trouble in Sussex county. Typically, Thomas Rodney used the term "Tories" for both, but he was not being fair. The moderates, that is the supporters of George Read and Charles Ridgely, might better be called cautious patriots. They supported the American cause in general, yet strongly disapproved of what they considered the Whigs' headlong rush to revolution and, at least until the signing of the Declaration of Independence, had hoped to work out some form of reconciliation with Britain. The Loyalists, on the other hand were true Tories, outright supporters of the British and intent on undermining the American cause.

Depressed by his defeat, Caesar asked McKean, who went to the convention as a delegate from New Castle county, to keep a wary eye on the proceedings. McKean was outraged at his friend's downfall, and vowed that the newly appointed convention should have no power except the narrow task of framing the government. Specifically, he vowed never to consent "to their appointing delegates [to Congress]" and was "determined *they* shall turn [Caesar] nor no one Else out." If they try, he vowed to "Try the strength of the County with *them* Even at the risk of the Court House.—"

George Read, as the acknowledged leader of the newly empowered moderates, served as speaker of the Delaware convention, leaving Caesar as the sole remaining Delaware delegate in Philadelphia. He agreeed to stay on in Congress solely to "prevent our Colony suffering while they were imployed on other business—" adding, somewhat petulantly, that he is "determined that the folly and ingratitude of the people Shall not divert my attention from the public Good. . . ." Nevertheless, he is bone tired, and writes Tommy that "—I have seen Independence declared, and when I See this Campaign well Ended and Regular Government Establish, Then I intend to leave the public, and take the private paths of Life. . . ."[11]

Typically, Caesar did not let his personal defeat affect his friendship with George Read, but wrote him regularly about the doings in Congress and the conduct of the war. Meanwhile, under Read's leadership, the convention turned their attention to the task of writing a sound government constitution. Delaware's, in fact, was the first such document in the union written by a body elected for that purpose.[12] Contrary to McKean's worst fears, they made no attempt to renege on the declaration, or to unseat McKean and Caesar from the Continental Congress. Nor did they oppose the war. On the contrary, they specifically provided for the "raising, equipping, and marching of the quotas of militia required from the State by Congress, appointing, promoting and commissioning officers, and settling their accounts, and borrowing money."[13]

In view of the worsening crisis with Britain, it was decided not to seek a public referendum on the new government; instead it went into effect immediately after the new legislature was elected in the fall. The new state of Delaware now had a bicameral legislature for the first time: an upper house called the Legislative Council and a lower house called the House of Assembly. The proprietary governor was officially replaced by a president, elected to a term of three years by a joint ballot of both houses. In the most controversial measure of the new constitution, he was aided by a privy council consisting of two members from each house.

The upper legislative council had nine members, three from each county. Each served a term of three years, but the terms were staggered so that only one member from each county came up for election each year. The lower house of assembly had twenty-one members, seven from each county, who were chosen annually. An amendment to exclude the clergy from holding office was rejected after considerable debate, but one stating that "No person in future imported from Africa ought to be held in slavery, and no Indian, negro, or mulatto slave ought to be brought into Delaware for sale, from any part of the world, under any pretence" was approved.[14] To be eligible to vote, a man must own at least fifty acres, twelve of which were cleared for farming, or equivalent property worth forty pounds.

The first election was held on October 21, 1776. On October 10, a sharp criticism of the new constitution appeared under the name of "Philo-Alethias." While conceding that there are "some good things in the Delaware Constitution, . . . evidently borrowed from the Pennsylvanian," the author scoffed that they are "mangled like a school-boy's abridgement of a *Spectator* paper." Nor did he approve of "Some of their Bill of Rights" which he claimed "might prevent [an] all American defense." The fact that "Justices of the Peace may also be Assemblymen, i.e. 'Make and execute laws which destroy all liberty!' " also worried him, but his strongest objection was to the four distinct legislative bodies: the assembly, legislative council, president, and his privy council. "All these opposite and incoherent powers, in that small and greatly divided handful must produce endless jars and confusions, till one of these powers becomes an aristocracy, and like Aaron's serpent, swallow up all the rest or betrays [them] to some foreign power."[15]

It is possible that this was McKean speaking. He had had a hard few weeks. His sister died in September, and his son had been seriously ill. On top of that his voice had not been heeded and his suggestions defeated by the majority at every turn. His argument for a December election on the grounds that two battalions of militia, "being absent . . . exposing their lives for their country," would not return until then was ignored. (The militia had gone to Perth Amboy, New Jersey as part of a "flying camp" of ten thousand men from the middle colonies with orders to stave off a British threat until regular forces could be mobilized.) "I might as well have harangued the walls," McKean complained to Caesar, "The matter had been settled out of doors. . . ." He scoffed that he "can almost name you every officer in the new Government, and will venture it when I see you" and railed against a suggestion that the new general assembly meet in Dover rather than New Castle as "fixed by acts of Assembly." In his view, it had been made for the sole purpose of increasing "their popularity in that county before the grand election." He also protested a move to "choose new Delegates, Council of Safety, and in short to do anything & everything." He told Caesar that "Doctor Ridgely was to be in your place [as delegate to Continental Congress], this is a fact; but I think it will not do. . . ." So disgruntled was the veteran Whig McKean that he "told the President that I could not with honor, nor in conscience, sit any longer in such an Assembly, and took my hat and withdrew. . . ."[16]

Caesar reported to Tommy in a letter dated September 25 that

"The Convention is dissolved; made a plan of Government it seems, and ordered an election . . . Quer[y]: Do their late opponents intend calmly to submit, or try again to rally?"[17] Tommy can only reply that "The Whigs intend to be active, but have formed no plan yet. . . ."[18]

17

Haslet's Delawares in New York

THE WAR, MEANWHILE, WAS NOT GOING WELL. AS EARLY AS MAY 18, Caesar had written Tommy that he had received "the disagreeable intelligence, That 2 men of war, 2 frigates & (I think) one sloop of war had arrived in Quebec" and that a thousand men under the British general Carleton had "sallied out against our troops . . . [and] compelled them to retreat."[1]

After Brigadier General Richard Montgomery was killed during the battle of Quebec in January, Benedict Arnold and his men had hung on in the north, enduring months of bitter cold, disease and deprivation. Now Arnold lay injured from a fall from his horse, and his army, reduced to fewer than a thousand able-bodied men, was fleeing southward. In spite of the arrival of badly needed reinforcements, they were defeated again in a battle at Trois-Rivières on June 8. By July, the Americans had retreated to Fort Ticonderoga, while the British general John Burgoyne had amassed eight thousand British regulars, Hessians and Indians near Lake Champlain ready to march south to New York City.

Incredibly, the British and Americans would spend the next four months building a fleet of warships on Lake Champlain. Arnold, with only four ships to begin with, built more from scratch, felling trees and importing the craftsmen needed to fit them. The British, on the other hand, were forced to dismantle their ships in order to get them by the rapids on the Richelieu River and rebuild them on Lake Champlain.

Arnold, then thirty-five years old, was the chief advocate of the Canadian campaign. It had been Arnold who convinced Ethan Allen and his Green Mountain Boys to attack the weakly defended Fort Ticonderoga in the spring of 1775. Their victorious assault had secured for the Americans both a strategic position and a valuable cache of arms.

However, Congress' idea that the "unhappy" Canadians would flock to their cause proved to be naive. It was based on the fact that the Quebec Act, one of the notorious "Intolerable Acts" of 1774, had denied the Canadians the right to govern themselves. Yet, far more important to the conservative French of Quebec, was the fact that the act had allowed them to remain Roman Catholic.[2] (The Americans, of course, were also incensed at the appropriation of large tracts of land along the Ohio River previously claimed by Virginia, Connecticut, and Massachusetts.)

Just when when things seemed at their worst in Canada, the American cause was given a welcome boost by a small band of South Carolinians who, from a makeshift fort of sand and palmetto logs, managed to keep the British from opening a southern offensive. The British fleet carrying the forces of generals Clinton and Cornwallis arrived off Charleston on June 28. Covered by the firing of the ships' cannon, twenty-five hundred British troops were put ashore on Long Island. Their plan was to ford a narrow inlet called "the Breach" and attack the American fort on Sullivan's Island; a low sandy spit that guarded the northern entrance to the city. Meanwhile, three of the British ships were to sail up an inlet behind the island and attack the fort from the rear. To everyone's surprise, the plan went disastrously wrong. The Breach proved to be some seven feet deep and impossible to ford; the three flanking ships ran aground, one so badly she had to be scuttled; and the spongy palmetto logs seemed to absorb the force of the British cannon balls, allowing the Americans to inflict far more damage than they received. After ten hours of incessant firing, the British withdrew and reluctantly set sail for New York.[3]

New York, of course, was the linchpin of the British military strategy: the capture of the city would allow them to finally sever the tie between New England and her sister colonies. Aware of the danger, Washington had moved his army there in April, soon after Sir William Howe had left Boston harbor for Halifax. All during the month of June, while Congress debated the question of Independence and Whigs and Tories squabbled in Delaware, the people of New York waited for the arrival of the British fleet.

The frigate carrying General Howe and seven army transport ships were finally sighted off Sandy Hook on June 25.[4] Colonel Gunning Bedford, in New York with the Delaware regiment, described their arrival to George Read:

We have just received intelligence of a fleet being seen in the sound, about sixty or seventy miles from this place, to the eastward, which will cut of the water-communication with the Eastern colonies. It has been long expected. Since our being here, every tide has given us expectation of the enemy's approach. . . . We must have a large army here and on Long Island, but I believe not so many as is generally said. They talk [of] twenty-five or thirty thousand. The Eastern regiments in general are very small. The works here are strong and extensive, and will require many men to occupy them.[5]

To the Americans' surprise, Howe did not immediately launch the expected assault on Manhattan, but remained encamped on Staten Island throughout the month of July awaiting the arrival of additional troops.[6] By the end of July, he had amassed more than thirty thousand men, including Clinton's force from South Carolina and nine thousand Hessian mercenaries, as well as a fleet that included ten ships of the line, twenty frigates and three hundred transport and supply vessels. Apparently, Howe hoped this impressive show of force would convince the Americans to surrender without a fight.[7]

In Delaware, Colonel Haslet was under orders to "station to Companies of the Battalion under my Command at Cape May, to replace two Companies formerly there, now ordered to Canada." This was the order he had found so "embarassing . . . [because] we have no arms fit to be depended on. . . ."[8] By August 8, however, Caesar was able to report that "The Delaware Battalion is . . . compleatly armed [with as many] Guns as you could wish to see."[9] Haslet's Continental troops went to Long Island to join Washington. Meanwhile, a regiment of militia, commanded by a miller from Christiana Bridge named Samuel Patterson, was sent to Amboy, New Jersey, as part of the so-called "Flying camp" that was to protect Philadelphia and the Delaware River valley.[10] They were not eager to go. "The whole," Patterson wrote George Read, "almost lay down their arms, [and] swore they would not go without a bounty such as others got in Pennsylvania. . . ." In fact, one of the companies "deserted in the night, [all] but eleven men."[11]

Caesar, like many Americans, was optimistic about the impending New York engagement. On August 14, he wrote Tommy that while "The English Army is supposed to be upwards of twenty thousand strong: ours is better than thirty thousand, in high spirits, and eager for action. . . ."[12] On the twenty-eighth, unaware of the bloody battle that was already taking place, he again reported that "Washington is in high spirits; says they have over Stayed their time, That he is now Ready for them—the sooner the better. . . ."[13]

Caesar was correct: Washington's army did equal Howe's in number. Yet most of his men were hastily recruited and undertrained; hardly a match for the disciplined British. Nor did Washington, at this early stage of the war, have anything like the military experience of his opponent.

As it happened, neither Colonel Bedford nor Colonel Haslet were with their men when the British finally attacked. Both were helping officiate on a court-martial in New York city.[14] On September 1, Bedford reported what happened to George Read:

> Eight days ago I wrote . . . informing you we were ordered to Long Island. Immediately on our going there, intelligence was received that the enemy were advancing in three large bodies. Our brigade, under Lord Sterling, [American General William Alexander, his claim to the title Earl of Stirling was disallowed by Parliament, but honored by his American friends][15] was quickly ordered out to meet them. . . . We found their numbers were three to one, with a large train of artillery, and [they] had possessed themselves of the most advantageous situations and passes. . . .[16]

The British landed twenty thousand men on Long Island between August 22 and 26.[17] The Americans, with about eight thousand in their advance position, had stationed twenty-eight hundred at each of the three main roads that led northward from the British landing spot, sending only five sentries to watch a minor road farther east. The bulk of the American army remained at Brooklyn Heights, further inland.

However, Howe did not center his attack on one of the three main roads as expected, but moved his main force to the east, where they easily overwhelmed the men guarding the fourth road, and penetrated well to the rear of the Americans.

To divert the Americans' attention, the British also launched two smaller attacks. The first, under the British General James Grant, encountered John Haslet's Delaware regiment and a regiment of Marylanders under Colonel William Smallwood along the road nearest the coast. They were under the command of Lord Stirling. The second, led by the Hessian, General Philip von Heister, faced the American, Major General John Sullivan. In the battle that followed, many Delaware men were killed.

Colonel Bedford described it to George Read:

> General Sullivan and Lord Sterling were taken prisoners, Lord Sterling not until the last, as he kept Colonel Smallwood's and our regiment four hours after every other regiment has retreated from the field, drawn up for battle in sight of five brigades of the enemy, who were surrounding us fast, when we received orders to retreat. On our retreat our regiment filed off [to] the left in pursuit of a small detachment of

the enemy, which we made prisoner,—a lieutenant, twenty-three gren-
adiers and three Hessians. Smallwood proceeded on, and fell into a am-
buscade of a least double their number. They engaged them, and lost
near three hundred men, killed and taken prisoners. . . .[18]

The Americans, finding themselves surrounded and attacked
from both front and rear, retreated into a fog-shrouded marsh,
while a small contingent of Smallwood's Marylanders tried to divert
the British.[19] Afterward, John Haslet wrote Caesar that the Delaware battalion "effected a most Noble Retreat up to the Middle thru
a Marsh of Mud, and brought off with them 23 prisoners."[20]
Haslet didn't mention that many of his men had been shot as
they slogged through a pond and more than a dozen others had
drowned.[21] The British troops, particularly the Hessians, had been
whipped into a passion by British anti-American propaganda, and
pursued the defeated Americans with a passionate ferocity, shoot-
ing and bayoneting them where they fell until even their own officers were horrified at the sight.[22]
After Long Island, the Americans were thoroughly demoralized,
yet Howe did not immediately press his advantage. He took two full
days to move on to Brooklyn Heights. Meanwhile, Washington, who
had watched as Stirling's men repeatedly attacked and were driven
back, was painfully aware that he had been out-maneuvered. "My
God," he reportedly cried as his men fell in battle, "what brave men
I must lose this day!"[23] Now, he took advantage of Howe's delay by
sending the survivors out of danger across the East River to Manhattan during the night, ferried to safety by a Massachusetts regiment of Gloucester fishermen.[24]
Now, Haslet expected "every moment Orders to March off to
King's Bridge, to prevent the Enemy Crossing the East River and
Confining us on another Nook. . . ."[25] He was right. Within the
week, the Delaware troops were at King's Bridge on the Hudson
river, where, Haslet complained, they were "exposed to wind,
Weather & the Enemy, who appear to have it nearly as much in
their Power to cut off our Communication as ever." Thoroughly
discouraged, he wrote Caesar that, in his opinion, the American
army's "Immensity of Labor and Expence [was] thrown away in for-
tifying L. Island . . . [and] N York [will] soon be in the same situation
. . . the superior Number of the British Troops, & the advantages of
their Fleet [make] the city indefensible. . . . Had Long Island been
rendered Useless to the Enemy, N. York laid in Ashes . . . [and] the
Heights between [here] and Connecticut Properly Occupied, the
Enemy must [have] attacked at disadvantage [and] we at Liberty to

fight when we pleased. . . ." As it was, "everything [has been] almost sacrificed . . . for the Preservation of N. York. . . ."[26]

Haslet was quite right; the city of New York was impossible to defend without a strong navy. Not only was it vulnerable from both land and sea, but most of the property in the city was said to be in the hands of Tories; a fact that was not lost on General Howe. For this reason, many of Washington's advisors had urged him to evacuate and burn the city to keep it from being used as winter quarters by the British. Washington, however, bowed to pressure from Congress, and did not do so.

The British landed on Manhattan on September 15, 1776, in the vicinity of what is now East 34th Street. At the sight of such an overwhelming force, the courage of the American militia failed. As an army chaplain, Reverend Joseph Montgomery (formerly pastor of a Presbyterian church in New Castle County), described it to Caesar: "the appearance of only a few of them made two or three regiments of Americans retreat. Retreat did I say, it [ought] to be *run away*, nothwithstanding all the solicitations, prayers, and I might say tears of General Washington." He added, somewhat pompously, that "These were not southern troops."[27]

The British gloated. So sure were they of victory that, after securing the Boston Post Road, the only route that ran the length of the island, they stopped to wait for a second division. Meanwhile, General Howe was distracted by the "crafty hospitality" of a prominent New York lady.[28] In the lull, the American general Israel Putnam was able to hurry three thousand men up the footlanes and farm paths along the west side of the island.

Before abandoning the city altogether, Washington lured a company of Hessians and British light infantry into his fire at Harlem Heights (now 125th Street), outflanked them and finally forced them to retreat. To quote Reverend Montgomery once again:

The Maryland and Virginian troops . . . with undaunted bravery . . . marched up, when a smart engagement ensued. Fresh troops were poured in upon both sides, the contest [was] obstinate and long. Finally our heroes forced them from three different grounds, at which they retreated leaving behind them three field peices and many slain. . . .[29]

General Howe was apparently so discouraged by this setback that he once again failed to press his advantage and retired to the west side of the Harlem River where he stayed for nearly a month.[30]

After Major General John Sullivan was taken prisoner at Long Island, the British tried to use him as an intermediary to Congress.

Caesar reported to George Read that Sullivan had been aboard the British ship *Eagle* and had a "private conversation with Lord [Admiral Richard] Howe. The Substance of Which Was, that his Lordship declared he had Ample power (together with the General [William Howe]) to settle matters between Great Britain and the Colonies. . . ." Claiming his rank made it impossible for him to talk directly with Washington or the Congress, Lord Howe suggested a "Conversation of an Hour or two with Some of the Members as private Gentlemen. . . ." The Admiral, rather unctuously, claimed he had stayed in England longer than necessary to be sure he had the power to negotiate, during which time the Declaration of Independence had, unfortunately, been passed, but that "he had many friends & Acquaintance here, and that he Should be pleased to See them, etc., etc. . . ."

Caesar's reaction was succinct: "You Sir may be desirous to know what Congress think of this Message delivered by Sullivan at the request of Lord Howe—To satisfie your desire I think I may Venture to say that a verry great Majority of the Members look on it as an Insult. . . ."[31]

The Congress did eventually send a delegation to hear Howe's proposal. They went, however, "with a view to satisfie some disturbed minds out of Doors, Rather than an Expectation of its bringing about Peace, They . . . [will] repair to New York with powers to Confer with Lord Howe, to know the Extent of his powers, and the Terms he Shall propose. . . ." Caesar, no fool, was well aware that "if Lord Howe Receives the Committee thus sent, he Acknowledges the Congress, and of Course the Independency of the States, Which I am Convinced he will not do. . . ."[32] He later wrote Tommy that "you will see by this method the Congress hold out to the people their willingness to put an End to the war, whenever it Can be done on principles of Liberty and Safety. . . ."[33]

The delegation, which consisted of Benjamin Franklin, John Adams and Edward Rutledge, travelled to Amboy, New Jersey, where Lord Howe sent a boat to ferry them across to Staten Island. Caesar reported to George Read that Howe himself, met them "at the water-side, and in a very polite manner conducted them up to the house, where he had a dinner and plenty of good wine for them, and that after dinner they had a conference, which, with the time they were dining, was about three hours. . . ." As Caesar expected, it turned out that Howe actually had "no power to make a peace, or even to order a cessation of arms . . . [but could only] hear what they had to offer, and report to his Majesty, but that previous to anything else we must return to and acknowledge obedience to his

Majesty. . . ."[34] The meeting had come to nothing. As Caesar put it to Tommy: "This jaunt was only to prove what [the committee] knew before, [and was conducted] purely for the Satisfaction of the Tories."

In the same letter, Caesar urged Tommy to send their sloop to Philadelphia "imediately for the purpose of haveing her Sold. . . ." The Americans, with no navy to speak of, depended on privateers to prey upon British shipping. Consequently, ships of all kinds were so in demand that "John Bell has Sold both his for more than a hundred pounds more than he Ever thought of Asking—in short more than they Cost him at first. . . ."[35] On hearing this news, Tommy immediately sent the sloop "away without staying for any loading, least she should not git up in time." He, too, was anxious to sell her for she "does not suite the creek & will want a good deal to be layed out on her next spring . . . £250 will do if no more can be had, but . . . she may perhaps bring £350 or more." However, he

Photo "Loading Wheat—Delaware," December 1889, by Arthur Stanley Logan. Item B-12, M6247. A. S. Logan Collection, Pennsylvania State Archives, Harrisburg.

thought a second Rodney boat, a schooner, should be sold only if you "could git such a price as would induce you to it . . . as freight will be plenty, on account of so many of the vessels being sold. . . . People are gitting very anxious (since the price has rose) to send their grain. . . ."[36]

18

Dark Days of Winter

Haslet was still in King's Bridge at the beginning of October, and wrote Caesar that he had "been nearly a month confined by the Dysentery, from our Exposure on Long Island to cold & damp Lying on the Ground."[1] He also reported that the British warships, "Roebuck, the Phoenix, & the Repulse" had control of the Hudson, having "moved up the River with all the Ease & Unconcern Imaginable, & passed the Chevaux amidst the thunder of our artillery from [Fort] Washington. . . ."[2] Haslet worried that Howe might send his ships up the East and Harlem rivers as well. If so, he could "draw a line behind us from River to River, [so that] We [will be] completely Surrounded. . . ."[3]

The under-trained American troops continued to be erratic and unreliable. While Haslet, like the Reverend Montgomery, told Caesar that "the Eastern Troops . . . are not like the Children of the South," he was also highly critical of "Some officers [who] have poured [on] much contempt . . . [and] sown the seeds of discord. . . ."[4] Nevertheless, the "Eastern troops" rose to the occasion on October 18 when "one hundred Sail ships of War & Transports sailed up to Frog's Pt (Throg's Neck) [they] were repulsed by 5000 men from Massachusetts and New Hampshire." Haslet continued:

> On Monday night [October 21] Lord Stirling ordered me with 750 men to attack the enemy's outposts ten miles from this place, at the village of Mamaroneck. . . . The party we fell in with was Colonel Rogers', the late worthless major. On the first fire he skulked off in the dark. His lieutenant and a number of others were left dead on the spot. Had not our guards deserted us on the first onset he and his whole party must have been taken. . . .[5]

Colonel Rogers was Robert Rogers, leader of a Loyalist regiment known as the Queen's American Rangers; Haslet's attack was the first time two American military units were pitted against one another in the war.[6] Afterwards, Haslet reported, Lord Stirling was "so highly pleased with our success that he thanked us publicly on the parade."[7]

A week later, he was once again in the thick of it, asked by Washington to command a regiment of militia near White Plains, New York. "We had not been many minutes on the ground," he told Caesar, "when the cannonade began, and the second shot wounded a militia-man on the thigh, upon which the whole regiment broke and fled. . . ." After rallying the militia with much difficulty, Haslet "went up to the top of the hill . . . to reconnoitre the enemy. I plainly perceived them marching to the White-Plain in eight columns and stop in the wheat-fields a considerable time. I saw their General Officers on horse back assemble in council, and soon their whole body faced about, and in one continued column, march[ed] to the hill opposite to our right. . . ." Haslet had begged his commanding officer, General McDougall, to move his or Colonel Smallwood's Continental regiment forward "for there was no dependence to be placed on the Militia. . . ." Haslet, himself, helped drag the artillery "along the rear of the regiment. While so employed, a cannon ball struck the carriage, and scattered the shot about, a wad of tow blazing in the middle. The artillerymen fled. . . ." Meanwhile, while "the Maryland battalion was warmly engaged, and the enemy ascending the hill . . . the Militia regiment behind the fence fled in confusion." With the militia deserting on all sides, even Smallwood's and Haslet's Continentals were finally forced to retreat, but "not till . . . The left of the [Delaware] regiment . . . twice repulsed the Light Troops and Horse of the enemy. . . ."[8]

This battle involved only advance brigades from both sides. Washington's main force was massed behind them, waiting for an British attack that never came. Instead of chasing the Americans northward, Howe had turned back to attack Fort Washington, where, in deference to the wishes of Congress, Washington had left a garrison to guard the Hudson River. It was a poor decision. Although a heavy downpour delayed the assault, the Hessian general Von Knyphausen eventually captured the fort on November 16, including a large store of ammunition and over twenty-six hundred men.[9] Among them, in Haslet's view, were two "as good officers as any of their rank in the Army; and all to defend a place in itself indefensible and not worth 100 men; they were attacked by 12,000."[10]

Meanwhile, Benedict Arnold's newly constructed fleet of ships had been destroyed in the battle of Valcour Island on October 11, giving Lake Champlain to the British as well. Caesar tried to put a good face on the defeat in a letter to George Read: "[despite] the Loss the Continent hath Sustained . . . I cannot but be much pleased with [the] behaviour of that Brave officer and his men."[11] Yet, all that really could be said of Arnold's effort was that took up so much time that the British had to abandon the idea of moving on to Fort Ticonderoga before retiring to their winter quarters in Canada.

At the "flying camp" in New Jersey, Colonel Samuel Patterson was also having problems. Disease was rampant among the Delaware militia. Three of his men had died and "about seventy now sick." George Read had suggested sending a second battalion, but Patterson could not "see the propriety of such an attempt, when mine is not near full. . . ." Besides, he added, "If any such should come, they must be mostly of the Militia kind; and half a month will cure them forever [of] going again and persuade others not."[12]

Supplies were woefully short for both militia and Continental troops. George Read had asked Caesar to call the Council of Safety together and "collect blankets and every species of Cloathing . . . that every encouragement may be given to the Soldiers in ye Delaware Battalion to continue in the Service." The men, he said, were sick and "suffer much for want of Medicines & many other things. . . ."[13] Caesar apparently received little support from the other members of the Council, for he bought what he could out of his own pocket. "Since I came to Kent I have purchased and paid for Corse Cloths to the Amount of near two hundred pounds. They come verry dear, but What is Worse, I have little or no Expectation That many more can be Got—The Shops throughout this County seem to be Intirely drained. Part of those I have are Homemade—Be pleased to let me know whether . . . [you can] Raise an Amount against this State for these Articles . . . or Whether I must look Elsewhere to be reimbursed."[14]

Caesar sent Haslet "the plan of the Delaware Government" in early October, which, he said, "whether you like it or not You are bound to Swallow. . . ." After their disastrous defeat on October 21, the Whigs had "given up all pretentions by their Conduct . . . not satisfied with Great numbers of them having necessarily gone to the Camp . . . many others have wantonly Gone, as if for no good Reason but to be out of the way."[15] Haslet, incensed by this news, wrote "Nocol[as] Van Dyke a most flaming Letter, runing O'er with Patriotism, praying him not to let the People attend the Noxtown fair rather than ye Election & sell their Birthright for a piece of Ginger Bread."[16]

Caesar's term in the Continental Congress expired on October 27. "If Health and Weather permits," he wrote Haslet, "I set out This day for Kent, and don't Intend to return to Congress soon again, at least not in the present Reign. . . ."[17] On November 10, 1776 both he and McKean were replaced by George Read, John Evans and John Dickinson, although both Dickinson and Evans subsequently refused to attend. George Read was also chosen speaker of the new Delaware legislature.

At the first meeting of the new government, the members seemed primarily concerned with choosing a great seal for their state. The first idea, a silver medallion depicting Britannia and Liberty with the words "Go to America" between, was abandoned after Thomas McKean and James Sykes reported that no engraver would do the work. In the end, a less controversial design was chosen: "a sheaf of wheat, an ear of Indian corn and an ox . . ." to be flanked by "an American soldier under arms on the right an a husbandman with a hoe in his hand on the left."[18] This design still adorns the Delaware state flag.

Congress had called for the raising of eighty-eight additional battalions, of which Delaware's quota was one battalion of eight hundred men. Privates and noncommissioned officers who agreed to serve throughout the war were paid twenty Continental dollars and given one hundred acres of land. "There is also a Bounty in Land to the officers," Caesar informed Haslet. "You will no doubt wonder that the Congress have not Raised the pay of the Officers. I Confess it is Strange that they have not—But depend on it (between you and I) their pay will be raised verry soon, and verry Considerably too. . . ."[19]

As each state was required to supply their own men with "arms, accoutrements and clothing," the Delaware legislature sent a delegation to the camps of Haslet and Patterson to assess their needs. They were also authorized to sign up whatever officers and men would agree to the new conditions. It was decided that Haslet's Continental regiment would have first choice of officers.[20]

The new legislature adjourned without electing a president, apparently because the new constitution did not specify how the ballot should be taken.[21] As a result, Caesar, as chairman of the Kent county Council of Safety, immediately became that county's chief executive by default.[22]

Haslet's regiment was among the half of Washington's army that left northern Manhattan in November. They crossed the Hudson near Peekskill, New York. The other half of the army remained in New York under General Charles Lee with orders to prevent a further British advance. Unfortunately, Fort Lee, Fort Washington's counterpart on the New Jersey side of the river, fell to the British general Cornwallis on November 20. The American general Nathanael Greene managed to escape with most of his men, but a great store of equipment and munitions were left behind. The British now had firm control of both sides of the Hudson.

Howe then sent Cornwallis after Washington with a large force of British and Hessian soldiers. Having lost so many men at Fort Washington and with half his remaining army still in New York, Washington had little choice but to retreat as slowly as possible while fighting a rearguard action.[23] One of the officers with Cornwallis described the chase across New Jersey: "As we go forward into the country, the rebels flee before us, and when we come back they always follow us, 'tis almost impossible to catch them. They will neither fight, nor totally run away, but they keep at such distance that we are always above a day's march from them. They seem to be playing at Bo Peep."[24]

To make matters worse, Washington was woefully short of supplies. As winter approached, the militia were deserting in droves, and the terms of enlistment of many of his Continentals would expire at the end of the year. Desperate, he ordered General Lee to leave New York and come to his aid. Lee's forces did cross the Hudson, but stopped at Morristown, New Jersey, where Lee proceeded to ignore the orders that Washington sent almost daily. Lee, apparently, wanted Washington to fail, believing that Congress would then appoint him as the next commander in chief of the American army.[25]

Trenton fell to Cornwallis on December 8, and Washington crossed the Delaware River to Pennsylvania. To prevent the British from following, he took or destroyed every boat he could find for several miles up and down stream. Haslet was still with him, but his Delaware regiment now numbered only fifteen officers and ninety-two men, down from twenty-eight officers and nearly three hundred men in early November.[26] With his own term due to expire at the end of the year, Haslet had reenlisted. Caesar informed him on December 14 that "Imediately on the Rect of your Last I wrote as usual to Mistress Haslet, and have to tell you that . . . She is verry Hearty but much troubled about your ReEntering the Service. . . ."[27]

New Jersey was lost. So was Newport, Rhode Island: the British General Clinton had captured the harbor in early December. It now seemed only a matter of time before Philadelphia would fall as well. The city was already under martial law; General Israel Putnam had been named the state's military governor on the day Washington crossed into Pennsylvania. According to a contemporary account, all the shops had closed and "people . . . of all ranks [are] sending all their goods out of town into the country." A curfew was also established; anyone on the streets after ten would be arrested.[28] On December 12, the members of the Continental Congress dumped full military powers on General Washington, sent all remaining munitions out of the city to Delaware, and gathered up their papers and fled to Baltimore. The American cause seemed doomed.

In an ironic twist of fate, the renegade General Lee was captured on December 13th, by a detail of British dragoons from the very same regiment that he, himself, had once served. He was having breakfast near Morristown at the time and writing a letter to his colleague, General Horatio Gates, condemning Washington as "damnably deficient."[29] The command of Lee's division passed to John Sullivan, who had been exchanged after his capture at Brooklyn Heights for a British prisoner of similar rank. Sullivan, with two thousand men, promptly set out to join Washington.[30] His arrival increased Washington's force to about five thousand, later bolstered to six thousand by the arrival of Generals Horatio Gates and John Cadwalader with some Pennsylvania volunteers. It was still a pitifully small force to face the British army.[31]

Meanwhile, Howe, under the impression that the war was won, offered a "free and general pardon" to any who would take an oath of loyalty to the king, and retired to winter quarters in New York, leaving a string of outposts across central New Jersey. When Howe's soldiers, forced to live off the land, began pillaging the countryside, the Pennsylvania Council of Safety reported that "sixteen young women . . . fled to the woods to avoid their brutality [but] were . . . seized and carried off. Furniture of every kind [was] destroyed or burnt, windows and door broke to pieces . . . every horse, cow, ox, hogs and poultry carried off. . . . A blind old gentleman near Pennytown [was] plundered of everything, and on his door wrote, "Capt Wills of the Royal Irish did this."[32]

On December 14, Thomas Rodney set out from Dover to join Washington's army. Long afterward, he claimed that while praying for his country's cause, he had had a vision of opposing armies and an archangel had appeared before him saying that if God found one perfect man, he would save America.[33] Did Tommy assume that he was that perfect man? Apparently so; however, when he described his vision to his brother, Caesar was said to have remarked dryly that he'd better take his militia company with him. (Only thirty-five men, less than half of the total company, agreed to go.) Tommy also claimed that while crossing the Christiana bridge on his way to Philadelphia, he met some members of the Continental Congress en route to Baltimore and tried "to rouze and animate them."[34]

On the sixteenth, Tommy and his militia arrived to find the city both demoralized and deserted. Again writing long afterward, Tommy claimed that while dining with his wife Betsy's uncle Joshua Fisher and family, who were "Quakers and great Tories," he was told that Washington had sent for terms of reconciliation. According to his account, the Fishers promised him money, property and a high position in government if he agreed not to interfere with the peace negotiations. Insulted, Thomas said he retorted that he would "march tomorrow morning for camp and . . . not return until we have recovered all Jersey from Brunswick to the Delaware."[35]

Tommy's version of these events was written in the 1790s, and paints an exaggerated, not to say delusionary, picture. There is no record that Washington ever sued for peace at the end of 1776. On the contrary, with General Lee out of the way and Sullivan's newly arrived reinforcements, he was now determined to attack the British at Trenton.

19

Trenton and Princeton

WASHINGTON PLANNED TO CROSS THE DELAWARE RIVER ON CHRISTMAS night and launch an attack on Trenton, a village of about a hundred houses. The British had left fifteen hundred men there under the Hessian colonel Carl von Donop with fifteen hundred more divided between Bordentown and Burlington, a few miles downstream. Their largest force was twenty-seven miles to the rear at New Brunswick. In spite of persistent rumors on the American side of the river that the British "intend to attempt crossing on the ice," Howe was in New York and Cornwallis planned to return to England; both were certain that the cold winter would bring what was left of the American army to its knees.[1]

While Washington saw these remnant British detachments as highly vulnerable, he was also aware that if the British succeeded in trapping his own army with the river at his back, it would be disastrous. His plan was to have his main force of about twenty-five hundred men cross the river nine miles north of Trenton. At the same time, two thousand under Colonel Cadwalader would cross near Bristol, Pennsylvania, and divert the attention of a Hessian garrison near Mount Holly. A third detachment of seven hundred under Brigadier James Ewing was to cross just south of Trenton to prevent the Hessians from retreating in that direction.[2]

Thomas Rodney was with Colonel Cadwallader. He had arrived on Christmas Eve, and was staying in "a most convenient and comfortable room" at Mr. and Mrs. Allen's at Shamany Creek, about four miles from Bristol. He and and his Dover light infantry were among the first to cross the river on Christmas night only to be brought back when Cadwallader decided that the "great bodies of floating ice" made it impossible to get the artillery across.[3] "It was as severe a night as ever I saw," Tommy wrote Caesar, "and after two battalions were landed the storm increased so much and the river was so full of ice that . . . we had to walk one hundred yards on the ice to get on shore. General [Colonel] Cadwalader . . . ordered the whole to retreat again, and we had to stand at least six hours under arms—first to cover the landing and [again] until all the rest had retreated again. . . ."[4] Ewing, meanwhile, took one look at the frozen river, and made no attempt to cross at all.

Washington, however, refused to be daunted and his men responded to his leadership. They began the embarkation at dusk on Christmas Day using shallow draft boats, forty to sixty feet long and eight feet wide, propelled by twenty-foot poles. The boats were manned by Colonel John Glover's fishermen from Massachusetts, the same regiment that had taken Washington's men across the East River after the battle of Long Island. "The ice continually stuck to the boats, driving them down stream," wrote one soldier afterward, "the boatmen endevering to clear off the ice pounded the boats . . . they all set to jumping at once with their [poles] flying up and down, soon shook off the ice. . . ."[5] Not until three in the morning did the last man reach the Jersey shore and it was another hour before all the artillery was across.

Just before dawn, Washington's men began their march through a driving sleet storm, some with only rags covering their bare feet. They were divided into two columns, each proceeding along a parallel road to Trenton, where fourteen hundred Hessian troops were sleeping off a night of feasting and drinking. The Hessians were attacked from four directions at once, Greene, Stirling and Mercer from the north, and Sullivan from the south. John Haslet, who was with General Mercer, wrote Caesar afterwards that "a party of Virginians formed the van Guard & did most of the fighting—Lord Stirling's Brigade [which included Haslet's Continentals] had the honor of fighting 1000 Hessians to a surrender—We should have gone on, & panic struck they would have fled before us, but the inclemency of the weather rendered it impossible. . . ."[6] The American attack was executed so quickly and flawlessly that "Washington took nine hundred and ten prisoners," wrote Tommy, "with six pieces of fine artillery, and all their baggage. . . ."[7]

Driving their prisoners before them, Washington's army returned the way they had come. After marching more than thirty miles in driving sleet and snow, they had sustained only six casualties; four wounded in the battle and two who froze to death while recrossing the icy river. Haslet was nearly one of them. "On our victorious return from Trenton," he wrote Caesar, "I fell into the Delaware at 3 O'Clock in the morning, up to my middle—have had the piles and swelled legs ever since—but no matter, if we drive them to New York."[8]

After failing to follow orders on Christmas night, Colonel John

Cadwalader was so elated by reports of Washington's victory that he took it upon himself to take his men across the river the following day. "I received orders to be in Bristol before day;" Tommy wrote, "and about nine o'clock began to embark . . . about three o'clock in the afternoon got all our troops and artillery over, consisting of about three thousand men, and began our march to Burlington . . . We got there about nine o'clock, and took possession of the town, but found the enemy had made [a] precipitate retreat the day before . . . in a great panick." Proceeding on to Bordentown, about eleven miles away, they captured "a large quantity of the enemy's stores, which they had not time to carry off."

Tommy was exhilarated. "The enemy have fled before us in the greatest panick," he boasted, "Never were men in higher spirits than our whole Army is; none are sick, and all are determined to extirpate them from the Jersey . . . Jersey will be the most Whiggish Colony on the Continent: the very Quakers declare for taking up arms."[9]

Cadwalader's move came as an unwelcome surprise to Washington, who had just managed to get his men safely back on the Pennsylvania side of the river. Deciding that it would be foolish to order Cadwalader's return, however, he wearily took his men across the icy water for the third time on December 30.

Howe, stunned by the news from Trenton, immediately cancelled Cornwallis' leave. Cornwallis then took his army across New Jersey with incredible speed, arriving at Princeton on the evening of January 1, 1777. His progress slowed, however, when he set off for Trenton the following morning. Not only had heavy rain during the night turned the frozen roads into a morass of deep mud, but he was continually harrassed by small bands of American troops.[10] One of these skirmishes was led by General Hugh Mercer and included Colonel John Haslet and his Delaware Continentals.[11]

It was late afternoon before the British advance approached Washington's main line of defense on the south bank of the Assunpink Creek near the Delaware river. Cornwallis, certain that he had Washington in a trap, allowed his tired army to stop for the night. He would attack in the morning.

Washington, aware that he had neither the time nor the boats to cross safely into Pennsylvania, made a bold decision. As Caesar described it to George Read: "Washington with his army Lay in the field and woods between the town creek and the River till about two Oclock in the morning and after having Caused the Fires to be well made up Marched his Army Round the head of the Creek into the Princetown Road. . . ."[12] Washington, his cannon wheels muffled with rags, silently moved his army around the enemy's flank, leaving a few hundred men behind to tend the campfires so the British would think they were still there. Thomas Rodney and the Dover militia were in the vanguard of the escaping troops.[13]

As the army neared Princeton, General Mercer's brigade, which now included Haslet's Continentals and Thomas Rodney's militia, were left behind at a small bridge with orders to delay the expected pursuit from Cornwallis.[14] They reached the bridge at sunrise, too late to stop the first regiment of British infantry from crossing. A second British regiment followed about a mile behind; both under the command of British lieutenant colonel Charles Mawhood. Realizing that they had the American's trapped, the advance column of British turned and charged back toward the bridge. A fierce battle ensued. General Mercer was bayoneted and left for dead and, a few moments later, Colonel John Haslet was killed instantly by a shot through the head.

Only a few days before, he had written Caesar: "If I return it will be to salute you, if not we shall meet in Heaven—Your Goodness will give Mrs. Haslet such news as you think proper. . . ."[15] Caesar, devastated by the loss of his friend, wrote William Killen that ". . . so Long as the Inhabitants of this American World Shall Continue to be a free people, So long . . . will the name of . . . Haslet be held in Honorable Remembrance . . . We [have] Lost a Brave, open, Honest, Sensible Man, One Who loved his Country's more than his private Interest. . . ."[16]

After Haslet's death, his men fled in disarray despite the best efforts of Major Thomas Macdonough, a doctor from New Castle County, to rally them.[17] Tommy's militia, meanwhile, was ordered to hold the left flank, but only fifteen of his men would go with him; the firing was so dreadful that he "could not keep them all there. . . ." Nevertheless, although "grazed by three balls," he and his little group with "about 30 of the Philadelphia infantry" managed to successfully hold the line.[18]

Then, General Washington, himself, galloped onto the field. A tall, impressive figure on a great white horse, he rode through the smoke of battle to within thirty yards of the British line, entreating his men to stand firm until General Sullivan's column arrived with reinforcements. Whereupon Mawhood, realizing he would soon be outnumbered, charged through the American line and escaped down the road to Trenton. The entire battle had taken only fifteen minutes.[19]

Tommy's militia was still in the vanguard of Washington's army as they moved on through Kingston and down the Millstone River toward Somerset Court House. At one point they managed to break up a plank bridge immediately in front of a party of British horsemen.[20]

Washington's quick and decisive action had dealt the British a decisive blow and given new life and energy to the American cause. When his men went into winter quarters in Morristown, New Jersey, on January 6, his reputation as a military leader was secure. His troubles, however, were far from over. Plagued by disease as well as a shortage of food, clothing and shelter, many of his most seasoned soldiers left for home, Tommy's militia among them. The Dover light infantry had fought bravely and well. They had also been incredibly lucky. Yet their leader, perhaps responding to Washington's efforts to keep his army intact, complained to Caesar that: "My Company has Stained those Glorious Lorrels which they gained in four weeks [of] Severe duty—Most of them were in the Hottest of the Battle at Prince Town without receiving a wound or loosing one life—But on the tenth of this Instant their Time Expired & they determined to go home. . . ."[21]

20

Militia and Other Matters

CAESAR, STILL IN DOVER IN THE DARK DAYS OF LATE DECEMBER 1776, had written Tommy that:

> I think it absolutely necessary that Howe Should be Routed from the Jersey this Winter, and the sooner it is done the better. But am afraid our General has not yet got Force enough to do it. Ever since you left, I have been doing everything in my power to draw the Militia of this County to Join the Army. . . . Some days ago I proposed Marching myself with such as Should be willing, and have [proposed that we meet] on Thursday next. . . . Some people are of opinion that many will turn out, some others that they will not. . . . My present determination is to Come at all Events. . . .[1]

And come he did. Caesar had already arrived in Philadelphia when Tommy, not realizing he had left Dover, begged him to reconsider: "I must Press my advice upon [you]," he wrote on January 14, 1777, "not to Come into the field. Your Present State of Health is not fit to Encounter the Severity & Difficulties of a winter's Campain."[2] Caesar, however, was feeling quite well. "[I] Have the pleasure to inform you," he wrote George Read at the end of January, "that I have not been in the least unwell since I left Home, not even with the Astma—In short I . . . grow Fatt. . . ."[3] By that time, of course, the American victories at Princeton and Trenton had brightened the picture considerably.

Meanwhile, Howe, certain that he could easily capture Philadelphia in the spring, sent his army into winter quarters in New Brunswick, Amboy, and Raritan where it could be easily supplied by boat from Staten Island. As the winter wore on, however, the British found that ice on the rivers often forced them to bring in their supplies overland, giving the newly energized Americans ample opportunity to attack the wagons. Individually and in small groups, the Americans also preyed on British outpost and foraging parties. In one such incident a British "Forraging party Consisting

147

of two thousand" ran into four hundred Virginians. After retreating initially, the Virginians obtained enough reinforcements to "beat the Enemy back to their Lines at Brunswick with the loss of all the Cattel Horses etc. they had been pillaging. . . ."[4]

As Washington continued to lose his most seasoned soldiers, Caesar was sent to Trenton by Lord Stirling. His job was to forward replacements, both Continental and militia, to Washington in Morristown, as well as to Major General Israel Putnam at Princeton, and Brigadier General Philemon Dickinson (John Dickinson's brother) on the Raritan River. "I am now not only playing the General but Commander in Chief" he wrote George Read on January 23.[5] Four days later he reported to William Killen that: "Since My arrival I have Sent forward Near two Thousand. . . . Among [them] the Delawares Who first Went to Princetown and Then were sent by General Putnam to the Main Army to Convoy forty or fifty Waggons. . . ."[6] This was Colonel Thomas Collins' brigade of Delaware militia, "The Strength of [which] is two hundred & thirty-eight including Officers. . . ."[7]

Caesar soon grew impatient with administrative duties and requested that he be "Removed to Headquarters to Join My Brigade. . . ."[8] After receiving permission from General Putnam to do so on January 26, he "got a waggon, packed up All my Baggage and set out." However, he had only "Got about four miles on my way [when he] met orders from him to return to this Post." General Putnam had changed his mind "upon second consideration." A few days later, the disappointed Caesar dined with his commander, Lord Stirling, who "promised that as soon as he got to Headquarters . . . he wou'd prevail upon General Washington to call me."[9]

Despite these efforts, Caesar was still at his desk in Trenton on February 5, when he complained to Philemon Dickinson that if General Washington didn't allow him to come soon he was "affraid I Shall have no Brigade to Join." The Delaware men had "begun to be Homesick" and were agitating to return home.[10]

In fact, they had already left. An exasperated Washington, "finding that he could do nothing with them" and under the impression that Caesar was commanding a brigade under Israel Putnam at Princeton, had sent them there on the fourth. Putnam, in turn, sent them on to Trenton, where despite Caesar's best efforts, they refused to stay. "To my Great Surprise, and their everlasting Shame," he wrote Lord Stirling, "the last of the Delaware Militia that I, with much pains, brought out to Serve the Cause, passed through this town, the day before Yesterday, on their way Home. . . . They Spent near . . . Three weeks in marching up to Head

Quarters, stayed There about one week without Rendering a Single Copperworth of Service to the Public—and then, Tho Solicited by the General to Stay only two weeks more, Shamefully set off. . . ."[11]

He tried to put a good face on it for Tommy, who had also returned to Dover despite boasting previously that "the Gen'l Has requested Me not to leave him notwithstanding my men being gone."[12] "To do the men Justice who came from our County," Caesar wrote, "Col Collins says he is convinced every man of them would have staid provided those from Newcastle and Sussex would, but that they were determined against it."[13]

A disgusted Caesar promised Lord Stirling that he would "Continue Here, Until ordered to some other Post, or discharged—If I have given Satisfaction, and can be longer usefull Here or Elsewhere, I shall, with the greatest Chearfullness Stay on—If not, Shall Expect a discharge."[14]

Meanwhile, he enjoyed himself in the local society. "I have now a Set of acquantance here, both Gentlemen and Ladies, that do everything in their power to make my time agreable, and will I am Convinced, part with me, when Obliged to do it, with great Reluctance," he wrote Tommy on February 12. With tongue firmly in cheek, he added: "You may think strange how this should come to pass. However I am certainly a man of Consequence here, tho of ever so little in my own State, and they have got it in their heads, tho ever so strangely, that I am a gentleman as well as a Whig."[15]

On February 18, Caesar received a highly complimentary letter from General Washington containing his expected discharge. "The readiness with which you took the field at the Period most critical to our affairs," the General wrote, "the industry you used in bringing out the Militia of the Delaware State, & the alertness observed by you in forwarding on the Troops from Trenton, reflect the highest Honour on your Character . . . [and] claim my Sincerest Thanks . . .—Circumstanced as you are, I see no necessity in detaining you longer from yr family & affairs. . .—You have therefore my Leave to return." The General then added a note of caution. "From the Enemy's maneuvres of late, especially their reinforcing Brunswic, I fear yr Militia will be wanted again—You will therefore be pleased to keep them in readiness, till I call for them.[16]

During Caesar's absence, the Delaware legislature had finally managed to choose their first president. Having previously omitted to specify the "mode of taking a ballot" in the new consitution, they eventually decided that each member of the house and council could propose a candidate. The names were written out and "left on the table. . . . After they had slept a night the joint convention would re-assemble the next day and proceed with the ballot."[17]

By this method, Dr. John McKinly was elected by a vote of twenty-three to nineteen on February 12. Fifty-six years old, McKinly had been born in Northern Ireland, but had lived in Wilmington for thirty-five years. Although a Presbyterian and a militia officer, he was no revolutionary firebrand.[18] Tommy, for one, bitterly dismissed him as "the only man that could so fully represent The Whig & Tory Complexion of this State . . . I make no doubt all their appointments will be of a piece with this and that the State will Continue in the same shackling condition . . . without affording the least aid to the Union except the private influence of a few individuals. . . ."[19]

In the following weeks, as the legislature filled other state offices, Tommy was relieved of his seat on the orphan's court and court of common pleas. Although obviously piqued, he boldly asserted that he was "well Pleased that I now Can Say I am Truly a Free Man being neither the Servant of the King nor People. . . ."

The new conservative government had also, Tommy reported to Caesar, "gone Great lenths to Strip you but were Too Timerous to do all they wished. . . ."[20] Actually, Caesar was appointed a Justice of the newly organized state supreme court, a post which he later declined, and reappointed "Brigadier General of the Two Battalions of Militia in Kent County & of the Western Battalion of Militia in Sussex County."[21] The latter was commanded by General John Dagworthy.

Caesar also continued to serve as trustee of the Kent county loan office. It cannot have been an enviable position. Delaware's fiscal condition was chaotic. The expense of running the new civil government as well as fulfilling their obligations to the war effort had put severe pressures on the state treasury. In an effort to remedy the situation, the new legislature issued £15,000 in bills of credit "to be let out on loan" and a further £10,000 to be used for the defense of the state. They also made the Continental currency legal tender in a futile effort to infuse value into the vast sums of essentially worthless paper that had been issued by the Continental Congress.[22]

These fiscal uncertainties surely had an adverse impact on the Rodneys' private finances as well. Tommy, perhaps rashly, had recently bought "about 1200 Acres of Land at a very low rate Chiefly in Marshy hope, which I can Contrive to pay for very readily . . . as I have Great part of the money . . . & can Collect the rest in time." Caesar could not have been reassured by the news that his brother

had already been offered any "sum of Continental money at Philadelphia, without Interest," to pay for it. Nor could he be certain
"that the advantage will be very Great as Land will Certainly rise
Shortly to a great price every thing it produces being Extravigant
already."[23] Inflation had already spun out of control. According to
Lieutenant Colonel Charles Pope, now in charge of Haslet's old
regiment, the depression of the currency is such that "five days pay
of a subaltern will now only purchase a Dinner—& other necessaries of life are equally as extravagant."[24]

To make matters worse, Boaz Manlove, one of the signers of bills
issued in January 1776, had just absconded with ten thousand
pounds of the state's money to cast his fortunes with the English
king.[25] He was only one of a number of loyalists who continued to
cause trouble on the lower Peninsula. On February 16, there was
also a "rising of the Tories to the amount of 2000 in Summersets
[Somerset County, Maryland] who upon the arrival of Colonel
Hooper with about 500 men, all dispersed & fled, but he Took about
40 of the Principle ones and sent them to Annapolis."[26]

On February 22, the same day they approved the issuing of the
money, the Delaware legislature passed a "Treason Act." Tommy
immediately sneered that "one of their fast friends in Mispillion
says they have made a law to hang their best friends."[27] Actually,
they were after Manlove and his compatriot, the notorious Thomas
Robinson. Manlove and Robinson had been in hiding since January. On a stormy night in March, "with a party of eleven," they
would paddle across Rehoboth Bay to board a British ship.[28]

Around the same time, Captain Smythe, an Englishman touring
America, arrived in Sussex county where he was informed by a
messenger that eleven hundred loyalists had cornered three hundred rebels near Salisbury, Maryland, and wanted him to take command. Concluding that the loyalists were both unarmed and
undisciplined, Smythe decided that success was unlikely and sent
them a message to that effect hidden in the hollow handle of a
whip.[29]

These were but a few of the incidents that occurred that winter
and spring. In April, Caesar was alerted by President McKinly as to
"the imminent Danger of an Insurrection in the Counties of Somerset and Worcester [Maryland] . . . & that the Insurgents may be
joined by dissafected Persons in . . . Sussex. . . ." He added that "as
the Western Battalion of that County belongs to your Brigade . . . I
do earnestly request that you wou'd make a speedy and full
Enquiry. . . ."[30]

The British ships in Delaware Bay, having interrupted normal trade routes between the lower Peninsula and Philadelphia, were now enticing many on the Peninsula to trade with them instead. In May, McKinly reported that "enemies' ships of War were lately seen on shore near Mispillion Creek & seemingly made welcome by some persons there. . . ." Also, "some parties of men from the said ships have landed near Jones' Creek in your Co. & have Killed several cattle & done other damage to the inhabitants." He wanted Caesar to "order a sufficient number of the Militia under your command to keep guard where it may be probable that they will land again, to give them a proper reception. . . ."[31]

By July, the problem was even worse. President McKinly promised a reward of two hundred dollars for the capture of anyone caught trading with the enemy, adding that anyone who agreed to supply information regarding such practices would be pardoned. It must have had some effect. On the eleventh, Caesar reported that he had apprehended one John Willson, a resident of New Jersey, as well as Jonas Edingfield and John Ashworth of Bombay Hook, and John Conner of Thoroughfare Neck. All were in "Dover Gaol", having been accused of "having Supplied the Men of War with Stock, etc." John Conner was also accused of piloting barges from the Men of War up into Duck Creek [Smyrna]. "This Evil is growing so verry fast," Caesar warned President McKinly, "That if not verry Shortly put a Stop to by Some Exertion of Government we Shall be Overwhelmed, We are most Certainly, Even now, in Eminent danger." In fact, the people in Mispillion Neck had "so generally got into the Tradeing Scheme with the men of War That it would be dangerous for any Man Who's property lay among them to say a Word, or do any Act in opposition to it." In Sussex, "they have got to so daring a pitch . . . as to put forth a Proclamation in opposition to yours . . . offering a Greater Reward than is in Yours, for the Apprehending all those who Shall attempt to oppose them."[32]

Besides dealing with these problems, Caesar had been ordered to raise enough militia to counteract the expected British invasion. As early as April 7, 1777, McKinly told him that Congress had advised "[us to] be prepared to defend ourselves, in case of a[n] . . . attack." McKinly also wanted Caesar to "plan a guard at Lewes Town . . . to protect the persons employed as Pilots, & such property of the good subjects of the United States. . . ."[33]

Things had become even more tense by the end of the month. It was thought "from several circumstances that Genl Howe will . . . make an attempt upon Philadelphia, both by land & water . . . the Aid of the Militia [will be] absolutely necessary for about 6 weeks [until] General Washington (who is now very deficient but whose army is daily increasing fast) will have a sufficient number of continental Troops under his command. . . ."[34]

Caesar was having a great deal of difficulty getting anyone to serve. He had already told McKinly that "from the best Information I Can get Great Numbers of the people are likely to decline Associating, Thinking it much Cheaper to pay the penalty than Equip themselves, attend Musters and lay themselves liable to be called into actual Service." "The penalty," he added, "ought to have been so high as to have Compelled them to Associate."[35]

Nevertheless, by May he was able to report that "The Officers who have met & been consulted are of Opinion that the Quota of this Country may be raised" and urged McKinly to "exert" himself to prepare a place for their arrival, suggesting "a fine healthy pleasant & convenient piece near Naamans Creek" in Brandywine Hundred.[36] (Caesar was not impressed with McKinly's zeal; he often implored him to "exert" himself as well as to "animate those under your command.")[37]

In the end, Caesar escorted the Kent county militia to the camp at Naaman's Creek himself.[38] Since their term of enlistment lasted only three weeks, he was once more back in Dover by the middle of June attempting to raise their replacements.[39]

Meanwhile, Washington was puzzled. The British lieutenant general John Burgoyne was in Canada with an army of nearly eight thousand men and, by mid-June, had begun to move toward Fort Ticonderoga. Yet General Howe, after a series of small offensive attacks in New Jersey, had withdrawn to Staten Island, and did not seem to be preparing a move up the Hudson to join him.[40]

On July 26, Caesar received "a Newspaper with the Account of the late unhappy Affair at Ticonderoga" from John McKinly.[41] During the night of July 4, the American major general Arthur St. Clair had been forced to evacuate the Fort by Burgoyne's forces who were firing down on him from adjacent Sugar Loaf Mountain. St. Clair, recognizing his danger, had opted to save his men, but a number of cannon and many valuable supplies were left behind.[42]

Instead of following up on Burgoyne's victory, however, Howe's fleet of transport ships carrying fifteen to eighteen thousand British troops left New York on July 5, only to become stranded for two weeks by a lack of wind.[43]

On July 30, Caesar sent an urgent letter to John Hancock, president of the Continental Congress: "Just now by Express from Lewes, I am Informed that two hundred and Twenty Eight of the Enemy's ships have appeared in the offing—I have sent a fresh man and a Horse that this Inteligence may be the Sooner with you—I believe our Militia . . . will Turn out Imediately pretty Generally but . . . we are in great Want of Arms, Amunition & Camp Utensils . . . pray provide us with those things. . . ."[44]

Caesar then ordered Colonel William Rhodes of the second battalion of Kent militia to "report to me of the Strength of Each and Every Company in Your Battalion . . . [and to] Secure . . . all Boats and Water Craft whosoever within your Limits, in such Manner, as to Prevent any Inteligence being given to . . . the Enemy's Vessels. . . . Place a Constant Guard of Six Men . . . at the Cross-Roads near Craiges Mill on that side next Dover—for the purpose . . . of Examining all travellers.[45]

Then, inexplicably, the British fleet disappeared. On August 2, Caesar received word that:

> On Wednesday we first discovered them & in a little time we could make 23 sail from the Light-House; they had every Appearance of coming into our Bay [since they had put a] small Vessel in the Tail of the Hen & Chickens [reef] with a large flag as a Beacon . . . [as well as] a Ship anchored in the Channel. . . . [In] the Evening . . . a large Ship which we took to be the Admiral fired a gun & immediately the whole Fleet tacked and stood off. . . . The Admiral with three or four others . . . lay close to the Cape 'till Thursday Morning & about Ten o'clock fired a signal Gun . . . immediately the whole Fleet changed their Course to about ESE . . . at about four o'clock P.M. they were out of sight; whether bound to New York or Virginia is not in my power to tell."[46]

Washington had assumed Howe was heading for Philadelphia, but he could not be certain. Perhaps he was trying to draw the American army to the south, so he could reverse course to join Burgoyne unopposed. Cautiously, Washington moved his army, which now numbered nearly nine thousand men, toward the Delaware River, prepared to march either north or south if need be. He also sent a message to the American troops near West Point to keep a lookout for Howe's return.

Washington's first guess had been correct. Howe, for reasons of his own, had decided as early as April to abandon Burgoyne in favor of attacking Philadelphia. The city, as he saw it, was not only the seat of the Continental Congress; its forges and surrounding fields were a major source of guns and grain for Washington's army. His plan was to occupy the city by the fall of 1777 and then move south to Georgia and South Carolina.

McKinly wrote Caesar: "It may be supposed that [the enemy's vessels] are destined for Philadelphia, but it being uncertain where they may make a descent . . . it behoves all persons . . . to hold

themselves in perfect readiness . . . take care that all stock and provisions of every kind . . . that are not immediately wanted for the
subsistence of the inhabitants be removed to places of safety. . . ."[47]

Howe had, indeed, planned to sail up Delaware Bay, but changed
his mind after being convinced that the American fortifications, not
to mention the roving ships of the "Pennsylvania Navy," made that
plan too risky. Instead, he went down the coast to the mouth of the
Chesapeake Bay.

21

The War Comes Home

As THE BRITISH FLEET SAILED THROUGH THE OPPRESSIVE AUGUST HEAT down the coast and into the mouth of the Chesapeake, the atmosphere in Delaware and Philadelphia grew increasingly tense. No one knew where Howe had gone or what he planned to do next. Caesar, in Dover, was preparing the Kent county militia, and implored McKinly to "supply our Deficiences. . . ."[1] McKinly promised to "forward by waggon," at least "35 tents, & as many Camp Kittles, together with a sufficiency of Ammunition made up in Cartridges."

In return, McKinly asked Caesar to take over the command of the Sussex detachment. In his view, Caesar was the only one who had the requisite "Knowledge of the affairs of that distracted County, & of the character of Every individual of note," as well as their "party disputes, private views, & personal animosities. . . ."[2]

McKinly needed Caesar to smooth relations between Colonel W. Richardson, commander of a Continental regiment in Sussex, and the fractious citizens of that county. Two men, Thomas Lightfoot and Thomas Cockayne, had been caught circulating counterfeit bills and carrying "on a Correspondence with the Enemy prejudicial to the United States." According to law, Caesar had asked the High Sheriff of Sussex to arrest them. Colonel Richardson, however, had insisted that they be sent directly to Congress, as, in his view, "there is no great probability that Tory Judges will punish Tory Offenders however Atrocious their Offence." In Richadson's opinion, "a large Majority of the Inhabitants of this County . . . would . . . afford the Enemy every Aid in their power, except Personal Service in the Field, which [they lack] Spirit to do. They are a set of poor Ignorant Illectorate People, yet they are Artful and Cunning as Foxes. . . ."[3]

Meanwhile, Howe's intention to attack Philadelphia overland from the south became clear. On August 22, his fleet, "consisting of between 2 & 300 Sail," were sighted off the mouth of the Sassafras River in the northern Chesapeake Bay. The ships had been so delayed by summer calms that it had taken them more than three weeks to make the the trip from the Delaware Capes.

Supposing that "they intend to make a Descent in order to possess themselves of the Peninsula," McKinly immediately ordered Caesar to march "with the Militia . . . to such Places as may be most necessary to annoy the Enemy & prevent them from effecting their purpose. . . . You know You have a Right by Law to impress Waggons & Horses," he reminded him, "I shall order You Bread & as much other Provisions as needful . . . but should any be wanting You must procure [it]."

Caesar was also "to take care that they do not cut off your communication with the upper part of this state and by [timely] Removal prevent them from obtaining any cattle . . . Horses Carts or Waggons . . . Arms or Ammunition. . . ." McKinly then added that "Burgoyne has met with a fortunate Check . . . if we do our duty here I believe there is no danger from that quarter. . . ." (Burgoyne, abandoned by Howe, had been outflanked and defeated near Bennington, Vermont, on August 16.)[4]

Meanwhile, General Washington had moved his army through Philadelphia and on to Wilmington's Quaker Hill. His troops now numbered about ten thousand men, but they were a motley lot, with no uniforms except their burnished arms and a sprig of evergreen for their hats.[5] Then, on August 25, nearly six weeks after they had left New York, Howe's forces landed unopposed on Elk Neck, a peninsula between the Northeast and Elk rivers.

That same day, Washington, accompanied by General Nathanael Greene and the young Marquis de Lafayette, newly arrived from France, had ridden out to scout the land and learn what they could of the intentions of the British. After a heavy rainstorm forced them to spend the night in a nearby farmhouse, Washington returned to his troops on the morning of the twenty-sixth, and immediately formed them into a long defensive line stretching along the Red Clay Creek from Newport, Delaware into Pennsylvania. He also sent a corps of light infantry under General William Maxwell into the woods along the road between Glasgow and Cooch's Bridge to harry and delay the British.[6]

Washington thought Howe might attack Wilmington. He was also concerned that "a considerable quantity of Continental Stores" stashed near the Head of Elk was in danger of being taken. Through McKinly, Washington asked Caesar to "hurry the militia . . . towards the place as fast as possible."[7] Caesar immediately ordered the Dover and New Castle detachments to Middletown to "secure the Troops in the best Manner you can from any Surprize of the Enemy."[8] They were also to serve as local guides for General Maxwell's infantry. The men from Kent were in position by the end of August, yet only about "forty or fifty of the Newcastle Militia" had answered the call.[9] Colonel Mordecai Gist, and his 3rd Maryland Regiment were at the Sassafras River on Maryland's Eastern Shore, but so short of men and equipment, that Gist could only "keep up a line of communication & hope that any Movement of the Enemy . . . will be forwarded."[10]

Meanwhile, General Howe and the British division commanded by Lord Cornwallis, marched to Head of Elk (Elkton, Maryland) on August 27, and from there proceeded east toward Aiken's Tavern (now Glasgow, Delaware). A second division, under the Hessian general Wilhelm von Knyphausen, crossed the Elk River and moved into Delaware just north of Middletown. After sweeping the countryside of all available sheep, cattle and horses, von Knyphausen's men spent the night of September 2 near Lum's Pond, intending to join Howe and Cornwallis at Aikentown the following day.[11]

On Wednesday, September 3, Caesar was in Noxontown, "between two and three miles from Middletown . . . gaining what intelligence I [can] of the Enemy's movements." His brother Tommy was with him. He had been acting as Caesar's military aide since the previous June, keeping track of orders and movements of the troops in an *Orderly Book*.[12] John Dickinson was also there; as a private in the Kent county militia under Captain Stephen Lewis. At the time that he refused to sign the Declaration of Independence, Dickinson had been a colonel in the Pennsylvania militia. Subsequently, he had been forced to resign his commission and was now beginning his long climb back into favor. (Dickinson had already refused to serve as a delegate to the Continental Congress and, in the fall of 1777, would also refuse an appointment as a brigadier general in the militia. Nevertheless, he would eventually serve as Delaware's fifth president.)[13]

Caesar had sent a detachment to spy on von Knyphausen: "Last night a little after dark they were close in with the Enemy at Carson's Tavern (near Summit, Delaware) where they . . . exchanged some shott and allarmed their whole camp. From the best information I can get, they are moving up toward Christiana Creek. . . ." Caesar had promised Washington to "maintain the Post as long as I can and continue to give the enemy all the trouble in my power. . . ."[14] With only three hundred and seventy men, he eagerly awaited further reinforcements from New Castle.

Howe and Cornwallis arrived at Aiken's Tavern at nine in the morning on September 3, and, turning north, immediately ran into Maxwell's men in the woods along the road. In the British vanguard was a corps of Hessian "jaegers," expert scouts and riflemen. As soon as the Americans opened fire, the jaegars surged into the woods to retaliate. The Americans immediately gave ground, as they had been ordered to do, retreating to the vicinity of Iron Hill, a rugged promontory that protected them to the west. When the British moved to the east in an attempt to outflank them, they blundered into a deep morass known as Purgatory Swamp, "which forced them to retrace their steps."[15] The Americans continued to fire and fall back for over two miles, luring the British toward Cooch's Bridge, where the skirmish escalated into the vicious fight that is now known as the Battle of Cooch's Bridge. The Americans lost about forty men, killed or wounded at the Bridge; the British toll is unknown.

Afterwards, the British burned both Cooch's Mill and the Cecil county, Maryland, courthouse. They also "captured all the records and public papers of New Castle County and every shilling of the public money, together with the fund belonging to the trustees of Newark Academy [now University of Delaware]."[16]

Caesar and his militia were positioned several miles to the south. The following morning, he wrote General Washington that he had "two scouting parties of foot out, one of twenty, and one other of fifty . . ." and planned "to move to Middletown to Morrow. . . ." He was still hoping to be joined within a few days by the New Castle militia and Gist's troops from Maryland. The British, he added, "seem determined to push Immediately for Philadelphia. . . ."[17]

They did not, at least not immediately. After briefly chasing Maxwell's men toward Christiana, the British settled into camp near Cooch's Bridge for the next five days, apparently awaiting the arrival of further supplies from the ships. Lord Cornwallis was headquartered in the Cooch family's farmhouse, General Howe in Aiken's Tavern. Von Knyphausen was also nearby; his troops had arrived while the battle was in progress.[18]

On September 5, Washington wrote Caesar:

For the present you can do no more than keep Scouts and Patroles towards the Enemy to watch their motions, but as soon as you are joined by more force from this State (the expected New Castle militia), [and] by the Militia of the Eastern Shore of Maryland and by Richardson's Battalion, I would have you move as near the Enemy as you can with safety, that you may, if they move on towards Philadelphia, get between them & their shipping and cut off their Communication with them or at least render it difficult. You will endeavour to check any parties that the Enemy may send out to collect Horses, Cattle or Forage; and give me intelligence of any Occurrences that may come to your Knowledge.

He then added a postscript: "The Light Horseman who brought your letter informe me that the Enemy's Shipping all fell down from Cecil Court House last Tuesday and were out of Sight, be pleased to inform me whether this be true, and if it is endeavour to find out how low they have fallen down. . . ."[19] After unloading their supplies, the British ships had, indeed, left the northern Chesapeake, apparently intending to return to Delaware Bay to support Howe on his way to Philadelphia.

Meanwhile, Caesar received word of "the Embodying of Some Tories" by "the Methodists, Many of whose preachers are in that Quarter." He had also been told by a Methodist preacher named Freeborn Garrettson that a band of about three thousand "Revolutionaries" under "a backslider" named Cheney Clow were planning to join the British at the Head of Elk. It was also said that "four hundred of Enemy had Landed . . . at Town Point, the farthest point of land between the Elk & Bohamia [Bohemia River]. . . ." However, when a scout was sent to check this, he reported "that he was down on the point and all through that neck, and that there were none of the Enemy to be seen. . . ."[20]

While neither of these rumors proved to be true, there was, in fact, ample reason to believe that the British could have organized Delaware's Tories. After the war, Joseph Galloway testified in the House of Commons that "Mr. Thos Robinson, a gentleman of first weight and influence in those counties, told Sir W. Howe that if Britain would supply arms, he would raise men to disarm rebels . . . and meet Howe at Head of Elk."[21]

On September 7, Caesar heard from Tench Tilghman, Washington's military secretary. "The Enemy have . . . drawn their whole force on this side of the Town of Elk, having destroyed all the Grain which they found in Store there. This being the Case, the General desires that you . . . [move] nearer the Enemy than you are at present, in order to keep them from making excursions to collect Horses . . . to move their Artillery . . . [and] be ready to fall upon their Rear should they move towards us. . . ."[22]

It was the most important military assignment of his career, but Caesar was unable to comply. "I am here in a disagreeable Scituation," he wrote Washington on September 9, "unable to Render you and the States those Services I both wished & Expected." He continued:

A few days ago I moved . . . to Middletown in order to induce the New-castle Militia . . . to turn out—especially as by that Move, Most of their farms & property [would be protected]. However all this has answered no purpose, for tho' I believe most of their officers have been Vigelant, . . . verry few have Come in at all, and those few who made their appearance in the Morning took the Liberty of Returning, Contrary to their Orders, in the Evening, [thus] increasing the duty of, and Setting [a] bad . . . Example to the Troops from Kent, about four hundred in number, and the only Troops I had with me—[This has] brought about so General discontent and Uneasiness, [among the men from Kent] Especially as they were . . . defending the property of those people, [and has] Caused them in great Numbers, to leave me, Tho I must Say the Officers did all they Could to prevent it—

Finding this the Case [I] paid Col. Gist a Visit myself to know his Scituation and when it might be possible for him to Move forward with Col Richardson's Battalion and the Militia of the Maryland Eastern Shore. . . . [He] let me know he . . . would move forward as soon as he Should have it in his power—the two Upper Battalions of Newcastle County have never Even Assigned me a Reason Why thay have not Joined me. . . . Yesterday Evening I Sent a party of my Light Horse to take a View of the Enemy and Gain Intelligence. The Officer with his Men Returned this Morning and Reports, That he was in Aitkin's Tavern-House, passed Some Miles through the late Encampment of the Enemy Round about that place, Saw, and was among the fires they had left burning. That the Extreem part of their Right Wing Was at Cooch's Mill, Their left toward Newark—This Intelligence Makes me the More Anxious to Collect and Move forward Such a Body as would be able to Render you Signal Service by falling upon and Harrasssing their Right wing or Rear . . . As Soon as I can Set forward Shall advise you—God Send you a compleat Victory.[23]

Instead of marching toward Wilmington as Washington had expected, the British had struck off northward toward Kennett Square, Pennsylvania. At four in the morning on September 9, Washington responded by moving his army from Red Clay Creek to the Brandywine River, about nine or ten miles to the north.

The British had also, McKinly informed Caesar, "by way of decoy, & to amuse our Troops from pursuits, left a body of their's on a high hill, about 3 miles west of Newport, who shew themselves very feely both last Eveng & this day on the skirt of a piece of Woods." McKinly, like Caesar, is frustrated by the dismal performance of the New Castle militia. "Nothing would please me more," he asserted, "than that they would be made prisoners by the militia of this state, & I have no doubt had the . . . first & 2nd Battalion of this County, been now under arms, they could Easily have accomplished that desirable service by tomorrow morning; but they are dispersed. . . ."[24]

22

The British Occupy Wilmington

A THICK FOG HUNG OVER THE PENNSYLVANIA LANDSCAPE ON THE morning of September 11, 1777. Washington's army was encamped at Chadd's Ford; the point where the main road from Baltimore to Philadelphia crossed the Brandywine river. The general and his new young aide, the Marquis de Lafayette, had set up their head-quarters in neighboring farmhouses about a mile east of the river.

Washington's artillery occupied the high ground overlooking the creek. Below them, two of General Nathanael Greene's brigades lined the east bank of the river at Chadd's Ford, while a larger force under General Sullivan was positioned a few miles upstream. The Delaware regiment was with Sullivan.[1]

Pyle's Ford, some two miles downstream, was guarded by a thousand men of the Pennsylvania militia. A small cavalry force under General William Maxwell was also there, poised to cross the creek and delay the British advance. It seemed a strong position.

Howe, however, did not plan to cross at Chadd's Ford. Instead, he sent von Knyphausen and five thousand Hessians to keep Washington's main force engaged while he and Cornwallis moved the bulk of the British army, some ten thousand men, along the Great Valley road to the north. "The country was . . . full of Tories and Quakers—. . . [and] Howe, guided by [Joseph] Galloway, had all the intelligence he needed, [while] Washington . . . seemed to be only partially acquainted with the lay of the land."[2]

Nevertheless, Maxwell's calvary, by constantly harrassing von Knyphausen's men, managed to keep him from establishing a position in the hills west of Chadd's Ford until well after ten o'clock. Also around midmorning, a small detachment of American light horse had crossed the Brandywine at Jones' Ford (now Pocopson) where they stumbled upon Cornwallis' men marching up the road in the fog. They dispatched a message to General Washington who immediately ordered General Sullivan to cross the river and attack the British column.

Then, mysteriously, word came that the first report was false; there was no enemy force threatening Sullivan's right flank. Washington took this second report at face value and cancelled the plan for attack: it would prove to be a grievous mistake. Cornwallis' army crossed the Brandywine unopposed six miles above Chadd's Ford and moved into the hills behind Sullivan's right flank at about 2:30 P.M. where they broke ranks for a hour's rest, having marched over seventeen miles in the August heat and humidity.

When, at two, an excited farmer named Thomas Cheney rode into Washington's headquarters with the news that the British had crossed the river, he was not, at first, believed. Washington waited for confirmation before sending word to Sullivan to turn his right flank to the rear.[3]

At four the British began to move, marching straight across the valley toward the American lines. The men on Sullivan's flanks, unprepared to face such a powerful force, gave way in confusion. Washington, realizing the gravity of his situation, rushed General Greene and his brigade to Sullivan's aid, leaving only a small force under Wayne and Maxwell to defend Chadd's Ford. Seizing his opportunity, von Knyphausen immediately moved to cross the creek.

The Battle of the Brandywine was one of the bloodiest encounters of the war. The Americans fought grimly for over four hours but were eventually overwhelmed. Assailed on two fronts and outnumbered on both, a thousand patriots were killed, wounded or captured to about six hundred for the British. One of the wounded was the Marquis de Lafayette; he was hit in the leg by a musket ball after leaping from his horse with sword in hand in a vain attempt to rally the Americans.[4]

On the evening of September 12, a detachment of Howe's troops occupied the town of Wilmington and seized President John McKinly, taking him "from his bed at dead of night. . . ." The next morning they captured "a sloop that lay in the stream, loaded with valuables stolen from the people, a large quantity of public and private money, many of the public and private records and all the papers and certificates of the loan and treasury offices."[5] Four days before, John McKinly had moved these papers by wagon team from the house of Colonel George Craghead in Christiana Hundred to a sloop in the Christiana River in a desperate effort to keep them from falling into the hands of the enemy. (Fifteen years later some of these same papers, including accounts of the "Flying Camp" battalion and the minutes of the New Castle Council of Safety, would be found in South Carolina where they had apparently been sent on a British ship.[6] Unfortunately, many were then lost again.)

The British sent many of their wounded to Wilmington and commandeered local houses to serve as hospitals. The people were not entirely displeased, since "they were at least safe from bombardment" from the British ships *Roebuck* and *Liverpool* lurking in the Delaware River.[7]

On September 16, the armies clashed again near Warren Tavern, twenty-three miles west of Philadelphia. This was the encounter that came to be known as the "Battle of the Clouds" after heavy rain ruined the American supply of ammunition and forced them to withdraw. On September 18, the members of the Continental Congress, alarmed at the approaching British juggernaut, once again gathered up their papers and fled, this time to Lancaster, Pennsylvania. Two days later, on the night of September 20, the British launched the "Paoli Massacre," a vicious surprise attack on Brigadier General Anthony Wayne's camp at Paoli, where more than three hundred men were bayonetted.[8]

Everywhere the militia deserted in panic. On September 22, Caesar wrote Washington: "The Next Morning after the Enemy had taken possession of Wilmington We got Inteligence of it . . . by the Evening [we] had no More of the Delaware Militia than Sufficient to Conduct their Baggage Home, and these . . . were determined to go that Night . . . Eversince, but am sorry to Say, to no purpose [I have] been Trying to rouse and Get them to the field again. . . ."[9]

Washington agreed. "The conduct of the militia is much to be regretted." he wrote, "In many instances, they are not to be roused, and in others they come into the field with all possible indifference, and, to all appearance, entirely unimpressed with the importance of the cause in which we are engaged. [There is] a total inattention to order and to discipline, and too often a disgraceful departure from the army at the instant their aid is most wanted. . . ."

This letter was written on September 24, the same day Howe crossed the Schuylkill River at Swede's Ford (Norristown). The Schuylkill, Washington told Caesar, was "fordable in almost every part several miles below us; he will possess himself of Philadelphia in all probability. . . ."[10] Washington was right; five days later, on September 26, the British entered Philadelphia.

George Read had fled the city only a few hours before the British arrival. Read, as Delaware's vice president, had automatically become its acting president when McKinly was taken prisoner. Realizing he was needed at home, he had not gone to Lancaster with the rest of the Continental Congress. Now, he could not travel his usual route down the "the western side of the [Delaware] river, because the British occupied the whole pass[age] from thence into the peninsula . . . [but] was . . . compelled to take his journey along the Jersey shore . . . and brave the risk of crossing it."[11] It was a risk, indeed. The very next day the American ships, in a brave attempt to keep the British at bay, fought a heated engagement that resulted in the loss of the *Delaware*, one of only three American sloops of war.[12]

In Read's absence, Thomas McKean, as speaker of the lower house of assembly was next in line, and had assumed the office of president. He was in Newark, having "retired from [New Castle] . . . on hearing that some attempts were preparing for making [him] prisoner"[13] and wrote Caesar on September 25 that he had taken "the command on Monday, with no other view but to do all I can, in the worst of times, to save my Country."[14] One of his first acts was to promote Caesar to the rank of major general of the state militia.[15]

Meanwhile, Delaware's loyalists continued their illicit trade with the British ships. The payment in "hard money" they received "for cattle, grain, and vegetables was an almost irresistible temptation to illicit traffic in these articles." The state was "infested with spies, who furnished lists to the British of the most forward Whigs . . . [who] in the vicinity of the bay and river, were liable to be seized by armed parties from the English men-of-war, and carried from their beds to these floating prisons."[16] One of their victims was Thomas Clark of New Castle, who was "taken out of his house about midnight and carried on board" the frigate *Lizard*.[17]

Not surprisingly, hostilities between Delaware's Whigs and Tories were at fever pitch by the time of the annual election on the first of October. Caesar was in Dover when William Peery, a captain in the Sussex militia, wrote from Lewes that the loyalists, afraid that they would be drafted into the militia if the Whigs took control of the assembly, had come out "almost to a man . . . collected in Town [and] began their usual strain of drinking prosperity to King George, Damning the Whigs, and swearing there was not Rebels enough in Town to take them up etc. . . . ."

The Whigs retaliated by demanding that no one be allowed to vote unless they swore to renounce the king and to reveal all they knew of "Treasons, or Traitorous conspiracies." Initially, the sheriff supported this idea, but "some short time after told us he was threatened to be thrown Neck and Heels out of the Court-House if he tender'd any such Oath." The Whigs then took the idea to the election inspectors, who had also agreed, Peery reported, until:

Jacob Moore and John Wiltbank come in and oppos'd it which drew on a pritty warm debate between Moore and myself, in the course of which Moore said he had opposed any such Oath in the House of Assembly and always would, that he would take no such Oath, and if any Inspector refus'd his Vote he would bring an Action against him, and he would find one hundred and fifty more should do the same, whereupon our proposal was rejected. . . .[18]

Matters came to blows when Captain Peery instructed the sheriff to "Either adjourn the Election, or Administer the Oath prescribed, or I will make Lewes Town too Hot for Every Tory in it." The unfortunate soldier who delivered this message was immediately set upon by the Tories

who Beat him with their Fists, Clubs, and Stamped him, untill the Militia . . . was called to his relief. . . . The people Enraged to see [him] thus basely treated, Beat without distinction every one . . . who came in their way, one of them fir'd a Gun . . . which made the Tories fly to their Houses with all possible speed, some Jumping out of the Court-House Windows . . . the Soldiers pursuing and firing several Guns after them.[19]

A few days later, the British fleet under the command of Admiral Lord Richard Howe appeared off Lewes, having sailed up the coast from the mouth of the Chesapeake Bay. On October 5, Captain Peery informed Caesar that "36 sail of the Enemies Ships went past this Town up the Bay, and this Evening 47 more were seen from the Light House Standing in for the Cape . . . they have Anchored in our Road." Caesar immediately passed this information on to General Washington.[20]

He had already sent Samuel Patterson to St. Georges to rally the militia, but Patterson had little luck. There is "not a field officer here," he wrote, and he had "no hopes" of getting them to "Guard their Shore as long as the Enemy lay there . . . I don't much blame them," he added, "as all our big men have left us. I wish Sincearly you could come, if only your [light] horse, to give some heart. If no help, the few I have will disperse."[21]

It seemed vital to prevent the British armada from coming upriver to supply General Howe's forces in Philadelphia and Wilmington, yet the American defenses were pitifully weak: two sloops of war, the *Montgomery* and the *Fly*; two sets of chevaux-de-frise, guarded by Fort Mercer on the New Jersey shore and Fort Mifflin on the Pennsylvanian; and a number of armed row-gallies.[22]

Washington, meanwhile, had "received intelligence" that General Howe planned to attack these forts to help get his brother's ships up the river. To do so, however, Howe took most of the troops now stationed at Germantown, about six miles from the center of Philadelphia. Seizing his opportunity, Washington attacked the remaining force at five on the morning of October 4, sending in four American columns. General Sullivan's column, which included both Washington and the Delaware battalion, led the way.

The Americans appeared silently out of the dawn mist with bayonets drawn. At first, it seemed as if an easy victory was in their grasp, yet the unsteadiness of their own recruits and the arrival of British reinforcements would eventually bring them down. Many Delaware men were killed and their leader, Colonel Hall, badly wounded.[23] Washington, however, refused to be discouraged. "If the uncommon fogginess of the morning & the smoke had not hindered us from seeing our advantage," he wrote Thomas McKean, "I am convinced it would have ended in a complete victory: But we must not repine, on the Contrary should rejoice that we have given a severe blow to our enemies, and that our ranks are as full or rather fuller than they were before. . . ."[24]

The situation in Delaware, however, was grim. In Thomas McKean's words, she was a "poor & distressed State, without a head, without a shilling, public records & papers in possession of the enemy . . . the militia dispirited & dispersed, many of them fled out of the State for safety, and a majority of the rest . . . disaffected to the glorious cause we are engaged in. . . ."

No Whig, however, was ready to admit defeat; certainly not such an ardent one as McKean. He wrote Caesar on October 15, that in New York, "General Burgoyne's army of about seven thousand [are] surrounded in a swamp by Twenty thousand Americans, his retreat and all supplies cut off,—General Howe's army . . . [has been] reduced by the battle of the 4th . . . to about 6,000 [and will] soon be attacked again by General Washington & an army of more than double the numbers; the row-gallies, Batteries etc [are] playing their part most nobly indeed. In short a month more will, in my opinion, give us peace, liberty and safety."[25]

Two days before McKean wrote this letter, George Read had finally arrived to take over the reins of government.

[He] arrived with his family at Salem, New Jersey, and procured a boat to convey them across the Delaware, there about five miles wide. At this time there were several British men-of war lying at anchor off New Castle. The boat had almost reached the Delaware shore, when she was descried by the enemy, who immediately despatched an armed barge in pursuit of her. The tide being unfortunately low, the boat grounded so far from the beach that it was impossible for Mr. Read and his family to land before their pursuers were upon them. There was only time to efface every mark on the baggage which could excite any suspicion that Mr. Read was not, as he represented himself, a country gentleman, returning to his home. . . . The presence of Mr. Read's mother, wife, and infant children, gave sufficient probability to his story to deceive sailors . . . [so that] the honest and kind-hearted tars assisted, with great glee, in landing the baggage and carrying the ladies and children on shore.[26]

23

Howe Departs and Caesar Takes Charge

On October 16, General Howe marched his troops out of the city of Wilmington. A few days later, he pulled out of Germantown as well, consolidating his forces in Phildelphia where he could supply them more easily.[1] Howe was frustrated; Burgoyne's defeat at Saratoga had energized the Americans and diminished his own accomplishments. It had also impressed Britain's old enemy, the French. In fact, Howe's capture of the American capital city, in Washington's words, had brought "no solid advantage to their arms."[2]

Howe's immediate task was to get his brother's ships up the Delaware River with food and supplies for his army. To that end, he ordered Count Donop and a party of Hessians to attack Fort Mercer on October 22, while, at the same time, some of the fleet broke through the chevaux-de-frise to bombard Fort Mifflin. Donop, however, was killed in the assault and three British warships, the *Roebuck*, the *Augusta*, and the *Merlin* all ran aground while trying to manuever in the narrow river channel. Stranded and helpless, the *Augusta* was set afire and blown up by Commodore Hazlewood and his fledgling American navy on the following morning; an event that "was felt distinctly" in Wilmington. One citizen reported that as he "was sitting in Dr. Way's parlor . . . we were surprised to hear the bottles and other glassware in his shop rattling together. We could not tell the cause until information came of the event and of the time that it took place, and we were satisified it was the concussion of that blow-up that shook the doctor's glass. . . ." Subsequently, the *Merlin* was destroyed as well, burned by her own crew to keep her from falling into American hands.[3]

Undeterred, Howe continued to besiege Fort Mifflin. During the next few weeks, under cover of darkness, he constructed batteries on river islands that were little more than mud banks and, on November 10, brought in a floating battery as well. For the next six days the British pounded the fort at a range of six hundred yards or less. The Americans put up a brave defense, but after the arrival of still more British ships on the fifteenth, they were forced to evacuate.

Meanwhile, Cornwallis again crossed to New Jersey a few miles downstream and moved in to attack Fort Mercer with a force of some three thousand men. With only a few hundred men to defend it, the American commander, Colonel Christopher Greene finally ordered his men to abandon it on November 20, afraid if he did not do so, they would be trapped inside.

After losing both Delaware River forts, Commodore Hazlewood managed to drive twenty-five row-gallies and a sloop upriver to safety, but the rest of the American vessels were driven on shore and burned. The British were now in full control of the waterway all the way from Philadelphia to the Atlantic.[4]

Meanwhile, the Delaware legislature moved to the relative safety of Dover after October elections that were both confused and indecisive. There had been no vote in Sussex due to the riotous fighting at the Lewes courthouse. New Castle had returned a radical slate and Kent a moderate one, but many members were too intimidated by the presence of the British to attend the fall session. The Whigs, however, had gained strength. Thomas McKean was again speaker of the House of Assembly, while Read as speaker of the Legislative Council was acting president. In early December, the Whigs Caesar and McKean were also reappointed to the Congress, replacing Read and James Sykes; Nicholas Van Dyke was the only moderate delegate to be reelected. Caesar, however, did not attend, finding himself too swamped with other duties.

Due to the continuing impasse between Whigs and moderates, the new legislators "could not nor did not form a House to do Legislative acts." They could only agree, in view of "the critical Situation of the State having the Enemy on its borders without any Armed force to repel their Attacks" to raise six hundred militia. As "Commanding Officer of the whole Militia," Caesar was ordered to raise "the Quota . . . assigned for Kent County . . . appoint a Commissary to supply them . . . [with] 1 lb Meat, 1 lb Bread or Flour, and 1/2 a gill of Brandy or Whiskey per man per day 3 pecks potatoes for 6 men per week or other vegetables in proportion, 1 gill of salt per man per week and 5 lbs candles for 50 men per week. . . ." These troops were not only assigned to protect and defend the inhabitants of the state, but also to prevent "all Traffick or Intercouse with the Enemy. . . ."[5]

Caesar fell to the task, immediately ordering a company of militia to Duck Creek to "Cause all the shallops, Boats, or other Small

Craft to be so Secured as to prevent their Trading with the Enemy
. . . [and] to apprehend, secure and bring to Justice all such persons
as are Concerned in Such Trade. . . ."⁶ As time went on, he carried
out this assignment with such zeal and determination that Thomas
McKean was moved to write his wife that Delaware was "said to be
on the verge of total Revolution to Whiggism."⁷

The Delaware legislature also borrowed £750 from Vincent
Loockerman to buy clothing for the Delaware Continentals who
were "starving and destitute" at Valley Forge. The name of that
place alone is enough to conjure up an image of their suffering. For
the third year in a row, General Washington was forced to stand by
and watch his army fall prey to hunger, disease, death and deser-
tion.⁸

On December 19, Washington sent General William Smallwood
from Valley Forge to Wilmington with orders to "put the place in
the best posture of defense."⁹ According to George Read, Washington "had reason to believe that the Enemy mean to establish a Post
at Wilmington for the Purpose of countenancing the Disaffected in
the Delaware State, drawing Supplies from our country, and securing a post upon the Delaware River during the Winter. . . ."¹⁰ Besides his two Maryland brigades, Smallwood took the Delaware
regiment with him, now commanded by Lt. Colonel Charles Pope.¹¹

Caesar was delighted when the delayed election in Sussex returned a Whig slate. "These men," he wrote McKean, "Joined with
the Representation from Newcastle County . . . will produce not
only wholesome Laws and Regulation but Energy in the Execution
of them, and . . . rouse this little Branch of the Union from its heretofore Torpid State. . . ."¹²

When the Delaware legislature reconvened in March, they
elected Caesar Rodney as president for a term of three years. In
further testimony of his astonishing appeal across the political
spectrum, he received twenty votes of the the twenty-four cast by a
joint meeting of the assembly and legislative council.¹³ Tommy's
star was also rising; in early April he was appointed a judge of the
admiralty court for a salary of ten pounds a year and fees. A few
weeks later he was also appointed clothier to Charles Pope's Delaware regiment.¹⁴

Former President John McKinly, meanwhile, was a prisoner in
Philadelphia. An outraged McKean wrote George Read that "I was
told the other day that he lodged at widow Jenkin's along with his
old friends Robinson and Manlove, and seemed very *happy*."¹⁵ Typically, Caesar refused to condemn McKinly on such flimsy evidence. "It may be," he wrote his old friend and compatriot, "that

those traitors to their Country have Visited him, tho it be merely to Insult him in his unfortunate Scituation. But, Sir, I am well informed that Robinson has Lodged at Joshua Fishers ever since he first went to the City and that Manloves place of Abode is at one Snowdens over the Drawbridge. . . ." (Joshua Fisher was Betsy Rodney's uncle in Philadelphia, earlier described by Tommy as a Quaker and great Tory.) In Caesar's view, John McKinly "meant well tho he might have been deceived by many in whom he placed Confidence . . . [and never] discharged the Duty of that Station with that Energy that You and I Could have wished."[16]

The British continued to raid Delaware's trading schooners as well as farms along the coast. In March 1778, George Read reported that "a considerable body of the Enemy supposed to be 700 landed this morning about Listen's Highlands and were on their March up the Thoroughfare Neck. . . ."[17] This alarming news was later amended by Charles Pope, commander of Delaware's Continental regiment. He wrote Caesar from Duck Creek (Smyrna) that "30—or 40 mar[in]es landed & took of[f] some cattle etc, & returned . . . at eight oclock this morning the fleet consisting of about 35 sail weighed & stood Down the Bay."[18]

The most serious incident occurred in April, however, when Pope reported that "It is with a Certainty I can inform you that the report of the Tories having a fort built is a truth for this Day myself with a party of about forty was within gun shot of their works. . . ."[19] This was a group of loyalists under the command of the same Cheney Clow who had been suspected of aiding Howe at Head of Elk. Born in England, Clow was a Methodist who had come to Queen Anne's county, Maryland, as a child. He now lived on a farm in Kent county, Delaware, just east of the Maryland line. On April 24, Caesar described what happened next in a letter to Henry Laurens, then President of the Continental Congress:

On Tuesday the fourteenth Instant I Got information that About one hundred and fifty Insurgents under the command of one China Clow were Armed and Assembled on the western side of this County near the borders of Maryland. I . . . Sent About one hundred and forty of the Militia of this County, under the Command of Lt. Col'l Pope of the Delawares, against them.—The Insurgents had build a Fort which the Militia Surrounded on the Thursday night following, but Mr. Clow and his Gang, hearing of their approach, fled. The Militia burnt the Fort and secured all the Stolen Effects in and about it and Returned . . . Since when many of them have been taken and others Surrendered . . . in all, of about fifty . . . I hope to hear in a few days that the Villain Clow is taken.[20]

Clow was not "taken," but his uprising so infuriated the Delaware legislature that they passed a so-called Test Act in May. Modeled on the same oath that had caused so much trouble in Lewes, the Test Act required that "for the Further security of the State" all citizens take "an oath of fidelity to the Federal and State governments and imposed the duty of bearing arms upon all except members of the Society of Friends, who were, however, compelled to pay an equivalent for their personal service." However, an accompanying measure seems to reflect the firm but tolerant hand of President Rodney. While severely penalizing "anyone dealing with the British or furnishing them with supplies," it also granted amnesty to anyone who had previously done so, but was now willing to swear his allegiance under the Test Act.[21]

Cheney Clow steadfastly refused to do any such thing, but was not caught until four years later. At that time there was a fight at his house in Little Creek Hundred in which a member of the sheriff's posse named Joseph Moore was killed. Clow was tried for treason, but was freed after he produced his commission as a captain in the British army; a bona fide British officer could not be accused of treason nor tried in a civil court. Nevertheless, Clow was eventually hanged for the murder of Moore.[22]

By the spring of 1778, President Rodney had begun to exercise the firm leadership so sorely needed in chaotic Delaware. In addition, Caesar's reputation for fair-mindedness, devotion to duty, and courage in the face of physical adversity had traveled far beyond the borders of his own state. That he was also loved for his genuine modesty and warm personality is evident from the letter he received from a delegate to the Continental Congress from North Carolina.

My dear Caesar,
   Or if you rather choose the more sounding military epithets with which your Country has honoured you,

Most respected Major General

   I cannot omit this favourable opportunity to assure you that there is still in the land of the living a man who sincerely esteems you & numbers amongst the happiest moments of his life those that composed the short hours which he and you laughed away in Philadelphia together— May he hope that that friendship is mutual & flatter himself that this scrawl . . . may tempt you in return to say upon paper that you exist, for to know even this alone would add much to the happiness of My dear Sir

Your Friend & Obed. Serv.
Wm. Hooper[23]

24
President Rodney

THE FIRST TASK OF THE NEW PRESIDENT WAS TO SECURE THE SAFETY of Delaware's borders. In view of Delaware's "verry considerable water frontier, bordering on which are our best grass & farm Lands . . . and a number of Salt works" Caesar asked Congress to "Order an Independent Company of an hundred men . . . to be stationed in Kent at Such place or places as I shall from time to time direct. . . ."[1]

While, in his view, Delaware's newly elected legislature was "disposed to do whatever . . . tends most to support the American Cause," they were "most of them new members. They want a Pen [and] . . . they want Patience." Besides, Caesar told McKean, "We are Constantly Alarmed in this Place by the Enemy and Refugees, and Seldom a day passes but Some man in this and the Neighbouring Counties is taken off by these Villains . . . many, near the Bay, dare neither Act or Speak least they Should be taken away and their Houses plundered."[2] The so-called "refugees" were actually loyalists from other colonies. Apparently in consort with the British ships, they prowled Delaware's waters in small boats, attacked shallops, ventured up the creeks to steal goods stored at farm landings, and even plundered the farms themselves.

In pressing his case for the independent company, Caesar stressed that, while he was "in great hopes that in a few days we shall have a Militia Law . . . Calculated to bring forth the Militia on any Requisition of Congress . . . I have got to be Tolerably acquainted with Militia in general and particularly with ours, [and I] do know that so near to their homes they cannot be kept to duty . . . unless they are Joined and acting with Continentals."[3]

Caesar was also busy "Tory kitching," according to Charles Pope, who wrote him that he was "sorry to hear my Relation Stokely was so lost to Virtue as to be one of that number but you cannot Expect anything Else whilst the Executive Power of your State [was] so Relax. . . ."[4] It was no longer "so Relax;" as a result of the Test Act,

the assembly had voted to confiscate the estates of forty-six loyalists
and anyone else found guilty of actively aiding British unless they
recanted and asked for a pardon before August 1.[5]

However, when loyalists Thomas White, Charles Gordon and
others were arrested by Colonel Hall of the Delaware Continental
regiment, White shrewdly insisted that he be charged within the
state, sparking a controversy between the Delaware legislature and
the Continental Congress, now sitting in York, Pennsylvania. In defending Colonel Hall's action, his superior officer, General Smallwood, indignantly informed Caesar that "your Legislature must
apply for Redress [from Congress] if they conceive the [arrest] to be
an Infringement of their Internal Police."[6] In truth, neither Smallwood nor the Congress had much faith in the Delaware Assembly,
and were afraid White and Gordon might be "rescued out of Gaol
by the Enemy or the Tories. . . ."[7] Caesar, while admitting their
"suspicions . . . [were] too well founded," protested in his own defense that as "the people at large are generally directed by those at
the Helm, [he hoped] they [would] soon mend."[8]

This seems to have been an early conflict between a state government and Congress. As it happened, because White and Gordon
never appeared before Congress, they got off under the writ of Ha-
beas Corpus, which requires that an accused man be brought before a court to decide the legality of his detention. Afterward,
McKean told Caesar that, "Gordon has again joined the Enemy."[9]

Meanwhile, the Delaware Assembly had become increasingly
skittish. On May 8, Caesar wrote McKean that "I am Apprehensive
[they] will not Continue to Sit more than a day or two . . . they might
as well never have Met for all they are likely to do—I have been
furnished with but one Bill Yet to put the Seal to, Tho they have
been Setting near Three Months."[10]

Indeed, by early June they had "imprudently dispersed . . . without [appointing] even one Supreme Judge in the State . . . [and] for
the purpose of getting rid of John Cook, [they] Got both Killen and
him to resign."[11] This was part of a long controversy that arose between the council (upper house) and the assembly (lower house)
over the loyalty of John Cook. The assembly's stategy was, apparently, to get both men to resign, ostensibly because they were both
from Kent county, and then reappoint William Killen with fellow
Whigs David Finney of New Castle county and John Jones of Sussex. The plan stalled, however, after the council insisted that neither man could be removed without first being impeached.[12]

At the end of April, McKean had some surprising news: the British were sending a team to negotiate an end to the war. Their pro-

posal, as McKean later outlined it, was this: if the Americans agreed to "Suspend hostilities by sea and land immediately . . . [they would] join in supporting our Paper money, [and] agree that we shall govern ourselves . . . excepting matters of trade." Also, they would allow the Americans to appoint representatives to Parliament if the British could do the same in Congress.[13]

Clearly, this move was precipitated by France's formal entry into the war on the American side. Shortly after the treaty had been signed in February 1778, the French admiral Comte d'Estaing had sailed for America with a large fleet of French warships. The British had been losing merchant vessels to American privateers for some time; now it seemed that the French could seriously interfere with the movement of their troops along the eastern seaboard, and might even attack Britain herself.[14]

McKean, of course, dismissed Parliament's offer out of hand: "I have not a fear [that this will result in] an Acknowledgm't of our Independance, and an honorable peace," he wrote Caesar, "if British Honors, Offices and Gold do not tempt and corrupt your Members of Congress and . . . Officers of the Army." For his part, McKean was "determined never to give up the Independance of the United States, after so much expence of blood and treasure, whilst I have a breath to draw. . . ."[15] Caesar agreed. He thought the offer a "production of a King and Ministry hard pushed and wicked even to the last . . . they are trying to divide us."[16]

The envoys carrying Britain's proposal arrived in Philadelphia in early June, shortly after Lieutenant General Sir Henry Clinton had replaced General Howe as commander in chief of the British forces. Even though British warships of "upward a hundred & fifty Sail"[17] still controlled the Delaware River and Bay, it was clear that Howe's occupation of the city had neither destroyed Washington's army nor prevented the Continental Congress from carrying on its business.[18]

The delegation, Caesar reported to Tommy, came aboard the "Trident of 64 Guns, off New-Castle and immediately proceeded to Phildelphia in one of the Eagle's Tenders."[19] It consisted of "Frederick, Earl of Carlisle, Richard Viscount Howe, Sir Henry Clinton, Wm Eden Esquire (brother to the late Governor of Maryland) and Captain George Johnstone. . . ."[20]

As expected, their meeting with Congress came to nothing. On June 17, McKean triumphantly reported that "instead of Americans licking the dust from the feet of a British Minister, the tables are turned. . . ." Congress had, in fact, demanded that Britain acknowledge American independence and withdraw her "fleets and armies" before they would enter into any kind of treaty. A delighted McKean told Caesar that soon "you may expect to hear the Enemy have evacuated Phildelphia. . . ."[21]

McKean was right. Having been ordered to withdraw to the more easily defended port of New York, Clinton pulled his forces out of Phildelphia the very next day. The ministry in London was apparently far more interested in the southern colonies and the strategic ports of the West Indies than they were in Philadelphia. They wanted their forces consolidated, and were were also afraid that the ships needed to supply them might be trapped in Delaware Bay by the French. Also, the British fleet was far too valuable, in their view, to waste its power in harrassing local trade.[22]

Because of the approaching French, sea transport was considered too risky; only prisoners of war, including Delaware's former president, John McKinly, traveled to New York by ship.[23] The main British army marched overland; about nine thousand men and fifteen hundred wagons, including both Cornwallis' and von Knyphausen's divisions. They left the city at 3:00 A.M. on June 18, taking almost all of Phildelphia's loyalists with them.

Progress was very slow. Not only did the heavy wagons continually bog down in New Jersey's marshes, many of the roads were blocked and bridges across creeks destroyed, thanks to General Philemon Dickinson's New Jersey militia and Maxwell's Continental regiment, who had been sent by Washington to shadow and harass the British.[24]

On June 23, Washington, himself, crossed the river at Coryell's Ferry, some forty miles above Philadelphia. His army now numbered about 13,500 men, including those under Dickinson and Maxwell, and were stronger, more disciplined and far better equipped that ever before. The new recruits, as well as those who had survived the bitter winter at Valley Forge, had been training all spring under a German volunteer named Baron von Steuben and, for the first time, looked and acted like a real army.

Washington had ordered his second in command, General Charles Lee, whose force now included the Delaware regiment under Charles Pope, to attack the British rear guard at Monmouth Courthouse, while he brought the main force into position. Lee, however, failed to do so, allowing von Knyphausen's division to slip away.

A few days later, Lee again faltered, apparently after receiving conflicting intelligence reports, and lost control of his men. When

"Battle Between Farmers and Hessians" by Darley, Courtesy of the Historical Society of Delaware.

Washington, riding at the head of the main army, met Lee's retreating troops on the road, he refused, at first, to believe them, and even arrested one poor soldier for spreading false rumors. When he finally realized what had happened, Washington lost his temper and, according to one account, "Swore like an angel from Heaven!"[25]

Thanks to von Steuben's months of rigorous training, Washington managed to turn a disorderly retreat into a disciplined attack, despite temperatures of nearly a hundred degrees. The ensuing battle lasted all day, but Clinton finally withdrew about six in the evening.

Afterward, Caesar sent an account of the engagement to General John Dagworthy in Sussex: "You'l see we have gained the Field" he wrote. "I had it also by Express. It seems we have killed and taken upward of a Thousand of the Enemy, our Loss inconsiderable. Besides this, best accounts are, about three Thousand of the enemy deserted—Great News—"[26] In fact, it could only be called a draw. The British had about three hundred and fifty killed or wounded out of a total of 9500, while the Americans lost about the same number out of 13,500, many from sunstroke or heat prostration. Nevertheless, they failed to interrupt the British retreat from Philadelphia.[27]

General Lee was court-martialed for failing to exercise his duty, found guilty and suspended for a year. Later, after writing a rude letter to Congress objecting to his sentence, he was expelled from the army altogether.[28]

With the British safely out of the area, Congress returned to Philadelphia on July 2, 1778. Admiral d'Estaing's fleet arrived in Delaware Bay the following week. Caesar had a letter from David Hall in Lewes reporting that a "Captain Nicholson who came Passenger with the honourable S[ilas] Dean, [signer with Benjamin Franklin and Arthur Lee of the treaty with France] in the Admiral Ship Languidor . . . is on his way to Congress with Express from the Admiral. . . ."[29]

D'Estaing, unfortunately, had arrived too late to trap the British fleet. Nevertheless, Caesar could write William Patterson on July 11, that "As the enemy have now entirely left the Delaware, and [with] a large French fleet on our Coast, there does not appear to be that danger to this State . . . [as] when [the Assembly] passed the Act for establishing the independent company you were commissioned to command. . . . Therefore, . . . the said independent company for the County of New Castle is hereby disbanded. . . ."[30]

Meanwhile, after participating in the battle of Monmouth Court-house, the Delaware regiment "marched with Washington to his camp at White Plains. . . ."[31] In fact, both armies were back to essentially the same positions they had occupied in 1776: the British in New York City, Washington on the heights above the Hudson.

25

Politics

IN AUGUST OF 1778, JOHN MCKINLY WAS PAROLED TO WILMINGTON. CAE-
sar wrote the president of Congress, Henry Laurens, that "General
Clinton has Enlarged him, on Parole, for one month . . . in order to
Effect an Exchange for Mr. Franklin late [the] Governor of the
State of New Jersey."[1] Talk of exchanging McKinly for Benjamin
Franklin's illegitimate son, William, had been going on for some
time. William Franklin was an committed and outspoken Tory who
had been held by the Americans in house arrest for over two years.
Not surprisingly, the idea of trading him for McKinly was hotly op-
posed by some of the more fervent Whigs, particularly Thomas
McKean, who told George Read that Franklin could do far more
mischief than McKinly good if it should come to pass.[2]

Caesar, however, was more sympathetic. "[U]ntil he was taken
Prisoner," he wrote Laurens, "all his Letters and orders to me as
commanding officer of the Militia breathed the same Spirit of Patriotism—I cannot pretend to Judge of Mr. McKinly's Secret Intention or wish, But his public Services . . . induce me to wish him
restored to his Liberty. . . ."[3]

On the same day, Caesar wrote McKean and Nicholas van Dyke,
currently Delaware's delegates to Congress: "Tho I do not altogether approve his Conduct, I have wrote the President of Congres
Soliciting [McKinly's] Exchange . . . so far, as you think you can
with propriety, would . . . you . . . lend your aid in bringing it
about. . . . He is an old man and can Illy support himself under his
present misfortune." (McKinly, at the time, was fifty-seven years
old.)

It was a kind yet halfhearted defense. Caesar argued for the exchange of one of his own officers with far more conviction: "Silas
Snow, a Captain in the militia, [who] was taken in the dead of Night
out his warm bed by the refugees and Carried on board of Ship
without Clothes or money etc. . . . There are now prisoners of this
State . . . a Captain Nowls, a Captain Burrows and Mr. Young, a

181

merchant, why might not one of these be Exchanged for him? In short he was so Servisable That rather than not have him I would give them all. . . ."[4]

A month before, some of the "public papers belonging to this State that had been taken away by the English" had been found in Philadelphia by Samuel Patterson.[5] He wrote Caesar that he had "procured four chests of public papers, many of the books, half-used and torn. I found them in near a hundred places, barbers, Taylors Shops, etc., should have got many more if our old president had let them alone, but he gathered them to better Security as he thought. . . ." Also the Whigs' old nemesis, "Mr. T. Robi[n]son [had] laid hold of a number that he may make his peace I s[up]pose."[6]

Meanwhile, the French fleet had departed for New York, having arrived too late to trap the British ships in Delaware Bay. When the bar at the entrance to New York harbor was thought to be too dangerous to cross in the face of the British ships inside, d'Estaing moved on to Newport, Rhode Island to join General John Sullivan in a confused and uncoordinated effort to recapture that port.

No sooner had the French left Delaware, however, than the loyalists renewed their attacks on the local shallops and trading schooners. Bombay Hook had "a wicked Set [that had] carried on, for a considerable time, a most Villainous and distructive trade with the Enemy." In the effort to stop them, however, a Whig named Jonathan B. Smith had also had his "farm houses and other buildings" destroyed by "a party of Continental Troops from Wilmington Under the Command of Lt. Coll. Pope. . . ." Caesar wrote him a letter of apology: "I am Much Concerned Whenever the opperations of War are Such as Make it Necessary to Sacrifice the property of Whigs," especially as these "rascally Tories" he added, "are accumulating Wealth for Which They are Claiming, and indeed obtaining, The protection of that Government they Never Sought to Establish."[7] Apparently, Caesar was still angry over the legal maneuvers of White and Gordon.

In October, a strange thing happened. Laurens wrote Caesar that certain papers "said to be from the British Commissioners was lately thrown up by the Sea on the Jersey Shore, it contained one Package marked Delaware. . . ."[8] They apparently were from "the Preston British Man of War, [which] had been wrecked some days ago on the Coast of New Jersey. . . ." It is unclear exactly what was contained in the package, except that they were from the British peace delegation who, after being rebuffed by Congress, had promised to "Make an appeal to the People and treat there."[9] Laurens reported that when a similar packet marked Pennsylvania was offered to "the Vice President of this State [he] declined touching it."[10] Caesar did likewise. "I suppose there is little doubt that the package Marked Delaware, is filled with Manifestoes from the British [Peace] Commissioners, if so, I would not be at the Trouble of opening it. . . ."[11]

In the same letter, Laurens pleaded that Delaware "supply immediately a proper number of Representatives in Congress; for some considerable time past the State has been almost wholly unrepresented." In fact as early as June, McKean had urged that more members be appointed since "Mr. Vandike is not only a little unwilling to leave home so far, but much Engaged of late in the General Assembly."[12] Now Laurens reported that Nicholas van Dyke had "retired on account of the bad state of his health," and Thomas McKean, now chief justice of the state of Pennsylvania, was far too busy to attend.

As the year 1778 drew to a close, however, Caesar's primary concern was to pass the Articles of Confederation; the plan for a central government that had been originally drawn up by John Dickinson before his opposition to the Declaration of Independence had sent him to political Coventry. Dickinson had been asked to "prepare and digest the form of confederation to be entered into between these colonies." His proposal basically codified current practice; it assigned the functions of a central government to a Congress composed of delegates appointed annually by their respective states, giving them exclusive authority over some matters and concurrent authority with the states over others. Although flawed in many ways, Dickinson's articles were the first to call this country the United States of America. Later, they would serve as the basis for the Constitution.

When the articles had first come up for debate in 1776, all the colonies' old quarrels and jealousies immediately rose to the surface. Having just voted to free themselves from the excesses of an imperial Parliament, the delegates were highly suspicious of any central government, including, it seemed, their own Congress. When it became apparent that the only thing they could agree upon was their opposition to Britain, debate on the articles was quickly tabled for fear of fracturing that fragile unity.

On November 15, 1777, after many revisions, the articles had been passed by Congress and submitted to the states for ratification. Suspicious state legislatures, however, debated them endlessly, sending in amendment after amendment designed to further curtail what they saw as dangerous federal power.[13]

In the meantime, Congress was having trouble paying for the

war. The delegates had never given themselves the power to levy taxes, arguing that they did not have the power to do so, since they had been appointed by their legislatures rather than chosen by the people. Instead, they had assumed the authority to issue bills of credit. In 1775, they had issued some three million dollars of paper money, assigning to each state a share to be repaid in four annual installments beginning in 1779. In an effort to support the credit of these bills, the states were also asked to make them legal tender. Delaware did this on February 22, 1777, while, at the same time, issuing some twenty-five thousand pounds in bills of credit of her own.[14]

As the cost of the war increased, Congress continued to print money. With virtually nothing to back them, however, the bills quickly lost value. Public confidence sank, and prices rose. By the end of 1778, Continental money was considered so worthless that many of the nation's merchants and farmers refused to accept it. No wonder the British, in their aborted peace offer, had thought it an inducement to "join in supporting our paper money."[15]

In an attempt to shore up the nation's credit, the Articles of Confederation gave Congress the official power to requisition the states for funds, again legitimizing what they had already been forced to do. It soon became apparent, however, that Dickinson's document had failed to provide the means to enforce this or any other Congressional decision.

Due to the confusion surrounding the British occupation of Philadelphia, the Delaware Assembly did not receive their official copy of the articles for debate until July of 1778. By then, many of the most pressing questions had already been settled and every state except New Jersey, Maryland and Delaware had agreed to ratify. "Concerning the Confederation," Caesar complained to Henry Laurens on the thirty-first of that month, ". . . several of the members [have asked] why it was not taken in Consideration heretofore."

Nevertheless, Caesar assured Laurens that when the assembly convened on August 10, he would "urge them to as Speedy a determination as its Importance will admit. . . ."[16] As it turned out, it was not very speedy; not until October 27, could Caesar report that he had "laid [the Articles] before the General Assembly now setting. . . ."[17] Even then, nothing was accomplished. A week later Caesar had to confess that "by Some means or other in the course of Yesterday and today and Members of the House of Assembly have dispersed . . . without having Compleated any one peice of business laid before them. . . ."

As required by the Delaware constitution, Caesar called a meeting of his privy council in order to issue "Writs to Call the General Assembly to Meet." Even so, it seemed that they would not actually meet until "the fourth day of January Next. . . ."[18] When Laurens insisted on quicker action, an emergency session was finally called for "Monday the Twenty Third [of November]."[19] In pressing for quick action, Laurens added: "The State of Jersey have Resolve to Ratify, we trust that Maryland and Delaware will no much longer be delinquents."[20]

The sticking points in Delaware, as in other states, centered around two questions: the apportioning of expenses and voting power between the large and small states; and the control of western territories. The question of voting power had been more or less settled by the time the articles arrived in Delaware's General Assembly. In order to protect the small states from being continually outvoted by the large, decisions would be made by a simple majority with each state having one vote, although in some cases a nine state majority would be required.

How to apportion expenses and who should have control of the western territories, however, remained serious problems. On the question of expenses, the eighth article proposed that "the supply of a common treasury" should be calculated "in proportion to the value of land granted to or surveyed for any person, [including] the buildings and improvements thereon;" an idea that Delaware considered impossible to enforce fairly without "great expense of money and time. . . ." In their view, the money raised from each state should instead be calculated "by the number of its inhabitants, of every age, sex, and quality. . . ."[21]

The articles also stated that no state should be "deprived of territory for the benefit of the United States." Yet Delaware considered the claims of some states to western land "vague and extravagant . . . their claims for western limits have been to the Southern Ocean, including countries partially possessed by the kings of France and Spain." With no western territories of its own, it was not surprising that Delaware joined with Maryland and New Jersey in insisting that "for the peace and safety of the States . . . included in the Union . . . a moderate extent of limits should be assigned for . . . those States as claim to the Mississippi or South Sea. . . . ." In their view, Delaware should have "a right, in common with the other members of the Union to that extensive tract of country. . . ."[22]

The Delaware legislature continued to drag their feet well into 1779, causing one New Hampshire delegate to grumble: "All the

States are represented [in Congress]. I wish I could say they were Confederated, but our F[or]ward Sister Maryland and her little Crooked Neighbour [Delaware] still stand out."[23]

Both Maryland and Delaware feared that the economic attractions of Virginia's vast claim to the west would eventually drain both their treasuries and their populations. It was a legitimate concern, but it was complicated by the interests of private land speculators. These speculators came from states without western claims, such as Maryland and Delaware, and many were also headquartered in Philadelphia, the center of Delaware's mercantile interests. Some states, notably Virginia, had firmly denied any speculators access to their western territories. It was clearly in the speculators' interest, therefore, to have these lands declared a part of the United States as a whole.[24]

At the end of January 1779, after duly registering their objections, the General Assembly finally agreed that although the articles were "in divers respects unequal" and not in Delaware's best interest, "The interest of particular states ought to be postponed to the general good of the union." Expressing their hope that "the objectionable parts" would, in due time, be removed, they ordered their delegates to Congress to sign the Articles of Confederation.[25]

Caesar was so delighted he declared a holiday. Wednesday, December 30, was to be "observed as a day of Thanksgiving and praise Throughout this State." It was however, to be celebrated with dignity: "all recreations, Unsuitable to the purpose of Such Solemnity" were to be omitted and the people encouraged to "attend places of public Worship . . . [and] with decency and devotion becomeing good Christians, acknowledge their obligations to Almighty God for the Benefits they have received."[26] Even so, the articles were not officially signed by Delaware's delegates to Congress until February 12, 1779.

26

"Engrossing"

DELAWARE HAD ACTED, BUT MARYLAND HAD NOT. SHE REFUSED TO ratify until all the states relinquished their western claims. The articles could not yet be put into effect.[1]

In the meantime, inflation was out of control. In April 1779, Caesar wrote John Dickinson, one of that year's delegates to Congress, that "The prices now given and likely to be given for every kind of forage, and provisions together with the Expences of Transporting are so Enormous that I much fear they will . . . Effectually ruin one of the most glorious Causes a people ever engaged in."[2]

In an attempt to control inflation, prevent hoarding, and guarantee that the regiments would be adequately supplied, the Delaware Assembly put an embargo on all exports of wheat, rye, flour, Indian corn, bread, beef, bacon, and livestock except for shipments to the army. This action, however, did little to stop the "Engrossers," as speculators were called. Having cornered the market in many commodities, they continued to push prices to enormous heights. "It is difficult to know how these people manage their business," Caesar naively told Dickinson, "but it appears strange to me that they should necessarily be obliged to [charge] such Extravagant Prices, When there is no other market for those articles."[3]

Caesar may have felt financially pressed himself. In May he tried to sell one of his carriages, but he was told by Samuel McLane of Philadelphia that there were "Severall to be disposed of in this City and Coach makers & others Say they can give no Opinion of it unless they see it whether it would be likely to Sell. . . ." At the same time, McLane reported that "A Spirit of regulating the prices of goods & rising the Value of the Money have taken place here [that] alarms the Monopoliser. . . . God knows its time something is done to help the Credit of the Currency. . . ."[4]

It is not known exactly where Caesar was living at this time. He still owned property in Dover as well as a share of the site of the aborted Rodney's Burgh where he would later occupy the house

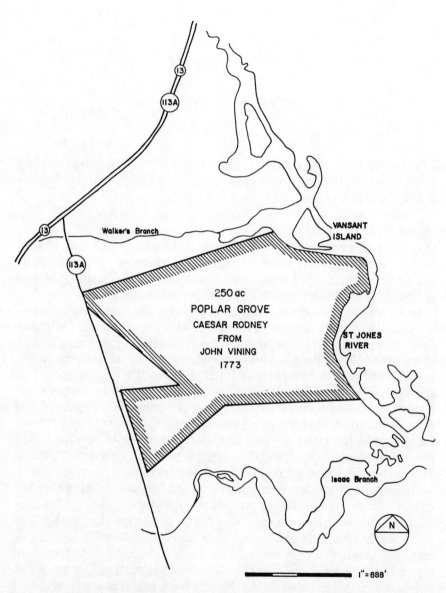

250 ac
POPLAR GROVE
CAESAR RODNEY
FROM
JOHN VINING
1773

Walker's Branch

VANSANT
ISLAND

ST JONES
RIVER

Isaac Branch

N

1"= 888'

Map showing location of Poplar Grove drawn by Jeroen van den Hurk according to information supplied by James B. Jackson.

known as Poplar Grove. Between 1776 and 1778, he was away from Dover so much that he may have found it more convenient to rent rooms in one of the two taverns on the Square, The Golden Fleece or the George Washington (formerly the King George). Now, in August of 1779, he mentions that his half sister Sally Wilson, who kept house for him, accompanied him on a visit to George Read's house in New Castle. Read, himself, was in Philadelphia at the time, once again serving as one of Delaware's delegates to Congress. In thanking him for his hospitality, Caesar teased that he and Sally "shall take up our Quarters with Misses Read and leave you, tho crowded with the great ones of the Earth to envy our happiness."[5]

Inevitably, the soaring prices charged by the "monopolisers" made it extremely difficult to supply the army. At the same time, the collapse of the national currency meant that each state now must outfit its Continental troops as well as its militia. Accordingly, George Craghead, the clothier general of Delaware, was given $12,000 in July with orders to fill "up the Delaware Regiment, and Supply the officers."[6] However, when he went to Philadelphia to purchase cloth for the officers' coats, he found it would not cover the "above and Two Shirts a Peice . . . What is [to] be done for Cash to Purchase the Remainder . . . particularly Shoes, Stockings & shirts, I cannot say. . . ."[7] Caesar immediately directed Samuel Patterson, now Treasurer of Delaware, to send him $1000 more.[8]

By August, the problem had become so severe that Washington implored the presidents of the eastern states to "interpose with their exertions . . . [or] the Troops may again experience . . . a part of those distresses, which were so severely and injuriously felt in past stages of the war." Particularly needed were "Blankets, Shirts, Shoes & Hats . . . The want of necessaries and of the means of procuring them at their present exorbitant prices have compelled a great many Officers, of good reputation and merit, to resign their commissions."[9]

In response, Caesar appointed a committee to take over "the directing of the prices to be given by the purchasing Commissaries" for Delaware's Continental regiment; a move welcomed by Francis Wade, deputy quartermaster general in Wilmington, "as . . . a means of stoping . . . the reflections thrown out against the department for raising the prices for the sake of the Commissioners . . . regulated prices . . . makes the business Exceeding Easy & no murmuring among the people. . . ."[10]

Everywhere, it seemed, "those termed Speculators are as thick and as industrious as Bees, and as Active and wicked as the Devil himself," and it wasn't long before the situation took a decidedly

ominous turn.[11] Samuel Patterson wrote Caesar in early October that "a party [of militia rose] . . . last Monday [in Philadelphia] against the merchants . . . a large number [of] both sides [were engaged] . . . some were killed dead on the spot & several badly wounded. . . . The poor [are] starving here and rise for redress."[12]
A few days later, he filled in the details.

On Monday morning a Handbill appeared for the Militia to collect on the Commons . . . to drive from the city, all disaffected persons, & those who supported them & . . . put [them] on board the prison ship to be sent to New York. . . . [One] they were after was James Wilson, the lawyer. . . . [Hearing the militia were coming, he] called in a number of his friends & armed, secured the doors . . . a fireing began . . . some say that one began first, & the others contradict it . . . four of the Mob & Negro boy were killed, in all 14 wounded. . . . In the meantime the Governor had ordered out the Light Horse of the city, who just came in time to save the lives of all in [his] House, for [the mob] had forced the doors, & the cry was blood for blood. . . . The Governor ordered them to charge with Swords,—they did—& after some cutting they broke them for that time. . . . At present there is a parley. The president, magistrates, & clergy of all denominations, met the militia & with very great difficulty, prevailed on them to lay their grievances before the Assembly . . . But he thinks it is not over. They will have blood for blood, & dreads the consequences yet . . . they are very numerous.[13]

Perhaps to forestall a similar uprising in Delaware, the assembly softened the embargo at their fall session. So as to "provide the people . . . with such manufactured goods . . . and encourage such trade as was possible in a country in a condition of invasion." Some grain and flour could now be exported if, in turn, the vessels brought in articles to be sold in the state.[14]

Nevertheless, all grain leaving the state for other colonies, or intended for use by the army and its French allies, had to be regulated. Accordingly, Caesar appointed a "person to Superintend the purchasing . . . [of] Flour" and gave him an order for $60,000 to begin his business with.[15] This "person" might have been Jonathan Rumford, Jr., a prominent Wilmington merchant and shipper, or it might have been Thomas Rodney, who, at one point, described his "peculiar duty . . . in Governm't to be . . . the Patron of Trade and Commerce."[16] Certainly Tommy had some authority in the fall of 1779, for he appointed George Latimer, a member of the assembly from New Castle, "as a deputy in Delaware for the purchasing of wheat and flour for the use of the United States."[17]

In any case, Thomas went into business with Rumford. By the

fall, he was looking for a house to buy in Wilmington and told Caesar that he was "not anxious to give what you may think an Extravagant price . . . but I would be willing to give from four to five thousand pounds hard money . . . provided from two to five years Credit could be obtained; I only mention this in Case any thing of this Sort Should fall in your way. . . ."[18]

Rumford had recently been accused of "dirty dealing" by Francis Wade for charging an exorbitant price for flour sent to John Holker, the agent for the French fleet in Philadelphia. When Wade also found problems with the accounts of an agent named George Evans, a man known for "taking and selling the people's cattle & retaining . . . the money," Evans immediately rose to his own and Rumford's defense by attempting to discredit Wade.[19]

Furious, Wade poured out his troubles to Caesar. "In the affair of Rumford," he wrote on September 14, 1779, "[Evans] . . . had the whole town ransacked for evidences against me & . . . encourage[d] . . . the most injurious insinuations . . . [but] when I called on him to support one sentence of what he advanced, he could not do it. . . . Mr. Evans declared [Rumford] to be as good a Whig as any in the States, altho' it is well known that he nor none of his family ever took up a fire lock in defense of their Country. . . ." Evans, according to Wade, worked "as the moles do under the surface . . ." first giving "out that [Rumford] had been guilty of dirty tricks before, which he no sooner discovered to be disagreeable to the opposite party, than he . . . joined Rumford . . . to attack me. Now," grumbled the insulted Wade, "Rumford, wants to take me by the hand after he has gained his end that of soaking my pocket."[20]

In a frantic effort to get control of the situation, Congress passed an act in November stating that "any State which had failed to limit the selling prices of such articles to twenty-fold the prices prevailing in 1774, should be charged . . . with the aggregate amount of the difference . . . after February 1780."

The Delaware Assembly hotly resented such interference in her "home affairs." Having done nothing to restrict their merchants, they would now have to pay "an enormous tax . . . for there were many staples of ordinary consumption that . . . cost forty or fifty times as much as six years previously." Reluctantly, they agreed to send George Latimer to a January meeting in Philadelphia that had been called to fix the price of "produce, merchandise and labor in each of the states." Latimer's instructions, however, were "to endeavor to procure its repeal."[21]

The meeting adjourned without action, having drawn representatives from only seven states. Subsequent meetings, although better attended, also failed to act and Delaware's General Assembly never passed any price fixing law despite ongoing complaints of "the Disorderly State of our Trade, Occasioned Chiefly by Forestallers, Engrossers, and Monopolizers"[22]

Meanwhile, Washington wrote Caesar that "The situation of the army with respect to supplies is alarming. . . . We have not more than three days bread . . . when this is exhausted we must depend on the precarious gleaning of the neighboring country. Our magazines are absolutely empty . . . our commissaries intirely destitute of money or credit to replenish them. . . . Unless some extraordinary and immediate exertions are made by the States . . . there is every appearance that the Army will . . . disband in a fortnight."[23] This was followed by a plea from Congress for "the most immediate & strenuous exertion of your State to forward a Supply of provisions . . . procure & forward with all possible expedition as much flour as can be obtained. . . ."[24]

Meanwhile, Caesar sent some business to Tommy and Rumford. He told John Holker in July of 1780, that "It will be necessary [that] . . . you should appoint some person as purchaser within this State . . . [so] I may . . . keep him within the line of his duty . . . [and] because this State has a Port and Market which it is . . . my duty to encourage. . . ." He then mentioned "Mr. Jonathan Rumford at Wilmington. . . ."[25] Later he also told the agent for the Spanish fleet to work through Holker, thereby directing him to Rumford and Tommy as well.

Rumford shipped 747 barrels of flour to the French fleet, but was once again accused of overcharging "relative to a quantity of flour purchased . . . thus contributing to the further depreciation of the currency of America."[26] Tommy, however, dismissed such accusations as "Trumped up . . . with the pretence of Injuring Rumford but with a More Vilianous & insidious intention of injuring You & My Self. . . ."[27]

On September 6, 1780, the schooner *St. Patrick*, arrived in Wilmington from the West Indies, earning the owners some £80,000 on the sale of her cargo of sugar, cocoa, coffee, and cotton.[28] Tommy immediately asked Caesar to suspend the embargo so that the *St. Patrick* could take out a load of Delaware flour. "The Owners of the St. Patrick . . . have requested that I would mention this matter to your self and some of the Gentlemen of the Council if necessary" he wrote. Arguing that the reasons for the embargo, that is "the fear of a Scarcity, and the fear of provisions falling into the hands of the Enemy" were no longer valid and that "the riches and prosperity of our State . . . greatly depends on Trade . . . the owners of the St Patrick think they may claim some favour. . . ."[29] That both Rodney brothers were among the "owners" is evident from a letter dated September 12, in which Caesar orders his "part of the St. Patrick's Cargo sold and the money arising therefrom carried to my account with the Ship's husband, Mr. Rumford. . . ."[30]

Nevertheless, Caesar, quite properly, dismissed Tommy's thinly disguised argument for their "private emolument." "I [too] . . . disapprove the scheme of embargoes—" he wrote, "But as the General Assembly . . . have, upon the requisition of Congress passed an Act for that purpose, I cannot think of voting for a suspension . . . in favour of the owners of the St. Patrick, or any other private purpose. More especially in a case Where I am personally Concerned. . . ."[31]

Writing many years later, Tommy claimed that in December of 1780, while serving as "Superintendent of Exportation of Flour to the Havannah," he had refused a bribe of some £30,000 to £50,000 to let merchants export flour in defiance of the embargo. He first said the offer had come from British agents, but later said it was from "J.R.," presumably Jonathan Rumford. While there is no solid evidence that such a bribe was ever offered, it is at least possible that it was related to Tommy's effort to get Caesar to clear the shipment for the *St. Patrick*. If so, Tommy failed to earn his money.[32]

Jonathan Rumford had a wharf between Orange and Tatnall Streets in Wilmington, where, it was said, "he leaned to Royalty, [but] never meddled with the affairs of state. . . ." Nevertheless, he became an anathema to the Whigs. In 1782, after he again got into trouble over a sale of grain, a mob broke into his house on Fourth Street and "snatching firebrands from the oven . . . abused his person in the most brutal manner." After the leader of the mob, a blacksmith, hit him on the head with a hammer, "Mr. Rumford lay apparently lifeless on the floor . . . everything was in the greatest confusion and his family panic stricken; no one dared to go to his relief. His wife was in deep affliction, having an infant, her only daughter ill with small pox . . . This infant then was in a dying state and soon sunk into a happy rest."

Although he was saved "from a violent death and his house from destruction," Rumford's "faculties were impaired and his capability for business so injured that in a few years, from a very rich man he died poor. . . ."[33]

A few months after this calamity, Tommy returned to Dover where he rented a house belonging to Mr. James Tilton. Later he would claim that he moved back only because his brother needed him. Perhaps so, but he was uncommonly lucky to escape unscathed from his ill-fated association with Jonathan Rumford.[34]

27

The War Moves South

THE WINTER OF 1779–80 WAS BITTERLY COLD. IN DECEMBER 1779, BEFORE he moved to Wilmington to go into business with Rumford, Tommy was busy overseeing the work on the Rodney farms. "The weather being bad," he wrote, "I was obliged to kept the boys gitting wood, so that I could neither go nor send to see if the corn was got in. . . . It began to snow this morning some time before light & has continued falling very fast since, so that it is now half [a] leg deep & falls as fast as ever. . . . The pork is to be in this week & the beef killed . . . if Warner brings wood to your house, as he has promised, on Munday, I will take Moses down to bring the beef up. . . ."[1]

Snow was also falling on Morristown, New Jersey, where Washington's army was again suffering from hunger and a lack of adequate clothing.[2] With the exception of some fierce skirmishes against bands of loyalists and Indians in New York and Pennsylvania, things had been quiet on the military front since "Mad Anthony" Wayne's astounding capture of a Hudson River fort the previous June. "Gen'l Wayne with 1200 Light Infantry . . . took sword in hand without firing a gun, . . ." Caesar had written Tommy at the time, "The whole garrison consisting of 500 fell into his hands, 15 pieces of Cannon & all the stores. . . . The above is one of the greatest strokes struck this war."[3]

With the exception of a similar coup led by Major Henry "Light Horse" Harry Lee at Paulus Hook, New Jersey, in August, the main thrust of the war had moved south. On September 25, 1779 John Dickinson had sent word to Caesar that "Count D'Estaing with a formidable Fleet has arriv'd at Georgia, with a very considerable Body of Troops on Board—one of the principal officers landed in South Carolina, held a Council of War there . . . and *if no Blunder* is committed the Event will be what we wish it to be."[4] The "event" was to be the recapture of Savannah, which had been in British hands since 1778. Unfortunately, a "blunder" *was* committed: the Americans gave the enemy almost two weeks to strengthen their position before launching an attack. When they finally moved in on October 9, they were repulsed with a loss of over eight hundred men, including Count Casimir Pulaski who was mortally wounded. The British lost about a fifth of that number and retained control of the city.[5]

Combining forces from Newport, Rhode Island and New York, the British general Sir Henry Clinton sailed for Georgia in December 1779, at about the same time that Tommy was worrying about getting his grain into storage. The American general Mordecai Gist described the scene to Caesar: "the embarkation [was] said to be of 8, or 10,000 troops . . . Supposed to be destin'd for the Southward, this fleet Consisted of 101 sail 91 of which were square Rigg'd Vessels."[6]

After "Storms scattered and impeded the fleet," they arrived at Tybee Bay, in the Savannah River at the end of January 1780. A week later they sailed northward into Edisto Sound to put the army ashore on John's Island, thirty miles south of Charleston. After receiving further reinforcements, "Sir Henry Clinton, by a slow and cautious march, proceeded to the Ashley River, opposite the city, while a part of the fleet went round by sea, for the purpose of blockading the port."[7]

The Americans had withstood an earlier British attack on Charleston in June of 1779. At that time, according to John Dickinson, "The Enemy attack'd our Lines at Charlestown, and were bravely repulsed—[when] a Column of [American General Benjamin] Lincoln's army appear'd in the rear of the Enemy, & immediatly falling upon them, put them to a total rout. . . ."[8] This report, however, was later tempered by one of General Lincoln's aides de camp. He reported that while the British had, indeed, been driven back "into their works, their works were so strongly Constructed, that our light field pieces Could make no Impression and . . . [because they were] Considerably reinforced from Johns Island dureing the Action, our troops were withdrawn from the lines. . . ."[9]

Now, in the spring of 1780, Charleston was threatened once again. Clinton's forces crossed the Ashley River at the end of March; a week later several British frigates arrived in Charleston harbor, effectively cutting off supplies to the city. There is little doubt that, from a military point of view, General Lincoln should have withdrawn from the city at this point; instead, apparently for political reasons, he was determined to defend it.

It was a hopeless task. Inevitably, despite his best efforts at fortification, Lincoln's army was trapped on the Charleston peninsula and under siege for nearly a month. Fort Moultrie, the Sullivan's

Island garrison which had so gallantly fought off the British in 1776, finally surrendered on May 6. Three days later, after enduring a night of continuous bombardment, Charleston fell as well. It was a devastating loss. Fifty-four hundred American soldiers were taken prisoner and three hundred and ninety guns and six thousand muskets handed over to the British. Leaving Cornwallis in charge, Sir Henry Clinton returned to New York, once more convinced that that the war was won.[10]

The American army was so decimated that Washington was forced to send an urgent call out to the states for more men. In response, a second Delaware regiment of the Continental line, to be offically known as Continental Regiment Number 38 was ordered into service "for the purpose of reinforcing the Army of the United States."[11] Caesar, however, was worried that "the great bounties given for men to fill [the militia] will effectually prevent our recruiting . . . the State Regiment which I am persuaded is of much more importance."[12] Nevertheless, by June 24, he was able to report to Congress "That the Troops, directed to be raised from the Militia of this State to form a Regiment, are under Marching Orders for Wilmington, Where I expect they will be verry soon Assembled in order to . . . Join the Army of the United States."[13]

Caesar, as governor, had the authority to choose the officers for this regiment "without being confined to any County for obtaining such gentlemen. . . ." Instead, in an effort "to serve . . . the expectations of the public" he asked the representatives from each county to pick their own officers. Imagine his chagrin when some of the chosen then refused to serve. "Is it not strange," he asked Samuel Patterson, "that any of these gentlemen, who were all well known and distinguished for their patriotism, and pointed out to me by their representatives, should refuse to accept their appointments?"[14] Even worse, when he went to Wilmington, himself, to find men to fill the vacancies, he found that some Sussex men "absolutely refused to March unless they were assured they should be Commanded by Captains from their Own County. . . ."[15]

The veteran first Delaware regiment had not been at Charleston, but they were in South Carolina, having gone south in April under Brigadier General Mordecai Gist. There, they had joined forces with the Maryland regiment under Brigadier William Smallwood and some militia units from Virginia and North Carolina. All were under the command of Major General Baron Johann deKalb, a German who had served in the French army with Lafayette.

Just before they had left Washington's camp in Morristown, deKalb had written Caesar that he was "much distressed [as to] how to bear the Expenses of so considerable a March . . . [now that] the Continental Treasury is quite exhausted" and begged him "to grant as ample a Supply to the officers of the Delaware Regiment as the Length of this march demands."[16]

As the men passed through Philadelphia and Wilmington on their way south, they were described by a woman bystander: "The shorter men of each company in the front rank, the taller men behind them—some in hunting-shirts, some in uniforms, some in common clothes—some with their hats cocked and some without, and those who did cock them, not all wearing them the same way, but each man with a green sprig, emblem of hope, in his hat, and each bearing his firelock with what, even to uninstructed eyes, had the air of skilful training."[17]

In what would prove to be a disastrous mistake, General Horatio Gates was brought in over deKalb in August 1780. "At this time," wrote Sergeant Major William Seymour of the Delaware regiment, "we were much distress for want of provisions; men were sent out to cut the grain [corn] for daily sustenance, but could scarcely get enough to keep the troops from starving . . . we lived chiefly on green apples and peaches, which rendered us weak and sickly."[18]

Gates' assignment was to capture the British garrison at Camden, the largest of a ring of outposts they had established in the northern part of the state after the fall of Charleston. Only a month after Gates took over the command, Tommy wrote Caesar that he had been "Totally defeated near Camden and lost the greatest part of his Army Killed and Taken prisoners. . . . Gates attacked to disadvantage by Too hasty a pursute, and the Malitia Giving way his Regulars were overpower'd. . . . If this account is True the Stroke is more Severe than that at Charles Town . . . [we] could not learn any particulars respecting the Dalawares. . . ."[19]

Gates, against the advice of deKalb and other officers, had chosen the wrong road. Instead of going by way of Salisbury, "a fertile country inhabited by a people zealous in the cause" he had taken a more direct route through the North Carolina pine barrens, a "sterile country" where his soldiers, already weak from lack of food, found little to eat but green corn on the banks of the Pee Dee river. This, they boiled with beef "collected in the woods . . . a repast, not unpalatable to be sure but attended with painful effects. . . . The officers, aware of the risk . . . restrained themselves from taking anything but the beef itself boiled or roasted. It ocurred to some that the hair-powder, which remained in their bags would thicken soup and it was actually applied."[20]

On the night of August 15, Gates' men ran into Cornwallis' army

Colonel David Hall's Delaware Regiment, 1777–1783, Plate #273 Military Uniforms of America, Courtesy of the Historical Society of Delaware.

by accident in a pine forest near Camden. When the British attacked, the weakened Americans found themselves hemmed in by
swamps and unable to maneuver. Most of the militia fled, leaving
only nine hundred Continentals and one militia unit to face over
two thousand well-rested and well-fed British soldiers. To his everlasting shame, General Gates joined his men in flight galloping
away from the scene of battle.

Although abandoned by their General, deKalb and Gist fought on
with great valour until a British calvary unit came up from the rear
to surround and slaughter them. Only a few managed to escape:
Gist was killed and General deKalb so badly wounded that he died
in captivity three days later. The war in the south seemed truly
lost.[21]

When the news reached Dover, Caesar was desparately anxious
about the fate of the Delaware regiment and particularly that of his
young half brother, John Wilson, a captain in the fifth company.
"These accounts have filled [all] the people . . . with deep concern,
but it is impossible to paint the distress of those who have friends
and connections in that little and brave Band of Officers. . . ." He
begged Tommy to let him know "whether Johnny Willson has fell
or not—Sally is greatly distressed and I think she could not suffer
much more if he certainly has. . . . I am disappointed in your not
writing to me on a matter of such importance before now."[22]

Not until the middle of September did the Rodneys finally receive "an Acct. of the Killed, Wounded, Missing and Prisoners. . . ."
Of the five hundred men and officers that went into battle, "there
remained four captains, seven subalterns, three staff officers, nineteen non-commissioned officers, eleven fifers and drummers and
145 rank and file."[23] Nevertheless, Tommy could report that "The
Dalawares . . . are in one respect very happy for there is not one
officer among them Killed, wounded or Missing. But Eight of Them
are Prisoners . . . Genl DeCalb [is] Killed . . . and a Considerable
number of Field officers . . . Taken Prisoners." He does not mention
John Wilson specifically, although he presumably survived, as he
was not listed among the captured. Neither Rodney brother expressed much concern about the 265 enlisted men who had been
lost.

Meanwhile, loyalist raiders continued to prowl Delaware Bay.
Colonel John Jones, of the Sussex county militia, wrote Caesar in
July 1780 that "Our situation here is truly alarming, the Enimy
being almost Constantly in the River. . . . We have neither Lead,
nor flints, Could you furnish us with a few of those Articles?"[24] In
reply, Caesar commissioned "Barges & Boats etc., to cruize in the

Bay & River." While assuring Jones that "the expences of Equipping the vessels and the wages of the Crews [would be] discharged by the State" he added that he would give every assistance to "any Gentlemen in your Quarter [who would] think [it] proper to Equip or cause to be Equipped and manned any such Vessel. . . . You all know that our Treasury is not presently in Cash. . . ."[25]

Once again, the people of Sussex proved unreliable. Caesar sent Colonel Pope to Lewes in September with "the Armed Vessel he commanded for the protection of our River Trade . . ." only to find that his plan was "totally defeated by the Whim or obstinacy of some Gentlemen in your Town."[26]

The legislature was proving troublesome as well. In June, after a majority of both houses agreed to give Caesar the power to impose martial law, they had adjourned without actually doing so. "I never was so deceived in my Politics, as on yesterday . . ." wrote a discouraged Samuel Patterson. "To my great surprize, when every moment I & others expected its appearance; the notice was, the Assembly was adjourned. . . . Nothing can be done without it. . . . I am tired with such complacency, & am almost determined never more to appear in that public body who cannot see the necessity of spirited measures. . . ."[27]

By August 1780, bands of the "disaffected" were once again "ranging about [Sussex] County disarming the well affected seizing the ammunition refusing to pay their taxes and in short openly avowing their intension of opposing the laws and threatening distruction to all that should oppose them. . . ." When "a party of horse" were sent out against them, six militiamen and one horse were killed. Afterward, General Dagworthy was "determined to march against them with what force he had Collected and after persuing them for three days and driving them from one Swamp into another have nearly dispersed them."[28]

Dagsworthy's militia was woefully short of supplies. According to Jones, they had "only rec'd 300 bushels of corn . . . 170 bushels of salt from Baltimore Hundred . . . [and] purchasing it is in vain . . . as the people . . . dislike the Certificates . . . as for wheat we have none in our county & very little corn."[29]

George Washington's army was also "reduced to an extremity of distress for want of provision. . . ." He had moved them from Morristown to Bergen County, New Jersey, "with a view of stripping the lower parts of the County of the remainder of its Cattle, which after a most vigorous exaction is found to afford between two and three days supply only, and those consisting of Milch Cows and Calves of one or two years old—when this scanty pittance is consumed, I know not what will be our next resource. . . ."[30]

28

An End to War

IN SEPTEMBER 1780 CAME THE SHOCKING NEWS THAT GENERAL BENE-
dict Arnold had committed treason, having apparently concluded
that the Americans could not possibly win the war. His plan to surrender the fort at West Point to the British was exposed when his
emmissary, Major John André, was seized with incriminating papers hidden in his boots.[1] André, to the consternation of many, was
summarily hanged, while Arnold, himself, escaped.

Another blow came on New Year's Day, 1781, when a group of
enlisted men from the Pennsylvania Line at Morristown marched
on Congress to protest their "want of pay, Clothing & Provisions . . .
no money having been receiv'd since the first of April last, very little
Clothing & many Times no Provision. . . ."[2] When this was followed
by a similar uprising in the New Jersey regiment, Washington immediately ordered their leaders seized and two were later executed.
Despite promises from Congress, however, the army's supply problems continued.[3]

A week later, Brigadier General Benedict Arnold, now of the *British* army, led sixteen hundred men up the James River to occupy
Richmond, Virginia, destroying warehouses and other buildings before withdrawing to the nearby town of Portsmouth. Things seemed
grim indeed.

Nevertheless, the tide was slowly beginning to turn. The first sign
of renewed hope had actually occurred the previous October, when
a makeshift army of patriot militia and "Over Mountain Men" from
beyond the Blue Ridge Mountains took on a army of Loyalist milita-
men and British regulars at King's Mountain, South Carolina, defeating one of Britain's most promising young officers. Afterward,
Colonel William Campbell, the leader of the Virginia militia was
able to report that "[British Major Patrick] Ferguson and his party
are no more in circumstances to injure the citizens of America."[4]

An even larger victory occurred on January 17, 1781; the Battle
of Cowpens, so called because it took place on a spot used to round

up stray cattle. There, a few miles west of King's Mountain, American forces under Major General Nathanael Greene, (Horatio Gates' replacement as commander of the southern army) managed to surround and defeat the notorious Lieutenant Colonel Banastre Tarleton, an able but merciless fighter whose massacre of defenseless prisoners had given rise to the term "Tarleton's Quarter." Once again, the Delaware regiment was in the thick of it. Under Brigadier General Daniel Morgan, they held the main line while militia units circled around to strike the British on the flank. The result was a major British defeat. "They lost one hundred killed, one hundred and fifty wounded, six hundred prisoners, three pieces of artillery, two stands of colors, eight hundred muskets, thirty-five wagons and baggage and one hundred cavalry horses."[5] By contrast, twelve Americans lost their lives and sixty-one were wounded.

When Lord Cornwallis, "who was not more than thirty miles distant from the scene of action" heard of Tarleton's defeat, he was determined "to pursue his retreating adversary, regain his captured troops and baggage, re-establish the royal government in North Carolina and press forward to [join] . . . the British troops under Arnold on the Chesapeake."[6] However, he was far too slow to catch the wily General Morgan who escaped into North Carolina to join General Greene.[7]

Keeping just out of reach, the Americans then teased the British into following them across North Carolina to the Virginia border, pulling them far from their base of supplies. At the same time, they suffered incredible privations of their own. "More than half our members," wrote General Greene, "are in a manner naked, so much so that we cannot put them on the least kind of duty; indeed, there is a great number that have not a rag of clothes on them except a little piece of blanket in the Indian form around their waists."[8] Meanwhile, some of the Delaware men were chosen to join a special force under Colonel Otho Williams to "harrass the enemy in their advance, check their progress, and, if possible, give us an opportunity to retire without a general action."[9]

After receiving reinforcements from Baron von Steuben's troops in Virginia, Greene turned south to meet Cornwallis in the battle at Guilford Court House, North Carolina, on February 10. Once again the Delaware infantry was in the fighting, striking the advancing British on the flank after three lines of infantry had fired and given way ahead of them. They stood their ground even when Cornwallis' gunners fired into the melee, hitting many of their own men as well as the Americans.[10]

The British managed to hold their line, but it was a hollow victory. According to Lieutenant Charles Magill, of the Virginia Regiment: "Such another dear bought day must effectually ruin the British army. From the nicest calculation seven hundred of the enemy were kill'd or Wounded."[11] The British had lost over a quarter of their men; the Americans about half that number.[12] A few months later General Nathancal Greene would write Caesar that "your troops without exception have behaved well . . . for their zeal and fidelity deserve the highest applause."[13]

In February of that year, Thomas Rodney was elected to the Continental Congress, along with Thomas McKean and the "moderate Whig," Nicholas Van Dyke. Tommy arrived to take up his post in Philadelphia just in time to celebrate the adoption of the Articles of Confederation. Maryland had finally agreed to ratify them, but only after the French Ambassador threatened to withdraw his protection from the Chesapeake Bay.[14] Among the festivities was a "collation" at the house of President Samuel Huntington, a man Tommy described as a "plain republican, not of shining abilities," and dinner at the McKeans "with an assembly of notables," followed by a show of fireworks at the State House and from Paul Jones's ship.[15]

Oddly, Thomas Rodney did not think much of Caesar's old compatriot Thomas McKean, now chief justice of the State of Pennsylvania. He called him "a man of talents—of great Vanity, extremely fond of power and entirely governed by passions, ever pursuing the object present with warm enthusiastic zeal without much reflection or forecast."[16] It seemed a clear case of the pot calling the kettle black!

Tommy was put on a committee on ways and means after he let it be known that he disapproved of the way Congress had handled the country's finances. He was certainly not alone in this opinion; as one member from North Carolina wrote: "Never was a poor fly more completely entangled in a cobweb than Congress in their paper currency."[17] While the committee accomplished little, Thomas' talent for self aggrandizement flourished. Once again writing many years after the event, he claimed that toward the end of April 1781, he and General Horatio Gates had come up with the same plan for government that was, afterward, attributed to Alexander Hamilton, and, in fact, it was they who had prevented Hamilton from having the army proclaim Washington king. He even took credit for the Constitution, boasting in the late 1790s, that "I have always Stood On the Democratic floor, Yet am Equally attached to the Presidental and Senatorial Order of Our Government & How can I be Otherwise Since its Form in Toto—Eminated from my own mind. . . ."[18]

On June 9, 1781, Tommy wrote Caesar that "Cornwallace joined Arnold about the 20th . . . at Peterborough [Petersburg], Virginia— The marquis [Lafayette] at the head of 1000 regulars & 4000 militia is giving them all the opposition he can—Gen Wain [Anthony Wayne] will join him in a few days and the malitia being now well armed are Turning out with great Spirit. . . ."[19]

Arnold had captured Petersburg in April, destroying many American supplies and vessels. Lafayette, meanwhile, had again lured Cornwallis northward with a series of minor skirmishes before joining General Wayne in Fredericksburg. Cornwallis was so frustrated by his inability to catch Lafayette, whom he dismissed as "the boy," that he sent Tarleton on a spite mission to destroy the seat of the Virginia legislature at Charlottesville.[20] With the Americans still on his heels, Cornwallis then crossed the James River and moved on to Williamsburg where he received a message from General Clinton rescinding an earlier order to send reinforcements to New York. Instead, Clinton directed him to occupy the deep water port of Yorktown and await the arrival of the British fleet. Tarleton, meanwhile, was to occupy the town of Gloucester on the opposite shore, so as to secure the mouth of the York River.

On August 14, General Washington was in New York planning an attack on General Clinton when he received the news that the French Admiral François deGrasse was on his way from the West Indies to the Chesapeake with three thousand French troops. Leaving Major General William Heath to defend the Hudson Highlands with less than twenty-five hundred men, he immediately began to march southward to join deGrasse. It was a bold decision. Washington knew well that with his main army gone, Clinton might finally succeed in gaining control of the Hudson River and isolating New England from the rest of the colonies.[21]

By the end of September, the American army had arrived in Virginia to occupy a position within a mile of the British outer line around Yorktown. Washington also positioned a force of seven hundred men and calvary on the opposite side of the river to keep Tarleton's forces confined at Gloucester. With the large number of French soldiers, Washington now had over sixteen thousand men in his command; Cornwallis had less than half as many, and had clearly not expected an attack from his landward side. Nevertheless, still expecting the British fleet to rescue him, he pulled back his outer line to be ready for their arrival. It was a fatal mistake: unbeknownst to Cornwallis, Clinton's ships had been driven back by deGrasse. The French fleet had completely blocked the entrance to the Chesapeake Bay and the York River.

Colonel Ephraim Blaine of the Pennsylvania militia, in charge of supplies for the army from the middle states, wrote Caesar from the Oxford, Maryland on October 4th: "Our heavy artillery . . . and our Engineers . . . have run a line . . . more than five hundred yards from the Enemy's Works . . . our army will advance by regular Approaches until they Subdue his Lordship with an Army of Seven thousand men which I have not the least doubt will be accomplished the course of twenty Days . . . for God's sake give me every Assistance. . . ."[22] The three hundred new recruits that had been sent from Delaware in the early months of 1781 were among the American and French soldiers that now moved in to bombard the city of Yorktown.[23]

After enduring a week of almost continuous shelling, Cornwallis made a desparate attempt to get his men across the river to Gloucester on the night of October 16. Only a few boats had made it across before a violent storm scattered those still on the river and removed any possibility of a further crossing. On the morning of the seventeenth, after British drums had signaled for a "parley," a British officer was taken, blindfolded, to the American lines to ask for an armistice. Two days later the British formally surrendered, marching out of Yorktown in gleaming red uniforms to the beat of "The World Turned upside Down." Tarleton, trapped on Gloucester point, also surrendered. The Delaware recruits returned home and disbanded in January of 1782.

Although the Yorktown surrender is now considered the end of the war, it did not seem so at the time. The Americans continued fighting in South Carolina under the "Swamp Fox," Brigadier General Francis Marion, for some time and the British did not relinquish Charleston until December of 1782. There were also continuing clashes between the British and French fleets in the West Indies.

According to Caesar, the British were still trying to make individual deals with various states a full seven months after Yorktown, despite the resignation of Lord North and the passage of a Parliamentary resolution to cease hostilities. As he wrote Tommy in May 1782, "bitter as the *Pill* is they must swallow it before long—Their present view is to unite Great Britain and America . . . they flatter themselves they shall succeed."[24] In fact, the final treaty was not signed until September, 3, 1783.

The final clash between Delaware's trading schooners and the raiding "refugee" boats occurred on April 8, 1782 when the American sloop of war *Hyder Alley* engaged and defeated the British sloop *General Monk* at the entrance to Delaware Bay.

Despite their great victory, many Americans, particularly in the smaller states, were uncertain about the future. Tommy, in Congress, expressed the doubts of many in a letter he wrote to Caesar on the day of the British surrender at Yorktown: "I wish the Legislature would consider seriously the importance of keeping up a well regulated malita. . . . This is not only necessary for our safety at present, but in future, least the neighbouring States seeing us weak and feeble may hereafter be tempted to invade our Liberties contrary to the Confederation. . . ."[25]

29

Caesar's Sand Runs Out

DUE TO THE ASSEMBLY'S DELAY IN ELECTING A SUCCESSOR, CAESAR'S term as president of Delaware did not expire until November 1781. Immediately afterward he placed himself under the care of Dr. Thomas Bond in Philadelphia. The never-ending demands for money from Congress combined with the continuing pressure to provide both men and supplies for the army had left him exhausted and dangerously ill. Sometime in the next few months, he wrote the following letter. We do not know to whom it was addressed.

The concern you express . . . with respect to the State of that Horrid and most obstinate disorder, the Cancer, which I now Labour under and am Endeavouring to have cured . . . [I will] give the most satisfactory answer in my power. . . . It is now four weeks since the Doctor first dressed me, which he has continued to do twice a day ever since. The Doctor declares with the greatest confidence that he shall perfect a cure. Many of those who have been under his hands, with similar complaints, but not half so bad, have been to Visit me, and . . . don't seem to have a single doubt . . . [I] hope they are right, but was I left to form a Judgement from my own feelings I should not be verry sanguine . . . However . . . I am determined to persevere, it is a matter of . . . no less than Life or Death . . . The Doctor must conquer the Cancer, or the Cancer will conquer me. . . .

He is also hard up for money.

When I left home I expected to [go] no further [than] Wilmington and there been attended by the Doctor for the cure of my Cancerous complaint, but on seeing him found I was under the disagreable necessity of repairing to Philadelphia where I have been between five and six weeks and where it is most likely I shall be detained many weeks more. I am necessarily at a verry considerable expence, my cash is running verry low, and, by means of the refugees, all communication between that part of the State where I live, and the market here is intirely cut off. Now Sir . . . if there is any money due to me which ought to come

207

through your hands, you will oblidge me exceedingly by . . . transmitting it to me . . . as soon as possible. I now begin to have some hopes that the Doctor will perfect a cure, but the disorder is extremely obstinate and . . . it will be a tedious as well a painfull business—However . . . I am determined to persevere. . . ."[1]

Meanwhile, his compatriots in the assembly, reluctant to let him go, had again appointed him to the Congress in February. "Yourself, Mr. McKean, Phill Dickerson [Philemon Dickinson] and Sam Wharton are appointed Deligates," wrote Tommy from Wilmington.

They were very odd choices. Caesar was, obviously, far too ill to serve; Thomas McKean had not lived in Delaware for years, and Philemon Dickinson was a resident of New Jersey. His only connection with the state was through his brother, John. Tommy is particularly incensed at the choice of Sam Wharton, calling it "Extraordanary indeed to appoint a man who has been all the war and long before residing in England intimate with ministerial and political men and has no knowledge of or connection with the affairs of this State . . . but this is a Sample of a new system of Politics now Extablished. . . ."[2]

Caesar's answer is typically wry. "I rather think the General Assembly have had in view the getting such as were most likely to serve for nothing. If so, they will find themselves mistaken as to me. . . ."[3]

In this same letter, Caesar asked his brother to help him convince the doctor to allow him to travel "at least as far as Wilmington," where Thomas has been living since his own term in Congress expired. Caesar, despite his illness, has not only settled the debts his brother had apparently left behind in Philadelphia but "sent all your things and all the papers, except the two books you mention, and have sent Caesar (Tommy's son, Caesar Augustus Rodney) tyed up in the foot of one of your worsted stockings, eleven stone marbles. . . ."

Caesar, worried about the neglect of their property in Kent county, begged his brother to "go to Kent . . . and . . . to let on the best terms you can, my Gibson place with the meadow. . . ." Having sent his carriage horses "down by Elisha," he also wanted Tommy to "to order proper care to be taken of them. I will gladly pay for the hay that may be purchased, as they will not be used. They cannot stand in need of much grain, if any at all."[4]

Tommy, in Dover, found Caesar's worst fears realized. "As to the meadow place . . . the house and meadow appeared in such order that . . . did not seem to deserve any rent. The house, though good frame, had the floors tore up and one half the weather boards off, and one half the meadow is over run with elders and briers, and at least one half the bank distroyed with the tide & muskrats." Tommy entered into an agreement with a black man named Jacob Armstrong to "weather board the house, clear up all the briers and elders out of the meadow, make up the bank . . . cut, cure & stack all the hay for you." In return Armstrong was given permission to live there for nothing on condition that "if he does not perform the agreement he is to pay £75 rent and in proportion for any part he leaves undone." "I know you do not like to have any of this colour on your land," Tommy told Caesar, "but . . . I have a good opinion of this fellow and think he will endeavour more to give you satisfation that any white person you could have got."[5]

Caesar, apparently, had no objection to the arrangement, but continued to worry about his other affairs. Still in Philadelphia at the beginning of April, he wanted desparately to get home for at least two weeks. "The scituation of my affairs seems to make this step necessary and I am in great hopes that about three weeks from this time I may venture to take this step without danger. . . ."[6] Caesar finally left Philadelphia for Dover sometime between May and September of 1782.

In 1783, he was once again elected to the state legislature and chosen speaker. This could only have been a gesture of respect. It had been nearly two years since he had first protested that "verry little Service can be expected of me in future, my constitution . . . is too much unhinged for me to discharge the duties in a public Station . . . my constitution requires Rest and my wish is to induge it."[7]

"My brother being on the decline desired my Company," wrote Thomas in 1784, "so I moved to his House then at Poplar Grove. . . ."[8] To accommodate Caesar's increasing weakness, the senate held its April 1784, session at Poplar Grove.

Soon afterward, the following notice appeared, written by Thomas Rodney as Executor of Caesar Rodney's estate.

Be it Remembered that the Hon Caesar Rodney Esq Speaker of the Legislative Council and Member of Congress, and President, Captn General & Commander in Chief of the Delaware State—Died at Poplar Grove near Dover and on the west side of the Dover River, his then place of Residence in the 57th year of his age on Saturday the twenty sixth day of June about seven o'clock in the evening 1784.[9]

The funeral was "at his late Dwelling place, on Monday Morning, eight O'Clock." (June 28, 1784)[10]

Let his own words serve as Caesar Rodney's epitaph: "When the contest between Great Britain and America first commenced, I stept forth among others in order to obtain a redress of Greivances. This and no other was my aim until absolutely refused. The Question then was Independence or the Bayonet, I was at no loss in determining which to chuse. Independence then and hope it will ere long be established, but Sir I always kept in View the good order well Being and Happiness of the people, more especially those over who I had lately the Honor to preside, and Trust That none who know me believe otherwise."[11]

EPILOGUE

An undated note in Thomas Rodney's "Commonplace Book" begun in 1773 reads: "Soon after I went to the Bastile in 1791, Byfield Farm the Mansion Plantation of the Rodney family where my brother Caesar and our Ancestors are buried, was Sold by the Sheriff of this County at Public Sale on the 4th of July. . . ."[12]

Thomas, in fact, lost his moorings after the death of his brother, and, as executor of Caesar's estate, soon found himself in grave financial difficulties. He had also lost his wife. Betsy Rodney had died the previous fall, on October 31, 1783, leaving him with two teenaged children. He moved into Caesar's house at Poplar Grove, boarding his children with either Sally Wilson or John Vining. (Caesar A. Rodney also seems to have lived for a time with Thomas McKean while he attended the University of Pennsylvania.)[13]

Thomas never achieved the stature of his famous brother, but he continued to serve in Delaware politics, both as a member of Congress and of the assembly, and was even elected speaker in 1787. After that, came financial disaster.

It began when he tried to collect £1500 for Caesar's estate from John Vining's estate, which Thomas claimed was owed after both men had served as cotrustees of the loan office. It was an effort that only succeeded in staining first Vining's reputation and then his own. Upon looking into the matter, the joint committee on finance of the assembly found that £1000 was missing and Thomas was subsequently accused of stealing. Whatever the correct explanation, by 1791, Thomas' affairs were a shambles. In March of that year, Poplar Grove was seized in foreclosure and Thomas moved to Ionia Farm in Jones' Neck. His wife's family, the Fishers of Philadelphia, then seized his furniture, livestock, three Negroes and a trading sloop in lieu of a debt owed to them. On June 13, 1791,

Rodney himself was thrown into debtor's prison where he stayed for fourteen months. Then Byfield was also sold, leaving only Ionia Farm to Caesar's heir, young Caesar Augustus Rodney. Thomas Rodney finally left Delaware about 1800 for the Mississippi territory where he was appointed to a judgeship by Thomas Jefferson. He died there on January 2, 1811.

His son, Caesar Augustus Rodney, had his own distinguished career. A respected lawyer, he served as both a United States representative and senator and eventually became an attorney general of the United States. He died in Buenos Aires, Argentina, in 1824 while serving as the United States' first ambassador to that country.

Meanwhile the cemetery at Byfield was left unmarked and unattended. In a codicil to his will, written in March 1784, Caesar ordered and directed that "my Brother Thomas Rodney to erect a good substantial brick Wall properly capd so as to inclose the Family Burial Ground at the old Byfield Farm in the same Manner as Burial Grounds are usually enclosed . . . and raise the money for erecting it out of the Rents and Profits of my real Estate. . . ." The only evidence that this was ever done is a note in Thomas Rodney's Account Book as executor of Caesar's estate that refers "to bricks of C. Rodney's grave." Over the years the location of this burial ground has been lost.

In the late 1880s, under the leadership of Chief Justice Joseph P. Comegys, a group of young men in Dover calling themselves the Rodney Club dug up what was thought to be Caesar's remains for reburial in the Christ Church Cemetery in Dover. This ceremony was performed even though there was considerable doubt at the time that any bones had been found. Eyewitnesses reported seeing only dirt and bits of metal fragments.

In 1978, Dr. Harold B. Hancock of Dover was preparing an article on Caesar Rodney, and asked James B. Jackson of Dover, a collateral descendant of Caesar's, to help him research the Rodney lands. After studying old maps and deeds, Mr. Jackson found that what the Rodney Club and Judge Comegys had thought was Byfield was, in fact a newer addition to the plantation. Mr. Jackson, by comparing old maps and sketches, found fourteen graves in a hundred-square-foot burial ground, untouched except for one collapsed brick vault that contained what was thought to be the bones and "skull of middle-aged man of delicate features." Further investigation, however, proved that they were, in fact, the remains of a woman. No other trace has since been found of Caesar's grave.

"Byfield" is now part of a corporate farm. There is no sign of the Rodney homestead. "Poplar Grove" is gone as well, replaced by a brick ranch house sometime in the 1960s.

Appendix I: Caesar Rodney's Bequests

CAESAR, IN HIS LAST WILL AND TESTAMENT, MAKES THE FOLLOWING bequests.

1st, to Caesar Augustus Rodney, his gold watch; 2nd, to the Wardens of Christ Church Dover, Delaware, one hundred pounds to inclose with a brick wall the burying-ground of Christ Church therein; 3rd, of a tract of land in Jones's Neck, Kent County, Delaware, commonly called "Byfield" to his nephew, Caesar Augustus Rodney, for his natural life . . . and after his death to his first son, and the heirs male of the body of such son; and he failing, to the third, fourth, fifth son, and all and every his sons, lawfully begotten succesively in remainder.

Caesar also directed his brother Thomas

To have his son, Caesar A. Rodney brought up in the form of religion commonly called the Church of England, and educated liberally in classical learning, Natural and Moral Philsophy, and every other branch of literature that has a tendencey to improve the understanding and polish the manners, as may reasonably be in America.

Should Thomas die in the minority of Caesar A. Rodney, this direction is to be performed by his brother, William Rodney, and if he also should so die, the testator earnestly requests his respectable friend, George Read, of New Castle, to see that this part of his will be judiciously executed.

Thomas Rodney, as executor of Caesar's will, submitted the following inventory of his possessions.

Photos of chests, tall case clock, chair, and silver by Delaware makers—probably similar to those listed in Caesar Rodney inventory. Courtesy of the Biggs Museum of American Art, Dover.

INVENTORY

"Inventory and appraisement of the Estate late of Caesar Rodney,
Esquire taken and made by us the Subscribers the 20th of July,
1784"[1]

In the Parlor Chamber:

1 picture of Queen Charlotte	£7
1 Silver mounted sword, a legacy	£5
1 bed, 1 pair sheets 1 pair blankets & bolster 2 pillows, 1 set Venetian Chintz curtains and mahogany bedstead with cornish	£20
1 field bedstead Madrass(?) and curtains	£4
1 mahogany droping table	£1 10/
1 walnut chest of drawers	£5
8 mahogany chairs with worsted damask bottoms	£8
1 walnut armchair with leather bottom	£1 15/
1 looking glass, 70/	
1 pair brass andirons, 40/	£5 10/
	£51 2/ (?)

In the passage upstairs:

1 looking glass, 70/ 1 dressing table, 25/	£4 15/
1 bed, 2 blankets, 2 sheets, 1 bolster 2 pillows a painted bedstead & furniture check curtains	£8
	£12 15/

In the passage below stairs:

1 mahogany tea table, 25/ a walnut desk, 40/	£3 5/
1 square walnut table 25/ 1 ditto, 25/	£2 10/
	£5 15/

In the Parlour:

8 mahogany chairs w hair bottoms @ 25/	£10
2 arm ditto 70/ 2 mahogany tables, £6	£9 10/
1 pair look glasses w gilt frames	£15
1 eight day clock and case	£14
1 small walnut table, 12/, tea board 10/	£1 2/

4 Venetian crimson harrateen(?) window curtains	£1 10/
1 pair andirons with brass fluted pillars	£3 10/
1 silver coffee pott with 53oz:6 pro(?): 12gh @ 12/oz	£31 9/10
1 ditto tea pott w handle 28:6:0 @12/	£16 9/6
2 ditto half pint creamers (?) 15:11:0 @12	£9 6/7
	£112(?)7/11p

Silver continued:

2 small sauce boats, 21oz 15du(?)0 gr @12/	£13 1/
1 sugar dish, 11oz 16du(?)0 gr @12/	£7 1/7
1 pint bowl 11oz 1du(?)12 gr @12/	£6 12/10
1 Carter(?)frame with topps 28oz 13du(?)0 gr @142	£20 9/
1 cream jug 3oz 10du(?)10 gr @8/6	£1 10/
1 pair salt cellars & shovels 5oz 16du(?)8 gr @12/	£3 9/8 1/2
1 punch strainer 1oz 14u(?)6 gr @12	£0 14/6
1 soup spoon 6oz 18du(?)0 gr @12/6	£2 17/5
12 table spoons 23oz 2du(?)0 gr @8/6	£9 16/11
13 tea spoons 4oz 16du(?)12 gr @8/6	£2 1/

5 pewter water plates	£1
Some china & Queensware plates a pair glass salts a china butter boat a cup and 2 small bottles	£15/
1 knife case very old & some knives & forks without handles	2/6
12 bone handle knives & 12 forks	7/6/
6 wine glasses 6/, 2 brass candlestands 10/	16/
1 tobacco box 1/, 4 coffee cups, 2 teacups 4 saucers 2/6	3/6
1 tumbler 1 mustard pot, 1 pint decanter & steel	4/
1 case and frame for fishing lines	1/
2 tinn canister 3/, 1 Case with 11 bottles 10/	13/
	£4 2/6

Books:

Blackstone Commentaries 4 vols	£2
1 old Bible imperfect	2/6
Robertson's history of Charles V 3 vols	15/
Bailys Dictionary	15/
A parcel of Pamphlets	5/
Hart's Table of Interest, 1 vol.	1/6
Prusiam Evolutions, 1 vol.	1/
Military Guides 2 vols	7/6
Chevelier DeValiers Art of War, 1 vol.	2/
Instructions to Field Officers, 1 vol.	1/6
Field Engineer, 1 vol.	2/6
On Wills and Testaments, 1 vol.	1/
Lord Summers of Kingdoms & Nations 1 vol.	1/6
	£4 6/ 0
	£189 8/ 10 1/2

In the Cellar:

127 Quart Bottles @3	£1 11/9
11 old casks Hogshead & Keggs	£1 15/
1 tin watering pot	7/
1 old box with about 2 doz candles	2/6
60 tallow and 2 earthen potts of parsnips	£2 1/6
	£5 17/9

In the logg House:

8 walnut chairs with damask bottoms	£3
2 arm ditto, 25/ 1 looking glass 30/	£2 15/
12 pictures framed w glass @2/6	£1 10/
1 bedstead, 2 blankets, bolster, 2 pillows	£3
1 pair brass andirons 25/, 2 gallon bottles 2/	£1 7/

In the same house upstairs:

1 bedstead, 2 blankets, and a bolster	£3
1 some (?)tub 3 pickle potts, 1 brush	6/6
5 walnut chairs w leather bottoms	£1 15/
5 ditto very old	5/
	£4 16/

In the Store House:

1 old wagon with Gear for 2 horses	10/
1 plow and Gear 30/, 4 hogsheads 7/6, 1 old Scritoire 10	£2 7/6
1 old woollen Wheel 5/, 1 old arm windsor chair 4/	9/
309lb bacon @9p, £11 11/9,	
109lbs dried beef @3p, £3 3/7	£14 15/4

Wareing Apparrell:

1 pair silver shoebuckles & 1 pair ditto knee buckles	£1 10/
1 pair gold sleeve buttons, 1 ditto stock buckle	£5 6/
1 gold watch, a legacy	£20
1 flesh brush 1/6, 5 napkins 7/6, 2 tablecloths 7/6	£16 6/
	£28 6/6

In the yard:

1 sow, 6 shoats 3 piggs	£3 17/6
2 bay horses	£40
2 cows, 1 bull	£9
12 old sheep and 6 lambs	£6 15/
1 old Phaeton and harness	£10
	£69 2/6

In the Kitchen:

1 pair andirons 25/, 1 dutch oven 7/6	£1 2/6
1 bell mettle skillet 15/, 2 pair sad(?) irons 10/	£1 5/
	£2 7/6
	£255 6/5 1/2

1 iron tea kettle 10/, 2 chafing dishes 2/	12/
1 tin candlebox or collender and 2 pans	7/6
1 wooden mortar and pestle 1/6, 2 cedar pails 2/	3/6
2 pair potthooks 4/, 1 frying pan 6/	10/
2 pair tongs 1 shovel 10/, 1 cedar tub 2/6	12/6

3 iron potts, 2 brackets 15/, 1 wheelbarrow 7/6	£1 2/6
3 hoes, 2 spades 15/, 2 old axes, a drawing knife 10/,	£1 5/
	£4 13/

In his will Caesar also directed:

I do give and bequeath to old Negro Charles and old negro Peg and negro Jude their Liberty forever, free and clear of me my Executors and and Administrator liberate all the rest of my Negro Slaves in manner and form following that is to say, all those that are Twenty one Years of age or upwards at the Time of my death shall have their full Freedom and Liberty at the Expiration of four years service after my decease, and all those that are not Twenty one years of age at the Time of my Death Shall have their full Freedom and Liberty when they attain the age of Twenty Five years and all that are Born after my death shall be free the instant they are born and it is my Express Order that none of those who are to be sold till they attain the respective ages aforesaid be disposed of to Persons residing out of this State but that they be sold within the state to Persons who will oblige themselves to keep them in this State during their respective Terms of servitude. . . .

They, and their values, were listed thus:

Shadrack, 4 years to serve	£40
Charles, 4 years	£40
Ezekel, 5 years	£50
Hannah, 4 years a breeding woman	£10
Cyrus, 3 years to serve till 25	£25
Ezekil, 3 months old, to serve till 25	£5
Kate, 5 years to serve a breeding woman	£10
Maria, 3 years to serve till 25	£15
Charlotte, 1 year to serve till 25	£7 10/
Bosman, 4 years to serve	£40
Pegg, 13 years old, to serve til 25	£40
Harry, 10 years to serve	£50
John, 17 years to serve	£25
Sal, 12 years to serve	£15
Beth, at Fields, 4 years to serve	£20

At the Meadow:

4 stacks of coarse hay supposed to contain 3/ tonn	£7 10/
1 cow at Joseph Fields'	
1 1 settee at Doctor Mollestons	£5
1 looking glass at Mr. Norths	£3 10/

A tract of land situate on Jones Creek said to contain 250 1/2 acres about 200 cleared the residue woodland	£563 12/6
A tract of land called Hartsfield situated in Jones Neck containing 107 acres	£700

Total Amount	£1932 1/11 1/2
Error on Plantation in the Forrest	

A note at the end of the inventory reads:

"Dr. Ridgely one of the appraisers died before this inventory was returned but James Sykes the surviving appraiser returned the originals into the office of which this is a copy." It is signed Thomas Rodney.

Appendix II: Caesar Rodney's Will
As recorded in the Office of Register of Wills
(Original in Delaware Public Archives)

I, CAESAR RODNEY OF THE COUNTY OF KENT IN THE DELAWARE STATE Esquire, Delegate in the Congress held at New York to solicit the repeal of the memorable Stamp Act, last speaker of the General Assembly of Delaware held under the Old Government, Delegate in the Revolution Congress held at Philadelphia, Signer of the Declaration of Independence, late President and Governor of the Delaware state aforesaid and eldest Son of Caesar Rodney deceased who was youngest son of William Rodney deceased who came from the City of Bristol in Great Brittain and was the first of our name in these Parts and Speaker of the first General Assembly of Delaware held under the Government after its seperation from Pennsylvania do make this my Testament and last Will for the disposal of all my real and personal Estate in manner and form following, that is to say I give and bequeath all my Silver Plate to my Brother William Rodney, my half Sister Sarah Wilson and my Niece Lavinia Rodney, (Daughter of my Brother Thomas Rodney) equally to be divided between them. I give and bequeath to my half Brother John Wilson my Silver-hilted Sword. I give and bequeath to my Nephew Caesar Augustus Rodney my gold Watch. I give and bequeath to Caesar Rodney Wilson, son of my half sister Sarah Wilson, Five Hundred Pounds lawful money of the Delaware State which sum I desire to be paid to his Mother to be held and enjoyed by her without Interest Till he is of the age of Twenty One Years. She giving Security as Guardian in the Orphans Court to pay the same to him at his said age. I give and bequeath to my said half Sister Sarah Wilson, One Feather Bed, Bedstead and Furniture and One Hundred Pounds lawful money of the Delaware State. I give and bequeath to my half brother John Wilson One Hundred Pounds lawful money of the Delaware State. I give and bequeath unto my Niece Letitia Rodney, Daughter of my Brother William Rodney, One Hundred pounds money aforesaid. I give and bequeath unto

Elizabeth Gordon, Daughter of my sister Mary Gordon deceased One Hundred Pounds money aforesaid. I give and bequeath unto Sarah Rodney, daughter of my Brother Daniel Rodney deceased One Hundred Pounds money aforesaid. I give and Bequeath to the Church Wardens of Christ Church in Dover in the said County of Kent and to their Successors One Hundred Pounds money aforesaid to be applied to the Walling in the Yard of the said Church with Brick, the same to be raised and paid as herein after directed. I do give and bequeath to old Negro Charles and old negro Peg and negro Jude their Liberty forever, free and clear of me my executors and Administrator and I do freely manumet and liberate all the rest of my Negro Slaves in manner and Form following, that is to say, all those that are Twenty one Years of age or upwards at the Time of my death shall have their full Freedom and Liberty at the Expiration of four years service after my decease, and all those that are not Twenty one years of age at the Time of my Death Shall have their full Freedom and Liberty when they attain the age of Twenty Five years and all that are Born after my death shall be free the instant they are born and it is my Express Order that none of those who are to be Sold till they attain the respective ages aforesaid be disposed of to Persons residing out of this State but that they be Sold within the State to Persons who will oblige themselves to keep them in this State during their respective Terms of Servitude. It is my will and desire that all my lands, Tenements, Hereditaments, and Real Estate, Situate lying and being in Jones's Neck in the said Kent County consisting of a large tract called Byfield, Part of a large Tract called Burton's Delight, Part of a large tract [called] Great Pipe Elm and three New Surveys one on Hog Pen Branch And two on the great branch and also of all the Marshes between the Ditches running from the mouth of the said Branches from the main Woodlands down to Delaware Bay shall hereafter be stiled [styled?] denominated called and known in the name of Byfield, a part of Burton's Delight called Hartsfield consisting of One Hundred and Seven Acres Or thereabouts being always first thereout excepted and taken and I do devise the same lands Tenements and Herditaments and real Estate in Jones's Neck, aforesaid Hartsfield excepted, to my Nephew Caesar Augustus Rodney son of my Brother Thomas Rodney for and during his natural Life without Impeachment of or for any manner of waste Subject to such Directions concerning the Management And Improvement of the same during the minority of the said Caesr Augustus Rodney or until his Death in his Minority and concerning the Application of the Rents Issues and Profits thereof during the said space of time, nevertheless shall be herein after given expressed or contained and from and after the Determination of that Estate to George Read of the town of New Castle in the said State Esquire and Fenwick Fisher of the said County of Kent, Merchant, and their Heirs during the Life of the said Caesar Augustus Rodney upon Trust to support and preserve the contingent Estates herein after limited from being defeated and destroyed and for that [purpose?] to make entries or bring actions as the case Shall require but nevertheless to permit and suffer the said Caesar Augustus Rodney after he attains his age of twenty one and his assigns during his life to receive and take the Rents Issues and Profits thereof and of every part thereof to and for his and their own use and Benefit. And from and after the Decease of the said Caesar Augustus Rodney then to the first Son of the said Caesar Augustus Rodney lawfully begotten and the Heirs Males of the body of such first son lawfully issuing and for default of such issue then to the second third fourth fifth sixth seventh eighth ninth tenth, and all and every other the son and sons of the said Caesar Augustus Rodney lawfully to be begotten severally successively and in remainder one after another as they and every of them shall in seniority of age and priority of Birth and the several and respective Heirs males of the Body and Bodies of all and every such son and sons lawfully issuing the Elder of such sons and the heirs males of his Body always to be preferred and to take before the younger Of such sons and the Heirs Males of their Body or Bodies issuing and for Default of such issue I give and devise the same, Hartsfield always excepted, as to one Moiety half Part thereof to my brother William Rodney for and during his Natural life Without Impeachment of or for any manner of waste and from and after the Determination Of that [land?] To the said George Read and Finwick Fisher and their Heirs during the Life of the said William Rodney upon Trust to support and preserve the Contingent Estates Herein after limited from being defeated and destroyed and for that Purpose to make End Tries and bring Actions as the Case Shall require nevertheless to permit and Suffer the Said William Rodney and his assigns during his Life to receive and take the Rents Issues and Profits thereof and of every Part thereof to and for his and their own use and Benefit and from and after the decease of the Said William Rodney to the first son of the said William Rodney lawfully begotten and the Heirs Males of the Body of such first Son Lawfully issuing and for Default of such issue then to the Second third fourth fifth sixth Seventh eighth ninth tenth and all and ever other the son and sons of the Said William Rodney lawfully to be begotten severally Successively and in remainder One after another as they and every of them shall be in Seniority of age and Priority of Of Birth and the Several and respective Heirs males of the Body and Bodies of all and every such Son and Sons lawfully issuing the Elder of such Sons and the Heirs males of his Body isssuing being always to be preferred and to take before the Younger of such Sons and the Heirs males of his or their Body or bodies issuing and for Default of Such Issue then to the Second third fourth fifth Sixth seventh eighth ninth tenth and all and every other the Sons and Sons of my Brother Thomas Rodney lawfully to be begotten severally Successively and in Remainder one after another as they and every of them shall be in Seniority of Age and Priority of Birth and the Several respective Heirs Males of the Body and Bodies of all and every such Son and Sons lawfully issuing the Elder of such Son and Sons and the heirs Males of his Body issuing being always to be preferred and to take before the younger of such Sons and The Heirs males of his or their Body or Bodies issuing and for Default of Such Issue to the aid Thomas Rodney for and during his Natural Life without Impreachment of or for any manner of Waste and from and after the Determination of that Estate to the Said George Read and Finwick Fisher and their heirs during the Life of the Said Thomas Rodney upon Trust to Support and preserve the contingent Estates herein after limited from being defeated and Destroyed and for the Purpose to make Entries and bring Actions as the Case shall require But nevertheless to permit and Suffer the said Thomas Rodney and his assigns during his Life to receive and take the Rests Issues and Profits thereof and of every part thereof to and For his and their own use and Benefit and from and after the Decease of the said Thomas Rodney to all and every the Son and Sons of Thomas Rodney who may happen to be born At such time or Times as to be incapable by Law of Taking all or any of the Continent Estate or Estates in the said Moiety herein before limited to the Son and Sons of the said Thomas Rodney on Failure of the Son or Sons of William Rodney and the heirs males of the Body and Bodies of Such Son or Sons of William Rodney respectively I say to such Son and Sons of Tomas Rodney lawfully to be begotten severally successively and in Remainder one after another as they and every of them shall be in seniority of age and Priority of Birth and the Several and respective Heirs males of the Body and Bodies of such Son and Sons lawfully issuing the elder of such Sons and the heirs males of his Body issuing being always to be preferred and to take before the younger of such Sons and the Heirs males of his or their Body or Bodies issuing and for default of such issue of the said Caesar Augustus Rodney as aforesaid I Give and devise the other

Moiety thereof Hartsfield always excepted, to my Brother Thomas Rodney for and during his natural life without Impeachment of or for any manner of Waste and from and after the Determination of that Estate to the said George Read and Fenwick Fisher and their Heirs for and during the life of the said Thomas Rodney upon Trust to Support and preserve the continent Estates herein after limited form being defeated and destroyed and for that Purpose to make Entries of bring actions as the Case shall reuire but Nevetheless to permit and suffer the said Thomas Rodney and his assigns during his Life to Receive and take the Rents Issues and Profits thereof and of every part thereof to and for His and their own use and Benefit. And from and after the decease of the said Thomas Rodney then to the first Son of the said William Rodney lawfully begotten and to the heirs Males of the Body of such first son lawfully issuing and for Default of Such Issue to the second third fourth fifth sixth seventh eighth ninth tenth and all and every Other the Son and Sons of the said William Rodney lawfully to be begotten Severally Successively and in Remainder one after another as they and every of them shall be in senoirity of age and Priority of birth and the several and respective heirs males of the Body and bodies of such son and Sons lawfully issuing the Elder of such sons and the heirs males of his Body issuing being always to be preferred and take before the younger of such Sons and the Heirs Males of the Body of such second son lawfully issuing and for default of such issue to the third fourth fifth sixth seventh eighth ninth tenth and all and every other the son and sons of the said Thomas Rodney lawfully to be begotten severally Successively and In remainder one after another as they and every of them shall be in seniority of age and Priority of Birth and the several and respective heirs lawfully issuing the elder of such sons and the heirs males of his Body issuing being always to be preferred and to take before the Younger of such sons and their heirs males of his or their body or bodies issuing and for default of such issue to the said William Rodney for and during his natural life without impeachment of or for any manner of Waste and from and after the Determination of that State to the said George Read and Fenwick Fisher and their heirs during the life of the said William Rodney Upon Trust to support and preserve the contingent estates herein after to Be limited from being defeated and destroyed and for that purpose to make entries and bring action as the case shall require but nevertheless to permit and suffer the same William Rodney and his assigns during his life to receive and take the Rents Issues and Profits thereof and of every part thereof to and for his and their own use and benefit and from after the decease of the said William Rodney to all and every the Son and Sons of the said William Rodney Lawfully begotten who may happen to be born at such time or times as to be Incapable by law of taking all or any of the contingent Estate or estates in the said Moiety herein before limited to the Son and Sons of the said William Rodney upon the death of Thomas Rodney I say to such son and Sons of William Rodney lawfully to be begotten severally successively and in Remainder one after Another as they and every of them shall by Seniority of age and Priority of Birth and And the several and respective Males of the Body and Bodies of such Son and Sons lawfully issuing the elder of such Son and Sons and the Heir Males of his Body issuing being always to be preferred and take before the Younger of such sons and the heirs males of his or their Body or Bodies issuing.

And the remainder of my estate in the whole of the same lands Tenements and hereditaments and real Estate in Jones's Neck (Hartsfield always excepted) I do give and devise in Manner and Form following that is to say the one sixth part thereof the whole into sixth equal parts to be Divided to Sarah Rodney Daughter of my brother Daniel Rodney deceased and to her Heirs and assigns forever but if she happen to die without issue living at her decease Then to my half sister Sarah Wilson her heirs and assigns forever And on other Sixth Part thereof to all and every the child and children of Mary Gordon deceased in Fee Simple as Tenants in Common and if any of them die before me the share and Shares of such to vest in the legal Representative of such so dying in the same Manner as if such person or persons had survived me. And one other Sixth Part Thereof to my half Brother John Wilson and his Heirs and assigns forever and If he die before me to vest in his legal Representative in the same manner as if He had survived me. And one other sixth part thereof to my half sister Sarah Wilson and her heirs and assigns forever and if she dies before me to Vest in her legal Representative in the same manner as if she had survived me. And one other sixth Part therof to my Brother William Rodney and his heirs and assigns forever and If he dies before me to Vest in his legal Representatve in the same manner as If he had survived me. And the Remaining sixth part to my brother Thomas Rodney his heirs and assigns forever and if he dies before me to Vest in his legal Representative in the same manner as if he had suvived me. And it is my Will that the same be divided Into the said six equal parts by five good Freeholders to be appointed by the person who Shall compose the orphans court when the said Remainder shall happen to be reduced into Actual possession the said division to be made according to Quantity and Quality and an Allotment to be made by the said Freeholders of each sixth as herein devised but not to be Subdivided among the Several Persons in whom the several six Parts may be Vested. And it is my Will and I do order that my brother Thomas Rodney have the management and Direction of the lands Tenements and Hereditaments and real estate herein Before devised to his son Caesar Augustus Rodney and that during the minority of the said Caesar or until the said Caesar die in his Minority and I do impower the said Thomas Rodney during the said Time to farm lease or [send] to the same to the best advantage And take and receive the Rents Issues and Profits thereof upon this special Trust and Confidence that he apply the whole of the said Rents Issues and Profits in the Improvement of the said Estate and the Education of the said Caesar Augustus Rodney paying nevertheless Thereout the legacy herein before bequeathed to Christ Church in Dover and that in three years at most after my Decease without Interest and reserving thereout a Sufficient Sum to purchase for the said Caesar Against the Time he arrives at the age of Twenty one years A good and compleat Law Library And it is my most particular Wish and desire that my Brother Thomas Rodney and those hereafter mentioned to Succeed him in the Powers Hereby given respecting the said Estate cause the said Caesar Augustus Rodney to be brot up in the Religion commonly called the Church of England and be Educated as liberally in Classical learning natural and Moral phosophy and every other Branch of Literature that has a tendency to improve the Understanding and polish the manners as may Reasonably be in America.

And in Case the said Thomas Rodney die during the Minority of his said Son I confer the aforesaid powers and the authorities on my Brother William Rodney. And in case of his Death during the minority of the said Caesar on George Read and Finwick Fisher afresaid earnestly requesting my respected Friend George Read to see That this article of my will in Judiciously put in Execution and fufilled.

And as to the Said tract of land called Hartsfield and all other my real Estate whatsoever not herein before devised and the residue of my personal Estate, it is my Will that my Executor dispose of the same for the best price that can be had as soon as reasonably may be and With the money arising from such sale and the Profits thereof untill such sale that he form a Fund for the Payment of my Debts and Legacies which I expressly charge on this and No other part of my Estate and I do impower my said Executor to make execute seal and deliver to all and every the Purchasor and Purchasors of the whole or any part of my said Real Estate good and Sufficient Deeds for the Conveyance thereof in Fee simple upon Payment of the Purchase Money or giving good security for the payment thereof—And the Rest and residue of the Money arising from the sale of my said Real Estate and of my personal Estate After Payment of my Debts and Legacies I do hereby divide into six equal Parts One Sixth whereof I bequeath to my Brother William Rodney and one Other Sixth to my Brother Thomas Rodney and another Sixth to my Niece Sarah Rodney and if she die without Issue living at her Death is my Half sister Sarah Wilson and one other Sixth all and ever the Children of my Sister Mary Gordon deceased equally to be divided Between them and another sixth to my half Brother John Wilson and the remaining Sixth Part to my half Sister Sarah Wilson. And it is my Will that if any of my Legatees (specific pecuniary_____) happen to die before me that in such case his/her or their legacy or Share go to and Vest in his her or their legal Representative in the same manner as if he she or they had Survived me unless the same are otherwise expressly limited over. If Caesar Rodney Wilson dies in his Minority see that the legacy bequesthed to him becomes the Property of any future Child of His Mother in my Will that his Mother enjoy the said Legacy during the Minority of such Child giving Security for the payment of the same without Interest to such child at its age of Twenty One as is directed with Regard to the said Caesar Rodney Wilson. It is also my Will and Intention that My Executor shall not be pressed unto any disadvantages by too early a Demand of the Primary and_____ herein given so as to oblige him to Sell Any Part of my Estate_____of him to be_____Under Value and therefore He shall have three years from my death to pay the said Bequests in during Which time he shall not have interest_____—nevertheless it is my desire that He may pay the Bequests as soon as he conveniently can especially those to my Half Sister Sarah Wilson and that he may the sooner be enable to do this I do hereby Oblige all the_____to take good Bonds or Bills assigned the goodness to be determined by the said George Read and Finwick Fisher and my Brother William Rodney instead of Money from_____legacies and their Respective shares of the_____of the Money arising from the sale of my Real and personal Estate directed to be sold as aforesaid. It is my Will and I do order that my brother Thomas Rodney make no charge against his son Caesar for mismanagement and Direction of the Estate tre_____to_____and or said or any Trouble on his Education. I do nominate constitue and appoint my Brother Thomas Rodney Executor of this my testament and last Will and instead or Commissions do bequeath him five on the Hundred on what he collects of my Personal Estate and of the money rising from the sale of my Real Estate that is Directed to be sold. And in Case of his Death appoint my Brother William Rodney my executor hereby giving him in all respects the same Powers as are Hereby before given to my Brother_____Executory and the like such of the Business as may be transacted by him the said William.

Lastly I Do hereby revoke make paid and renounce and revoke all other Wills by me heretofore made and do hereby lastly acknowledge pronounce and declare this present Testament consisting of four sheets of Paper and no other to be my Testament And last Will in testimony thereof I have herunto set my Hand and Affixed My Seal this Twentyeth day of January in the year of our Lord one Thouseand, Seven Hundred and Eighty Four.

Signed Sealed published pronounced and declared by the same Caesar Rodney Esquire as and for his Testament and last Will in the Presence of us who in his presence at his request have subscribed our names and witnesses to the same. The Word William in the last page of the Second sheet being first interested and the same being distinctly read to the testator.

[signed] Charles Ridgely, Wm. Molleston, Edward Tilghman

Codicil to Will of Caesar Rodney:

This is a codicil to the Testament and last Will of the Honorable Caesar Rodney of the County of Kent upon Delaware. Whereas I have lately purchased at Public Vendue of John Clayton, Esquire, Sheriff of the County aforesaid a certain tract or parcel of Land Containing Fifty acres More or less Situate in St. Jones's Neck being a moiety of One Hundred Acres formerly held by Randal Dons: Van [Donovan?] the Elder and willed by him to his son Randal and sold by the said Randal the son to a Certain John Stevens the Father of a certain George Stevens deceased as whose Property it was Seized and taken in Execution by the said Sheriff and a Part of a larger Tract called Great Pipe Elm Now it is my Will that the said Tract of parcel of Land with my Other lands in St. Jones's Neck (Hartsfield excepted) by called reputed and known by the name of Byfield and I do Give and devised the same Tract or Parcel of Land to the same Persons and Persons to who my real estate in St. Jones's Neck, Hartsfield excepted, is devised by my Testament and Will in the same manner a therin mentioned both in Possession reversion and Remainder Under the same uses Trusts Conditions

Provisoes Charges Incumbrances and Limitations in Every respect whatever as effectually to all Intents and Purposes whatsoever as well respecting the Application of the Rents Issues and Profits thereof as Otherwise as of every Clause and word in my said Will concerning the said real Estate (Hartsfield excepted) was in This my codicil particularly verbally and literally Set down and written again of about and concerning the said Tract or parcel of land it being my true intent meaning and Design to all the said Tract or Parcel of Land to my said real Estate in St. Jones's Neck (Hartsfield excepted) and limit it identically in every possible Respect as my said real Estate (Hartsfield excepted) in St. Jones's Neck is devised and limited in my said Testament and last Will and as if the said Tract or parcel of Land was included in my will in the enumeration of the said real Estate in St. Jones's Neck (Hartsfield excepted).

And I do order and direct my Brother Thomas Rodney to erect a good substantial brick Wall properly cap'd so as to inclose The Family Burial Ground at the Old Byfield Farm in the same manner as Burial Grounds are usually enclosed within Twenty Four months after my Decease and Raise the Money for erecting it out of the Rents and Profits of my real Estate which I have directed to be called by the name of Byfield. And I do declare this to be a codicil to my Testament and last Will and order and direct to be taken as Part of the same. In Witness Whereof I have ordered my Name to be signed herto and have affixed my seal, the Twenty Seventh Day of March in the year of our Lord One Thousand, Seven Hundred and eighty Four.

Signed by Edward Tilghman Junr in the presence of the Testator and by his express Directions and sealed promounced published and declared by the Testator as and for a codicil to his Testament and last Will in the Presence of us who in Presence of him and at his request have signed our Names as Witnesses theruntol the same being first distinctly read to the said Caesar Rodney—William Molleston, H. Matthews

I do hereby nominate constitute and appoint you, Thomas Collins, Esquire, to take hear examine and receive the Testimony and Evidence of the several subscribing witnesses to the Testament and last Will of the Honorable Caesar Rodney, Esquire, late of the County of Kent deceased for the Purpose and Intent that the same Will may be legally proven and exhibited. Witness my Hand and Seal ye 29TH June 1784

Nich. Van Dyke

Notes

CHAPTER 1. RODNEY ROOTS AND BEGINNINGS

1. Ryden, *Letters*, no. 87.
2. Fischer, *Albion's Seed*, 254.
3. Hansen, "The Paternal Ancestry," 104–06.
4. Gibson, *Essays*, 55.
5. Fischer, *Albion's Seed*, 236.
6. Ryden, *Letters*, 446
7. Ibid.
8. Hancock, ed. "Fare Weather and Good Helth" 18–19 October, 1727, 54.
9. Fischer, *Albion's Seed*, 346.
10. James B. Jackson, conversation with the author.
11. Hancock, ed. "Fare Weather and Good Helth" 66.
12. Ryden, *Letters*, 446.
13. Ibid., 3.
14. Thomas Rodney, *Commonplace Book* begun 1773. Rodney Collection, HSD.
15. Henkels Valuable Autograph Letters and Documents, 26 (See also Frank and Hancock, "Caesar Rodney's Two Hundred and Fiftieth Anniversary: an Evaluation" *Delaware History*, XVIII #2, 1978, 65.
16. Ryden, *Letters*, 447.
17. Sally was Mrs. Simon Wilmer Wilson. Her children were Caesar Rodney Wilson and Elizabeth Wilson. See Ryden, *Letters*, 446.
18. Thomas Rodney, Journal 1796–1797. AM/.1313. January 23, 1797, HSP.
19. Kent County, Delaware Deeds, X-1-162, DE State Archives, Rodney Collection, Box 6, Folder 7, HSD (quoted in Frank, & Hancock, 70.)
20. Hancock *Delaware Two Hundred Years Ago*, 86–87.
21. Ibid., 47.
22. Williams, *Slavery and Freedom* 4, 10–12.
23. Ibid, 16, 56.
24. Munroe, *Colonial Delaware*, 199.
25. Thomas Rodney Journal, September–November, 1769, Manuscript Books, Personal R, HSD
26. Munroe, *Federalist Delaware*, 40.
27. Munroe, *Delaware Becomes a State*, 8.
28. Letter from Caesar Rodney, Sr. addressed to "Casar Rodeney at the Latin School in Pilada," HSP. Quoted in Hancock, ed., "Fare Weather and Good Helth" 38.
29. Rodney Collection, folder 6, box 7, HSD. See also Frank and Hancock, 66.
30. Hancock "Personal Side," 188.
31. Ridgely *What Them Befell* 161–62.

Chapter 2. Delaware Life Under the Colonial Government

1. Brown Collection, box 18, folder 1 HSD, quoted in Frank and Hancock, "Caesar Rodney" 69.
2. Ryden, *Letters*, 23.
3. Fischer, *Albion's Seed*, 585.
4. "An Act Limiting the Time of the Sheriffs within this Government Holding Their offices and preventing Bribery and Corruption in the Election of said Sheriffs," in Cushing, *Earliest Printed Laws of Delaware*, 116.
5. Munroe, *Colonial Delaware*, 233.
6. "An Act for Regulating Elections and ascertaining the Members of the Assembly" in Cushing, *The Earliest Printed Laws of Delaware*, 93.
7. Munroe, *Colonial Delaware*, 231.
8. Cushing, *Earliest Printed Laws of Delaware*, 91.
9. Rowe, ed. "Thomas McKean's 'Biographical Sketches,' " 133.
10. Munroe, *Colonial Delaware*, 232.
11. Gibson, *Essays*, 195.
12. Munroe, *Colonial Delaware*, 223.
13. Ibid., 228.
14. Gibson, *Essays*, 34.
15. Ibid., 35.
16. Callister family papers, 1741–85, Maryland Diocesan Archives of Protestant Episcopal Church.
17. Rodney, *Colonial Finances in Delaware*, 23.
18. Ibid., 37–39
19. Gibson, *Essays*, 41
20. Ibid., 42
21. Ibid., 42
22. Jackson, *Golden Fleece Tavern*, 6.
23. Rutman, *Morning of America*, 134.

Chapter 3. Sugar and Stamps

1. John Biggs, III, esq., correspondance with the author 1997.
2. Munroe, *Colonial Delaware*, 230.
3. Stout, *Perfect Crisis*, 15
4. Ibid., 17.
5. Munroe, *Delaware Becomes a State*, 11.
6. Thomas Rodney, Commonplace Book begun in 1773, Rodney Collection, HSD.
7. Hamilton, *Thomas Rodney*, 6.
8. James B. Jackson, conversations with the author.
9. Scharf, *History of Delaware*, 1:144.
10. Stout, *Perfect Crisis*,17–19.
11. Dr. Carol E. Hoffecker, conversation with the author.
12. Stout, *Perfect Crisis*, 17–18.
13. Ibid., 18.
14. Handlin, *This Was America*, 44.
15. Stout, *Perfect Crisis*, 19.

16. Read, *Life and Correspondence*, 29.
17. Ibid., 29–30.
18. Scharf, *History of Delaware*, 1:184.
19. Munroe, *Colonial Delaware*, 236.
20. Ibid., 238.
21. Ryden, *Letters*, no. 6.
22. Hancock "Letters to and from Caesar Rodney," 58–59.
23. Scharf, *History of Delaware*, 1:185.
24. Coleman, *Thomas McKean*, 66.
25. Rowe, "Thomas McKean's 'Biographical Sketches'," 135.
26. Munroe, *Colonial Delaware*, 238.
27. Ryden, *Letters*, no. 8.
28. Stout, *Perfect Crisis*, 19.
29. Bevan, *History of Delaware*, 1:349.
30. Hancock, "Letters to and From Caesar Rodney," 59.

CHAPTER 4. MORE TROUBLES WITH TRADE

1. Stout, *Perfect Crisis*, 20.
2. Bevan, *History of Delaware*, 1:354.
3. Stout, *Perfect Crisis*, 21.
4. Ryden, *Letters*, no. 9.
5. Munroe, *Colonial Delaware*, 239.
6. Ryden, *Letters*, no. 10.
7. Ibid., no. 12.
8. Ibid., no. 13.
9. Ibid., no. 14.
10. Hancock, "Personal Side," 191.
11. Stout, *Perfect Crisis*, 22.
12. Ibid., 23.
13. Scharf, *History of Delaware*, 1:186.
14. Hancock, "Personal Side," 191.
15. Ibid., 190.
16. Ibid., 189–90.
17. Hansen, "The Paternal Ancestry."
18. Ryden, *Letters*, no. 16.
19. Minutes, House of Representatives of the State of Delaware, 1765–1770, Dover, 1931, 128.
20. Williams, *Slavery and Freedom*, 171.
21. Thomas Rodney, box 23, folder #24, nd. HSD Brown collection.
22. Rodney Collection, box 18, HSD. Quoted in Frank and Hancock, "Caesar Rodney," 69.
23. Thomas Rodney, Journal September–November 1769, Manuscript Books, Personal R. HSD.

CHAPTER 5. CLASHES IN THE NORTH

1. Stout, *Perfect Crisis*, 25–27.
2. Ibid., 22.

3. Scharf, *History of Delaware*, 1:186.
4. Stout, *Perfect Crisis*, 24.
5. Rutman, *Morning of America*, 162.
6. Stout, *Perfect Crisis*, 23–24.
7. Ryden, *Letters*, no. 17.
8. Ibid., no. 20.
9. Ibid., no. 19.
10. Hancock, "The Personal Side," 188–89.
11. Lewis B. Flinn Library, The Delaware Academy of Medicine, Wilmington.
12. Hancock, "The Personal Side," 192.
13. Hamilton, *Thomas Rodney*, 7.
14. Ryden, *Letters*, no. 21.

CHAPTER 6. PERSONAL PLANS

1. Caesar Rodney to Thomas Rodney, April 14, 1772, Chester. Rodney Collection, HSD see Hancock, "The Personal Side" 193.
2. Thomas Rodney to Caesar Rodney, April 19, 1772, Philadelphia. Rodney Collection, HSD. See ibid., 194.
3. Caesar Rodney to Thomas Rodney, April 14, 1772, Dover. Rodney Collection HSD see ibid., 193.
4. Thomas Rodney to Caesar Rodney, April 19, 1772, Philadelphia, Rodney Collection, HSD. See ibid., 194.
5. Caesar Rodney to Thomas Rodney, May 16, 1772, Dover. Brown Collection HSD. See ibid., 194.
6. Caesar Rodney to Thomas Rodney, May 16, 1772, Dover. Brown Collection HSD. See ibid., 194.
7. Thomas Rodney to Caesar Rodney, July 22, 1772, Philadelphia. Rodney Collection, HSD. See ibid., 196.
8. Thomas Rodney to Caesar Rodney, August 17, 1772, Philadelphia. Rodney Collection, HSD. See ibid., 197.
9. Thomas Rodney to Caesar Rodney, April 19, 1772, Philadelphia, Rodney Collection, HSD. See ibid., 194.
10. Thomas Rodney to Caesar Rodney, July 22, 1772, Philadelphia. Rodney Collection, HSD. See ibid., 196.
11. Thomas Rodney to Caesar Rodney, August 17, 1772, Phil. Rodney Collection, HSD See ibid., 197.
12. Thomas Rodney to Caesar Rodney, September 7, 1772, Philadelphia, Rodney Collection, HSD. see ibid., 197–98.
13. Thomas Rodney to Caesar Rodney, December 16, 1772, Philadelphia, Rodney Collection, HSD. see ibid., 199.
14. Caesar Rodney to Thomas Rodney, December 12, 1772, Dover. Brown Collection, HSD. See ibid., 198–9.
15. Thomas Rodney to Caesar Rodney, December 16, 1772, Philadelphia. Rodney Collection, HSD. see ibid., 199.
16. Caesar Rodney to Thomas Rodney, March 7, 1773, Dover. Rodney Collection, HSD. See ibid., 200.
17. Scharf, *History of Delaware*, 2:1032.
18. Leon deValinger, Map of Dover in Revolutionary Times, 1936, with notes by James B. Jackson.

19. Thomas Rodney to Caesar Rodney, August 17, 1772, Philadelphia. Rodney Collection, HSD. See ibid., 197.

20. Caesar Rodney to Thomas Rodney, March 16, 1773, Dover. Rodney Collection, HSD. See ibid., 201.

21. Thomas Rodney to Caesar Rodney, April 4, 1773, Philadelphia. Roberts Collection, Haverford. See ibid., 202.

22. James B. Jackson research on Rodney houses.

23. Thomas Rodney to Caesar Rodney, June 10, 1773, Philadelphia. Rodney Collection, HSD. See ibid., 203.

24. Note in Thomas Rodney's hand in Rodney geneology. See Hamilton, *Thomas Rodney*, fn 7.

CHAPTER 7. TEA

1. Stout, *Perfect Crisis*, 28.
2. Ibid., 29.
3. Munroe, *Colonial Delaware*, 243.
4. Hancock, *Delaware Loyalists*, 44.
5. Hamilton, *Thomas Rodney*, 16.
6. Rutman, *Morning of America*, 169.
7. Thomas Rodney to Caesar Rodney, June 10, 1773, Philadelphia, Rodney Collection, HSD. See Hancock, "The Personal Side," 203–4.
8. Ryden, *Letters*, no. 22.
9. Stout, *Perfect Crisis*, 31.
10. Ibid., 32.
11. Hamilton, *Thomas Rodney*, 8.
12. Ryerson, *Revolution Has Now Begun*, 14.
13. Munroe, *Colonial Delaware*, 243.
14. Stout, *Perfect Crisis*, 32.
15. Ibid., 32.

CHAPTER 8. BRITAIN ACTS: THE COLONIES REACT

1. Stout, *Perfect Crisis*, 42.
2. Willcox, *Papers of Benjamin Franklin*, 20:391 and 414.
3. Ibid., 42–46.
4. Ibid., 48.
5. Fischer, *Paul Revere's Ride*, 38.
6. Stout, *Perfect Crisis*, 42.
7. Ibid., 49.
8. Bevan, *History of Delaware*, 1:363.
9. Read, *Life and Correspondence*, 86.
10. Stout, *Perfect Crisis*, 112.
11. Ibid., 113.
12. Ibid.
13. Virginia state papers, 8:53 mss VSL. Quoted in Randall, *Thomas Jefferson*, 188.
14. Stout, *Perfect Crisis*, 115.

15. Munroe, *Colonial Delaware*, 246.
16. Stout, *Perfect Crisis*, 117.
17. Bevan, *History of Delaware*, 1:366.
18. Read, *Life and Correspondence*, 88.
19. Ryden, *Letters*, no. 27.
20. Scharf, *History of Delaware*, 1:217–218.
21. Ibid., 1:219.
22. Stout, *Perfect Crisis*, 53.
23. Ibid., 10–14.

Chapter 9. The First Continental Congress

1. Ryden, *Letters*, no. 30.
2. Bevan, *History of Delaware*, 1:373
3. Stout, *Perfect Crisis*, 131.
4. Bevan, *History of Delaware*, 1:373.
5. Ryden, *Letters*, no. 30.
6. Stout, *Perfect Crisis*, 134–35.
7. Ibid., 135.
8. Ryden, *Letters*, no. 34.
9. Stout, *Perfect Crisis*, 136.
10. Ryden, *Letters*, no. 32.
11. Ibid.
12. Ibid., no. 34.
13. Fisher, *Paul Revere's Ride*, 48.
14. Ryden, *Letters*, no. 30.
15. Ibid., no. 32.
16. Stout, *Perfect Crisis*, 137.
17. Ryden, *Letters*, no. 33.
18. Ibid., no. 33.
19. Hamilton, *Thomas Rodney*, 9.
20. Scharf, *History of Delaware*, 1:206.
21. Hancock, *Delaware Loyalists*, 44.
22. Ryden, *Letters*, no. 31.
23. Ibid.
24. Ibid., no. 33.
25. Ibid., no. 35.
26. Ibid., no. 38.
27. Ibid., nos. 36 & 38.
28. Ibid., no. 37.
29. Ibid.
30. Munroe, *Colonial Delaware*, 247.
31. Ryden, *Letters*, no. 37.
32. Bevan, *History of Delaware*, 1:373
33. Stout, *Perfect Crisis*, 140.
34. Ryden, *Letters*, no. 37.
35. Stout, *Perfect Crisis*, 140.
36. Bevan, *History of Delaware*, 1:374.
37. Ibid., 1:377.
38. Stout, *Perfect Crisis*, 171.

10. Hamilton, *Thomas Rodney*, 10.
11. Scharf, *History of Delaware*, 1:223.
12. Ryden, *Letters*, no. 41.
13. Scharf, *History of Delaware*, 1:223.
14. Ryden, *Letters*, no. 44.
15. Ibid.
16. Ibid., no. 45.
17. Ibid., no. 47.
18. Washington to George William Fairfax, May 31, 1775, Fitzpatrick, ed. *Writings of George Washington*, 3:291–92. See Fischer, *Paul Revere's Ride*, 280.
19. Fleming, *Year of Illusions*, 36.
20. Scharf, *History of Delaware*, 1:225.
21. Ryden, *Letters*, no. 45.
22. Thomas Rodney to Caesar Rodney, n.d. Rodney Collection, HSD. See Hancock "Personal Side," 204.
23. Ryden, *Letters*, no. 50.
24. Ibid., no. 45.
25. Ibid., no. 49.
26. Ibid., no. 45.
27. Morgan, *The Birth of the Republic*, 69.
28. Ryden, *Letters*, no. 48.
29. Hutchinson, *Diary*, 1:454–63. See Fischer, *Paul Revere's Ride*, 275.
30. Ryden, *Letters*, no. 49.
31. Ibid., no. 50.
32. Scharf, 1:223–24

CHAPTER 12. SPIES, STORMS, AND TORIES

1. Morgan, *Birth of the Republic* 69. See also Scharf, *History of Delaware*, 1:224.
2. Morgan, *Birth of the Republic*, 70.
3. Fischer, *Paul Revere's Ride*, 290.
4. Ryden, *Letters*, no. 51.
5. Hamilton, *Thomas Rodney*, 11.
6. Ibid., 12.
7. Ryden, *Letters*, no. 52.
8. Ibid., no. 53.
9. Roberts Collection, Haverford. See Hancock "Personal Side," 205–6.
10. Rodney Collection, HSD. See Hancock, "Personal Side," 206.
11. Scharf, *History of Delaware*, 1:225.
12. Ryden, *Letters*, no. 54.
13. Gibson, *Essays*, 45.
14. Scharf, *History of Delaware*, 1:225.
15. Bevan, *History of Delaware*, 1:387.
16. Ryden, *Letters*, no. 53.
17. Ibid., no. 54.
18. Higginbotham, *War of American Independence*, 113.
19. Ryden, *Letters*, no. 55.

Chapter 13. Battles in Delaware Bay

1. Higginbotham, *War of American Independence*, 150.
2. Ibid., 135.
3. Read, *Life and Correspondence*, 147.
4. Ibid., 147–48.
5. Ibid., 148.
6. Ryden, *Letters*, no. 60.
7. Scharf, *History of Delaware*, 1:226.
8. Ibid., 1:226–27.
9. Ryden, *Letters*, no. 64.
10. Ibid., no. 66.
11. Scharf, *History of Delaware*, 1:227.
12. Ibid., 1:227.
13. Ryden, *Letters*, no. 67.
14. Rodney Collection, HSD See Hancock "Personal Side," 208–9.
15. Williams, *Slavery and Freedom in Delaware*, 171.
16. HSP Sprague, William Buell, 1795–1876, Autograph Collection, 1749–1814. Volume III. Mss. # 623.
17. Ryden, *Letters*, no. 62.
18. Munroe, *Timoleon*, vi.
19. Note by Thomas Rodney in Munroe, *Timoleon*, 72.
20. Hamilton, *Thomas Rodney*, 15.
21. Ryden, *Letters*, no. 67.
22. Ibid., no. 76.
23. Munroe, *Timoleon*, ix.
24. Rightmyer, *Anglican Church in Delaware*, 117.

Chapter 14. Further Trouble with Tories

1. Ryden *Letters*, no. 71.
2. Ibid., no. 72.
3. Ibid., no. 71.
4. Ibid., no. 75.
5. Ibid., no. 71.
6. Ibid., no. 75.
7. Ibid., no. 76.
8. Ibid., no. 74.
9. Munroe, *Timoleon*, 12.
10. Ryden, *Letters*, no. 78.
11. Ibid., no. 81.
12. Ibid., no. 78.
13. Ibid., no. 81.
14. Ibid., no. 78.
15. Hamilton, *Thomas Rodney*, 19.
16. Ibid., 19–20.
17. Ibid., 20.
18. Scharf, *History of Delaware*, 1:229.
19. Ryden, *Letters*, no. 83.

20. Munroe, *Timoloen*, 15–16.
21. Ryden, *Letters*, no. 78.
22. Ibid., no. 87.

CHAPTER 15. INDEPENDENCE IS DECLARED

1. Bevan, *History of Delaware*, 1:402.
2. Ryden, *Letters*, no. 77.
3. Weslager, "Politics Behind Rodney's Famous Ride," 15.
4. Scharf, *History of Delaware*, 1:229.
5. Coleman, *Thomas McKean*, 170–71.
6. Read, *Life and Correspondence*, 161.
7. Jefferson's Writings, quoted in Scharf, *History of Delaware*, 1:229 and Read, *Life and Correspondence*, 162.
8. Ryden, *Letters*, no. 84.
9. Coleman, *Thomas McKean*, 177.
10. Ryden, *Letters*, no. 85.
11. Coleman, *Thomas McKean*, 164.
12. Weslager, "Politics Behind Rodney's Famous Ride," 20, quotes a letter Adams wrote to Timothy Pickering, no reference.
13. Ibid., 20.
14. Munroe, *Colonial Delaware*, 250.
15. Read, *Life and Correspondence*, 247. (Writings of John Adams)
16. Ibid., 163.
17. Ibid., 164. See also Ryden, *Letters*, n. 93.
18. Coleman, *Thomas McKean*, 173.
19. Ryden, *Letters*, no. 85.
20. Ibid., no. 90.
21. Scharf, *History of Delaware*, 1:231.
22. Ryden, *Letters*, n. 95.
23. Diary, Works of John Adams, vol. 2 (1850), 364. Quoted in Chinard, *Honest John Adams*, 76.
24. Coleman, *Thomas McKean*, 174.
25. Thomas Rodney, Draft Ionia Farm, May 15, 1793 to the chief justice of PA (Thomas McKean) in HSD, box 10, folder 9.
26. Thomas McKean to C. A. Rodney, Philadelphia. August (September) 22, 1813. Quoted in Munroe, *Federalist Delaware*, 14.
27. Ryden, *Letters*, no. 87.
28. Thomas McKean to C. A. Rodney, Philadelphia. August (September) 22, 1813. Burnett, *Letters*, 2:534. Quoted in Munroe, *Federalist Delaware*, 14.
29. Ryden, *Letters*, n. 95.
30. Ibid.
31. Munroe, *Colonial Delaware*, 252.
32. Ryden, *Letters*, no. 87.
33. Munroe, *Colonial Delaware*, 253.
34. Read, *Life and Correspondence*, 166.
35. Thomas Rodney's Journal 1796–1797. Am/.1313. March 12, 1797, HSP. Quoted in Hamilton, *Thomas Rodney*, 22.

CHAPTER 16. REACTION

1. Scharf, *History of Delaware*, 1:232.
2. Hamilton, *Thomas Rodney*, 22–23.
3. Bevan, *History of Delaware*, 1:405–6.
4. Thomas Rodney to Caesar Rodney, Dover, July 30, 1776. *Delaware History*, 3 (Sept 1948) 109–10. Quoted in Hamilton, *Thomas Rodney*, 23.
5. Ryden, *Letters*, no. 93.
6. Ibid., no. 95.
7. Ibid., no. 98.
8. Ibid., no. 95.
9. Ibid., no. 99.
10. Ibid., no. 100.
11. Ibid., no. 101.
12. Munroe, *Colonial Delaware*, 253.
13. Read, *Life and Correspondence*, 185–6
14. Ibid., 184.
15. Scharf, *History of Delaware*, 1:236.
16. Ryden, *Letters*, no. 117.
17. Ibid., no. 123.
18. Thomas Rodney to Caesar Rodney, Dover, September 29, 1776. See Hancock, "The Personal Side." 212.

CHAPTER 17. HASLET'S DELAWARES IN NEW YORK

1. Ryden, *Letters* no. 73.
2. Langguth, *Patriots*, 315.
3. Mitchell, *Decisive Battles*, 47–48.
4. Read, *Life and Correspondence*, 168.
5. Ibid., 171.
6. Ibid., 168.
7. Coleman, *Thomas McKean*, 168.
8. Ryden, *Letters*, no. 86.
9. Ibid., no. 96.
10. Ibid., n. 130.
11. Read, *Life and Correspondence*, 194.
12. Ryden, *Letters*, no. 98.
13. Ibid., no. 101.
14. Ibid., no. 106.
15. Ibid., n. 173.
16. Read, *Life and Correspondence*, 173.
17. Mitchell, *Decisive Battles*, 53.
18. Read, *Life and Correspondence*, 173.
19. Ibid., 170.
20. Ryden, *Letters*, no. 105.
21. Langguth, *Patriots*, 383.
22. Ibid., 384.
23. Mitchell, *Decisive Battles*, 56.
24. Ibid., 56–59.

25. Ryden, *Letters*, no. 105.
26. Ibid., no. 108.
27. Hancock, "The Personal Side," 211.
28. Mitchell, *Decisive Battles*, 61.
29. Hancock, "The Personal Side," 211.
30. Mitchell, *Decisive Battles*, 62–64.
31. Ryden, *Letters*, no. 106.
32. Ibid., no. 109.
33. Ibid., no. 110.
34. Ibid., no. 112.
35. Ibid., no. 115.
36. Hancock, "The Personal Side," 212.

Chapter 18. Dark Days of Winter

1. Ryden, *Letters*, no. 126.
2. Ibid., no. 130.
3. Ibid., no. 131.
4. Ibid., no. 130.
5. Ibid., no. 131.
6. Mitchell, *Decisive Battles*, 68.
7. Scharf, *History of Delaware*, 1:238.
8. Ryden, *Letters*, no. 136.
9. Mitchell, *Decisive Battles*, 71.
10. Hancock, "Letters to and from Caesar Rodney," 68.
11. Ryden, *Letters*, no. 134.
12. Ibid., no. 128.
13. Ibid., no. 129.
14. Ibid., no. 134.
15. Ibid., no. 127.
16. Ibid., no. 130.
17. Ibid., no. 127.
18. Scharf, *History of Delaware*, 1:240.
19. Ryden, *Letters*, no. 127.
20. Scharf, *History of Delaware*, 1:241.
21. Ibid., 1:241.
22. Ryden, *Letters*, n. 145.
23. Mitchell, *Decisive Battles*, 71.
24. Wright, *The Fire of Liberty*, 77.
25. Mitchell, *Decisive Battles*, 72.
26. Bevan, *History of Delaware*, 1:427.
27. Ryden, *Letters*, no. 139.
28. Gifford, *American Revolution*, 34
29. Mitchell, *Decisive Battles*, 72.
30. Ibid.
31. Ibid., 74.
32. Wright, *Fire of Liberty*, 78.
33. Thomas Rodney Journal, August 16, 1796–April 12, 1797, HSP. Quoted in Hamilton, *Thomas Rodney*, 25.
34. Ibid., 26.

35. "Letter to a Stranger friend who was anxious to know why my conduct appear'd so misterious to many," See Ibid., 25–26 (Mistakenly attributed to HSD).

CHAPTER 19. TRENTON AND PRINCETON

1. Thomas Rodney to Caesar Rodney, Shamany Creek, December 24, 1776. See Hancock, "The Personal Side," 214.
2. Mitchell, *Decisive Battles*, 75.
3. Gifford, *American Revolution*, 37.
4. Ryden, *Letters*, no. 143.
5. Wright, *Fire of Liberty*, 79.
6. Ryden, *Letters* no. 144.
7. Ibid., no. 143.
8. Ibid., no. 144.
9. Ibid., no. 143.
10. Mitchell, *Decisive Battles*, 82.
11. Hamilton, *Thomas Rodney*, 29.
12. Ryden, *Letters*, no. 149.
13. Hamilton, *Thomas Rodney*, 29.
14. Ibid., 29–30.
15. Ryden, *Letters*, no. 144.
16. Ibid., no. 151.
17. Scharf, *History of Delaware*, 1:238–38.
18. Hamilton, *Thomas Rodney*, 30.
19. Mitchell, *Decisive Battles*, 84–85.
20. Hamilton, *Thomas Rodney*, 30.
21. Ryden, *Letters*, no. 145.

CHAPTER 20. MILITIA AND OTHER MATTERS

1. Ryden, *Letters*, no. 142.
2. Ibid., no. 145.
3. Ibid., no. 149.
4. Ibid., no. 156.
5. Ibid., no. 149.
6. Ibid., no. 151.
7. Ibid., no. 150.
8. Ibid., no. 152.
9. Ibid., no. 156.
10. Ibid., no. 153.
11. Ibid., no. 156.
12. Ibid., no. 145.
13. Ibid., no. 156.
14. Ibid., no. 155.
15. Ibid., no. 156.
16. Ibid., no. 159.
17. Scharf, *History of Delaware*, 1:241.
18. Martin, *History of Delaware*, 2.

19. Ryden, *Letters*, no. 158.
20. Ibid., no. 158.
21. Ibid., no. 161.
22. Scharf, *History of Delaware*, 1:242.
23. Ryden, *Letters*, no. 158.
24. Ibid., no. 175.
25. Rodney, *Colonial Finanaces in Delaware*, 44.
26. Ryden, *Letters*, no. 158.
27. Ibid.
28. Carey, "The Tories of Delaware," 16.
29. Ibid., 5.
30. Ryden, *Letters*, no. 164.
31. Ibid., no. 171.
32. Ibid., no. 180.
33. Ibid., no. 162.
34. Ibid., no. 165.
35. Ibid., no. 163.
36. Ibid., no. 169.
37. Ibid., no. 166.
38. Ibid., no. 174.
39. Ibid., no. 177.
40. Mitchell, *Decisive Battles*, 89.
41. Ryden, *Letters*, no. 184.
42. Mitchell, *Decisive Battles*, 96.
43. Higginbotham, *War of American Independence*, 183.
44. Ryden, *Letters* no. 186.
45. Ibid., no. 187.
46. Ibid., no. 189.
47. Executive Papers, DE State Archives, see Hancock, "The Personal Side," 215.

Chapter 21. The War Comes Home

1. Ryden, *Letters*, no. 191.
2. Ibid., no. 192.
3. Ibid., n. 211.
4. Ibid., no. 198.
5. Bevan, *History of Delaware*, 1:434.
6. Munroe, "Battle of Cooch's Bridge," 14.
7. Ryden, *Letters*, no. 200.
8. Ibid., no. 203.
9. Ibid., no. 207.
10. Ibid., no. 204.
11. Munroe, "Battle of Cooch's Bridge," 14.
12. Ryden, *Letters,* no. 217.
13. Martin, *History of Delaware*, 37.
14. Ryden, *Letters*, no. 206.
15. British Captain Frederich von Muenchhausen, quoted in Munroe, "Battle of Cooch's Bridge," 15.
16. Scharf, *History of Delaware*, 1:244.

17. Ryden, *Letters*, no. 207.
18. Munroe, "Battle of Cooch's Bridge," 14.
19. Ryden, *Letters*, no. 209.
20. Ibid., no. 210.
21. Carey, "Tories of Delaware," 9.
22. Ryden, *Letters*, no. 211.
23. Ibid., no. 212.
24. Ibid., no. 213.

CHAPTER 22. THE BRITISH OCCUPY WILMINGTON

1. Scharf, *History of Delaware*, 1:245.
2. Ibid., 1:245.
3. Mitchell, *Decisive Battles*, 112.
4. Ibid., 109.
5. Scharf, *History of Delaware*, 1:246.
6. Munroe, *Colonial Delaware*, 255.
7. Scharf, *History of Delaware*, 1:246.
8. Mitchell, *Decisive Battles*, 115.
9. Ryden, *Letters*, no. 220.
10. Ibid., no. 222.
11. Read, *Life and Correspondence*, 274–75.
12. Scharf, *History of Delaware*, 1:246.
13. Read, *Life and Correspondence*, 275.
14. Ryden, *Letters*, no. 223.
15. Ibid., no. 224.
16. Read, *Life and Correspondence*, 278.
17. Ibid., 275.
18. Ryden, *Letters*, no. 225.
19. Ibid.
20. Ibid., no. 227.
21. Ibid., no. 221.
22. Scharf, *History of Delaware*, 1:246.
23. Ibid., 1:246–47.
24. Ryden, *Letters*, no. 228.
25. Ibid., no. 228.
26. Read, *Life and Correspondence*, 276.

CHAPTER 23. HOWE DEPARTS AND CAESAR TAKES CHARGE

1. Munroe, *Colonial Delaware*, 255.
2. Ferling, *First of Men* 221.
3. Scharf, *History of Delaware*, 1:247.
4. Ibid., 1:246–47.
5. Ryden, *Letters*, no. 229.
6. Ibid., no. 231.
7. McKean Papers, 4:11, McKean to John Adams, Philadelphia, 15 Nov 1813. Adams, *Works*, 10:81–87. In Munroe, *Federalist Delaware*, 88.

8. Scharf, *History of Delaware*, 1:247.
9. Ibid., 1:247.
10. Ryden, *Letters*, no. 235.
11. Ibid., n. 256.
12. Ibid., no. 244.
13. Scharf, *History of Delaware*, 1:247–48.
14. Hamilton, *Thomas Rodney*, 32–33.
15. Ryden, *Letters*, n. 254.
16. Ibid., no. 244.
17. Ibid., no. 246.
18. Ibid., no. 247.
19. Ibid., no. 253.
20. Ibid., no. 258.
21. Scharf, *History of Delaware*, 1:248.
22. Ryden, *Letters*, n. 259.
23. Ibid., no. 241.

CHAPTER 24. PRESIDENT RODNEY

1. Ryden, *Letters*, no. 256.
2. Ibid., no. 262.
3. Ibid., no. 256.
4. Ibid., no. 260.
5. Munroe, *Colonial Delaware*, 256.
6. Ryden, *Letters*, no. 251.
7. Ibid., no. 259.
8. Ibid., no. 257.
9. Ibid., nos. 257, 259.
10. Ibid., no. 262.
11. Ibid., no. 267.
12. Scharf, *History of Delaware*, 1:248.
13. Ryden, *Letters*, no. 269.
14. Ferling, *First of Men*, 242.
15. Ryden, *Letters*, no. 259.
16. Ibid., no. 262.
17. Ibid., no. 266.
18. Mitchell, *Decisive Battles*, 139–40.
19. Ryden *Letters*, no. 266.
20. Ibid., no. 269.
21. Ibid.
22. Munroe, *Colonial Delaware*, 256.
23. Martin, *History of Delaware*, 6.
24. Mitchell, *Decisive Battles*, 141.
25. Ibid., 145.
26. Ryden, *Letters*, no. 270.
27. Mitchell, *Decisive Battles*, 146.
28. Ibid., 147.
29. Ryden, *Letters*, no. 272.
30. Ibid., no. 273.
31. Scharf, *History of Delaware*, 1:248.

Chapter 25. Politics

1. Ryden *Letters*, no. 283.
2. Martin, *History of Delaware*, 6.
3. Ryden, *Letters* no. 283.
4. Ibid., no. 284.
5. Ibid., no. 289.
6. Ibid., no. 275.
7. Ibid., no. 280.
8. Ibid., no. 290.
9. Ibid., no. 275.
10. Ibid., no. 290.
11. Ibid., no. 291.
12. Ibid., no. 268.
13. Morgan, *Birth of the Republic*, 107.
14. Munroe, *Federalist Delaware*, 37.
15. Ryden, *Letters*, no. 269.
16. Ibid., no. 278.
17. Ibid., no. 288.
18. Ibid., no. 291.
19. Ibid., no. 294.
20. Ibid., no. 295.
21. Read, *Letters and Correspondence*, 347.
22. Scharf, *History of Delaware*, 1:249.
23. Burnett, *Letters* 4:6,7. quoted in Munroe, *Federalist Delaware*, 96.
24. Ibid., 95.
25. Ibid., 97.
26. Ryden, *Letters*, no. 300.

Chapter 26. "Engrossing"

1. Morgan, *Birth of the Republic*, 112.
2. Ryden, *Letters*, no. 315.
3. Ibid., no. 315.
4. Ibid., no. 321.
5. Ibid., no. 339.
6. Ibid., no. 325.
7. Ibid., no. 329.
8. Ibid., no. 331.
9. Ibid., no. 343.
10. Ibid., no. 338.
11. Ibid., no. 356.
12. Ibid., no. 354.
13. Ibid., no. 355.
14. Scharf, *History of Delaware*, 1:250.
15. Ryden, *Letters*, no. 357.
16. Ibid., no. 450.
17. Hamilton, *Thomas Rodney*, 34.

18. Ryden *Letters*, no. 366. See also Thomas Rodney Journal of Accounts 1780–81, Div of MSS, Library of Congress, in Hamilton, *Thomas Rodney*. n. 34.

19. Ryden *Letters*, no. 349.

20. Ibid., no. 349.

21. Scharf, *History of Delaware*, 1:251.

22. Petition of October, 1779, Legislative Papers. See Munroe, *Federalist Delaware*, n. 38.

23. Ryden, *Letters*, no. 368.

24. Ibid., no. 370.

25. Ibid., no. 422.

26. Patterson, "The Rumfords."

27. Ryden, *Letters*, no. 457.

28. Hamilton, *Thomas Rodney*, 35.

29. Ryden, *Letters*, no. 450.

30. Ibid., no. 447.

31. Ibid., no. 451.

32. Hamilton, *Thomas Rodney*, 35–36.

33. Montgomery "Remininscences of Wilmington," 168.

34. Hamilton, *Thomas Rodney*, 33–36.

CHAPTER 27. THE WAR MOVES SOUTH

1. Hancock, "The Personal Side," 217.

2. Mitchell, *Decisive Battles*, 158.

3. Ryden, *Letters*, no. 335.

4. Ibid., no. 353.

5. Mitchell, *Decisive Battles*, 156.

6. Ryden, *Letters*, no. 372.

7. Scharf, *History of Delaware*, 1:251.

8. Ryden, *Letters*, no. 324.

9. Ibid., no. 332.

10. Mitchell, *Decisive Battles*, 159.

11. Ryden, *Letters*, no. 396.

12. Ibid., no. 403.

13. Ibid., no. 418.

14. Ibid., no. 420.

15. Ibid., no. 423.

16. Ibid., no. 385.

17. Scharf, *History of Delaware*, 1:253.

18. Ibid., 1:253.

19. Ryden, *Letters*, no. 442.

20. Scharf, *History of Delaware*, 1:254.

21. Mitchell, *Decisive Battles*, 163.

22. Ryden, *Letters*, no. 443.

23. Scharf, *History of Delaware*, 1:255.

24. Ryden, *Letters*, no. 413.

25. Ibid., no. 415.

26. Ibid., no. 454.

27. Ibid., no. 399.

28. Ibid., no. 432.

29. Ibid., no. 434.
30. Ibid., no. 439.

CHAPTER 28. AN END TO WAR

1. Mitchell, *Decisive Battles*, 169–70.
2. Samuel Holden Parsons to Thos Mumford January 6, 1781. See Ryan, *Salute to Courage*, 205.
3. Ibid., 207.
4. William Campbell to Arthur Campbell, Wilkes County, Camp on Brier Creek, October 20, 1780. See Ibid., 232.
5. Scharf, *History of Delaware*, 1:258.
6. Ibid., 1:258.
7. Mitchell, *Decisive Battles*, 175–78.
8. Scharf, *History of Delaware*, 1:258.
9. Ibid., 1:258–59.
10. Mitchell, *Decisive Battles*, 185.
11. Ryan, *Salute to Courage*, 244.
12. Mitchell, *Decisive Battles*, 185.
13. Ryden, *Letters*, no. 521.
14. Morgan, *Birth of the Republic*, 112.
15. Hamilton, *Thomas Rodney*, 37.
16. Ibid., 38.
17. Ibid.
18. Ibid., 40.
19. Ryden, *Letters*, no. 505.
20. Mitchell, *Decisive Battles*, 188.
21. Ibid., 191.
22. Ryden, *Letters*, no. 526.
23. Scharf, *History of Delaware*, 1:262.
24. Ryden, *Letters*, no. 537.
25. Ibid., no. 527.

CHAPTER 29. CEASAR'S SAND RUNS OUT

1. Ryden *Letters*, no. 529.
2. Ibid., no. 530.
3. Hancock "The Personal Side" 218.
4. Ibid., 218.
5. Ibid., 220.
6. Ryden, *Letters*, no. 536.
7. Ibid., no. 529.
8. Thomas Rodney Commonplace Book, begun in 1773, HSD
9. Ryden, *Letters*, no. 542.
10. Ibid., no. 543.
11. Ibid., no. 529.

12. Thomas Rodney, journal, begun July 1773, Manuscript Books, Personal, R. HSD.

13. Hamilton, *Thomas Rodney*, 46–47.

APPENDIX I. CAESAR RODNEY'S BEQUESTS

1. Rodney Collection, Box 6, Folder 22. HSD.

Bibliography

Bevan, Wilson Lloyd, ed. *History of Delaware, Past and Present*, 4 vols. New York: Lewis Historical Publishing Co., Inc., 1939.

Callister Family Papers, 1741–85, Maryland Diocesan Archives of the Protestant Episcopal Church, Baltimore.

Carey, Alfred B. "The Tories of Delaware." Graduating essay, University of Delaware, n.d.

Carter, Clarence E., ed. *The Correspondence of General Thomas Gage*. 2 vols. New Haven, 1933. Reprint 1969.

Chinard, Gilbert. *Honest John Adams*. Boston: Little, Brown and Co., 1933.

Coleman, John M. *Thomas McKean, Forgotten Leader of the Revolution*. Rockaway, NJ: American Faculty Press, 1975.

Cushing, Henry A., ed. *Writings of Samuel Adams*, 4 vols. New York, 1904.

Cushing, John D., ed. *The Earliest Printed Laws of Delaware, 1704–1741*. Wilmington, DE: Michael Glazier, Inc., 1978.

Ferling, John E. *The First of Men: A Life of George Washington*. Knoxville: University of Tennessee Press, 1988.

Fischer, David Hackett. *Albion's Seed: Four British Folkways in America*. New York and Oxford: Oxford University Press, 1989.

———. *Paul Revere's Ride*, New York and Oxford: Oxford University Press, 1994.

Fitzpatrick, John C., ed. *The Writings of George Washington from the Original Manuscript Sources, 1745–1799*. Washington: U.S. Government Printing Office, 1931–44.

Fleming, Thomas. *Year of Illusions*. New York: W. W. Norton, 1975.

Frank, William P. and Hancock, Harold B. "Caesar Rodney's Two Hundred & Fiftieth Anniversary: An Evaluation." *Delaware History* 18 no. 2 (1978–79) 63–74.

French, Allen. *General Gage's Informers: New Material upon Lexington and Concord*. Ann Arbor, 1932.

Gibson, George H. *The Collected Essays of Richard S. Rodney on Early Delaware*. Wilmington: Society of Colonial Wars in the State of Delaware, 1975.

Gifford, Edward S. *The American Revolution in the Delaware Valley*, Philadelphia: Pennsylvania Society of the Sons of the Revolution, 1976.

Hamilton, William Baskerville. *Thomas Rodney, Revolutionary and Builder of the West*. Separate printing of biographical sketch from *Anglo-American Law on the Frontier: Thomas Rodney and His Territorial Cases*. Durham, NC: Duke University Press, 1953.

Hancock, Harold B. *The Delaware Loyalists*, Wilmington: The Historical Society of Delaware, 1940.

———. *Delaware Two Hundred Years Ago, 1780–1800*. Wilmington: Middle Atlantic Press, 1987.

———. "Letters to and from Caesar Rodney" *Delaware History*, 12, (1966–67): 54–76.

———. "Letters to and from Caesar Rodney: the Personal Side" *Delaware History* 20, no. 3, (1982–83): 185–221.

———. " 'Fare Weather and Good Helth' The Journal of Caesar Rodeney, 1727–1729" *Delaware History* 10 (1962–63): 33–70.

Handlin, Oscar. *This Was America, True Accounts of People and Places, Manners and Customs, As Recorded by European Travelers to the Western Shore in the Eighteenth, Nineteenth, and Twentieth Centuries*. Reprint, Cambridge: Harvard University Press, 1969.

Hansen, Col. Charles M. "The Paternal Ancestry of Caesar Rodney of Delaware, Signer of the Declaration of Independence." *The American Geneologist*, (April 1989).

Higginbotham, Don. *The War of American Independence, Military Attitudes, Policies and Practice, 1763–1789*. New York: Macmillan, 1971.

The Historical Society of Delaware, 505 market St., Wilmington, DE 19801 (HSD)

———. *Delaware History* Journal published semi-annually by the Society.

———. Brown Collection of Rodney letters and Journals

———. Rodney Collection of Letters and Journals.

The Historical Society of Pennsylvania, 1300 Locust St., Philadelphia, PA 19107 (HSP)

Hutchinson, Thomas. *The Diary and Letters of His Excellency Thomas Hutchinson, esq.* 2 vols. Boston, 1884.

Jackson, James B. *The Golden Fleece Tavern, The Birthplace of the First State*. Dover, DE: Friends of Old Dover, 1987.

Langguth, A. J. *Patriots: The Men Who Started the American Revolution*. New York: Simon and Shuster, n.d.

The Library of Virginia, 800 East Broad St., Richmond, VA 23219

Martin, Roger A. *A History of Delaware Through Its Governors, 1776–1984*. Wilmington: McClafferty Printing, 1984.

McCusker, John J. *Money and Exchange in Europe and America, 1600–1775*. Chapel Hill: University of North Carolina Press published for Institute of Early American History and Culture, Williamsburg, VA, 1978.

Minutes, House of Representatives of the State of Delaware, 1765–1770. Dover, 1931.

Mitchell, Joseph B. *Decisive Battles of the American Revolution*. New York: G. P. Putnam's Sons, 1962.

Montgomery, Elizabeth, "Remininscences of Wilmington, 1851." Wilmington: Historical Society of Delaware, n.d.

Morgan, Edmund S. *The Birth of the Republic, 1763–1789*. 3rd ed. Chicago and London: University of Chicago Press, 1992.

Munroe, John A. "The Battle of Cooch's Bridge." *Delaware Conservationist*, 21, no. 4 (Winter, 1977–78): 11–15.

———. *Colonial Delaware, A History*. Millwood, NY: KTO Press, 1978.

——. *Delaware Becomes a State*, Newark: University of Delaware Press, 1987.

——. *Federalist Delaware, 1775–1815*, New Brunswick: Rutgers University Press, 1954.

——. "The Philadelawareans: A Study in the Relations Between Philadelphia and Delaware in the Late Eighteenth Century." *The Pennsylvania Magazine*, Vol. 69. 146.

——, ed. *Timoleon: Biographical History of Dionysius, Tyrant of Delaware*, Newark: University of Delaware Press, 1958.

The New York Historical Society, 2 West 77th St., New York, NY 10024.

Patterson, Mary T. S., "The Rumfords." Family History File, Historical Society of Delaware, Wilmington.

Randall, Willard Sterne. *Thomas Jefferson, A Life*. New York: Henry Holt & Co., 1993.)

Read, William Thompson. *The Life and Correspondence of George Read*. Philadelphia: J. B. Lippincott & Co., 1870.

Ridgeley, Mabel Lloyd. *What Them Befell, The Ridgelys of Delaware and Their Circle in Colonial and Federal Times, Letters, 1751–1890*. Portland, ME: Anthoensen Press, 1949.

Rightmyer, Nelson Waite. *The Anglican Church in Delaware*. Philadelphia: The Church Historical Society, 1947.

Rodney, Richard S. *Colonial Finances in Delaware*, Wilmington: Wilmington Trust Co, 1928.

Rodney, Thomas to Caesar Rodney, July 30, 1776. *Delaware History* 3 (1948–49) 109–10.

Rodney, Thomas. Journal of 1797, Philadelphia: HSP

——. Journal September–November, 1769. Manuscript

Books, Personal R. HSD

——. *Journal*, begun July 1773, Manuscript Books, Personal, R. HSD

Rowe, G. S., ed. "Thomas McKean's Biographical Sketches." *Delaware History*, 26, no. 2, (1994–95): 125–37.

Rutman, Darrett B. *The Morning of America, 1603–1789*. Boston: Houghton Mifflin, 1971.

Ryan, Dennis P., ed. *A Salute to Courage, the American Revolution as seen Through the Writings of Officers in the Continental Army and Navy*. New York: Columbia University Press, 1979.

Ryden, George Herbert, ed. *Letters to and From Caesar Rodney, 1756–1784*. Philadelphia: University of Pennsylvania Press, for the Historical Society of Delaware, 1933.

Ryerson, Richard Alan. *The Revolution Is Now Begun: The Radical Committees of Philadelphia, 1765–1776*. Philadelphia: University of Pennsylvania Press, 1978.

Scharf, J. Thomas, *History of Delaware, 1609–1888*. 2 vols. Philadelphia: L. J. Richards and Co., 1888.

Shryock, Richard Harrison. *Medicine and Society in America, 1660–1860*, Ithaca and London: Cornell University Press, sixth printing, 1988.

Stout, Neil R. *The Perfect Crisis, The Beginning of the Revolutionary War*. New York: New York University Press, 1976.

Weslager, C. A. "The Politics Behind Rodney's Famous Ride." *Delaware Today* June/July, 1968.

Willcox, William, ed. *Papers of Benjamin Franklin*, 33 vols. New Haven and London: Yale University Press, 1976.

Williams, William H. *Slavery and Freedom in Delaware, 1639–1865*. Wilmington: SR Books, 1996.

Wood, Gordon S. *The Radicalism of the American Revolution*. New York: Random House, Vintage Books, 1991.

Wright, Edmund S. *The Fire of Liberty*. London: The Folio Society, 1983.

Index